Australia's Vietnam

MARK DAPIN is the author of *The Nashos' War*, which won the People's Choice Award and an Alex Buzo Shortlist Prize at the NIB Awards and was shortlisted for the NSW Premier's Literary Award for Non-Fiction. His most recent military history book, *Jewish Anzacs*, has been highly praised. His novel *Spirit House*, based on the experience of Second World War POWs on the Burma Railway, was longlisted for the Miles Franklin Literary Award in Australia and shortlisted for the Royal Society of Literature's Ondaatje Prize in the UK. Dapin is also the editor of the *Penguin Book of Australian War Writing*. He lives in Sydney, where he works as a journalist and historian.

Australia's Vietnam

Myth vs History

Mark Dapin

NEWSOUTH

A NewSouth book

Published by
NewSouth Publishing
University of New South Wales Press Ltd
University of New South Wales
Sydney NSW 2052
AUSTRALIA
newsouthpublishing.com

© Mark Dapin 2019
First published 2019

10 9 8 7 6 5 4 3 2 1

A catalogue record for this book is available from the National Library of Australia

ISBN   9781742236360 (paperback)
        9781742244525 (ebook)
        9781742248981 (ePDF)

Design Avril Makula
Cover design Peter Long
Cover image Vietnam war – Australian troops returned from Vietnam march through Brisbane, Queensland, 12 November 1970. National Archives of Australia, NAA: A1500, K26967
Printer Griffin Press

Contents

Abbreviations

1ALSG	1st Australian Logistic Support Group
1ATF	1st Australian Task Force
2AOD	2 Advanced Ordnance Depot
AATTV	Australian Army Training Team Vietnam
ABC	Australian Broadcasting Corporation
AIF	Australian Imperial Force
ALP	Australian Labor Party
ANZAC	Australian and New Zealand Army Corps
APWU	Amalgamated Postal Workers' Union
ARA	Australian Regular Army
ARVN	Army of the Republic of Vietnam
ASIO	Australian Security Intelligence Organisation
AWM	Australian War Memorial
CMF	Citizen Military Forces
CO	Commanding Officer
CPA	Communist Party of Australia
DLNS	Department of Labour and National Service
DVA	Department of Veterans' Affairs
nasho	national serviceman
NCO	non-commissioned officer
NLF	National Liberation Front
NS	national service
PAVN	People's Army of Vietnam
PMG	Postmaster-General's Department
POW	prisoner of war
PTSD	post-traumatic stress disorder
RAAF	Royal Australian Air Force
RAAOC	Royal Australian Army Ordnance Corps
RAASC	Royal Australian Army Service Corps
RAE	Royal Australian Engineers
RAR	Royal Australian Regiment
RNZAF	Royal New Zealand Air Force
RSL	Returned and Services League of Australia
RTB	recruit training battalion
SAS	Special Air Service Regiment
SDA	Students for Democratic Action/Society for Democratic Action
SDS	Students for a Democratic Society
SEATO	Southeast Asia Treaty Organization
SOS	Save Our Sons
SVN	South Vietnam
VAC	Vietnam Action Committee/Vietnam Action Campaign
VC	Vietcong
VVAA	Vietnam Veterans' Association of Australia
VVMC	Vietnam Veterans Motorcycle Club
WILPF	Women's International League for Peace and Freedom
YCAC	Youth Campaign Against Conscription

Dedication

This book is partially based on my doctoral thesis. My supervisor, Professor Jeffrey Grey, was probably the finest military historian in Australia. On the morning I submitted the final abstract of the thesis for his approval, Jeff died.

He was 57 years old.

When I first approached Jeff at the Australian Defence Force Academy (ADFA) he clearly thought I was an idiot. He only changed his mind when my novel *Spirit House* was longlisted for the Miles Franklin Literary Award. With this, I seemed to transform in his eyes from a complete idiot to a near-complete-idiot-with-one-single-redeeming-talent. This, I suspect, put me ahead of 90 per cent of humanity.

Jeff finally accepted me as a student but when I turned up to enrol, I couldn't find his office. I was discovered wandering vacantly around the campus by an academic from another faculty, who asked if I were a member of staff or a postgraduate student. When I told him Jeff was my supervisor, the stranger lightly touched my arm and said, 'You don't have to spend much time with your supervisor, you know. I hardly ever saw mine. You'll probably be alright.'

He pointed me towards the faculty building, where eventually I found Jeff sitting in a room with books packed on every shelf of every wall, and even more books piled high on his desk and table like towers of Jenga bricks, or a scale model of the New York City skyline. (When I texted a friend to tell him Jeff had died, he asked, 'Did his books fall on him?')

I told Jeff about my encounter with the other academic and he laughed, then gently probed me for identifying details so he could find him and, presumably, kill him. Once Jeff had accepted me, he was very kind. He guided me towards the right answers with a subtlety I only fully came to appreciate when I began work on my final draft. I wrote every sentence with Jeff in mind, and now he'll never read it.

I always attend funerals and memorials, even though I hate them. I was out of the country when my grandad died, so I never properly mourned him and he didn't truly seem dead to me. For years, my grandad came back to me at night in my dreams, telling me he was still alive and asking me to come out for a drink. For years, I would wake up in the morning and my heart would break once more.

I don't want Jeff in my nightmares, urging me to finish my thesis when I'm 80 years old, so I went to his memorial service at RMC Duntroon. I saw his father march sadly through the chapel, wearing his life story in ribbons across his chest. Major General Ron Grey had fought in Borneo, Korea and Vietnam yet still somehow outlived his son. It must be the most terrible thing in the world to see your children die before you. But in the military, more than anywhere, they know that.

It was a good memorial. At the front of the chapel was a table of books Jeff had written. They weren't actually for sale, but the display made me think that, when I pass on, it might be a good opportunity to flog off some of the remaindered copies of *Spirit House* that fill my attic with evidence of my commercial failure.

I wouldn't be able to sign them, though, obviously.

The moral of this dedication is: if you have a teacher you value, for God's sake don't hold them close, hug them, or tell them how much they mean to you.

Because Jeff would've really, really hated that.

1
'In the way of a good story' The myths I helped to make

Let our history be as factual, logical, reliable, and as documented as a history book needs to be. But also let it contain the dialogic history of its making, and the experience of its makers. Let it show how historians themselves grow, change, and stumble through the research and the encounter with other subjects.

– Alessandro Portelli [1]

As a journalist I first wrote about Vietnam veterans in 2007, when I spoke with members of the Queensland chapter of the Vietnam Veterans Motorcycle Club (VVMC) on the afternoon of their annual Bike, Trike and Hot Rod Show. I left shortly after dusk, at the end of the wet T-shirt contest but before the stripper they called 'the Vegetable Lady' mounted the stage with her groceries. I missed the ladies' gumboot-throwing contest and most of the men's keg-throwing while I spent six hours drinking icy Castlemaine XXXX with club members, under a coffin lid inscribed with the names of fallen soldiers, and I had the same mordant, bitter conversation over and over again. When they were on the cusp of adulthood, these men went to war, and it mangled their hearts and upturned their lives, then suddenly, 30 years later, it drove them out of their minds.

'We came back with the general consensus that we were a bunch of bloody idiots, bludgers, baby killers, morons,' said the VVMC's president, whose club name was Mutha. 'The government shit on us, the public shit on us.' Mutha was a stern, sonorous witness, a lion of a leader. His conversation prowled and snarled, and he faintly bared his teeth. Much of the time, he played a suspicious, resentful hard man, struggling to keep his anger under control but, at 58 years old, he was more thoughtful and articulate than the limits of that persona allowed.

It was the second time I had visited the VVMC clubhouse, built at the point where an industrial estate meets the bush on the fringes of Logan City, between Brisbane and the Gold Coast. On the first occasion, I walked in on the club's regular Friday night drinks, where members clutched stubby holders in the Bunker bar, or sat quietly around wooden tables on the deck, while their wives grilled hamburgers in the kitchen. I was told the veterans do not usually speak to the media, that club business is private and that they do not like outsiders at their drinks, then almost every man I met told me his life story and offered to buy me a beer.

The Queensland chapter held annual bike shows, tattoo shows and poker runs, all open to the public. It was recognised by the Department of Veterans' Affairs (DVA) as a veterans' support group, raised money for charity and was a patron of the local army cadet unit. However, it was not a weekend social club for older riders. VVMC members wore the ribbons of their war medals on their chests, took their colours seriously, and would fight to protect their mates.

On the afternoon of the bike show, Tiny the caretaker, a bulky, friendly, but slightly hesitant former infantryman, showed me around the sprawling clubhouse. The main building used to be a boatshed. In the five years before, veterans had cleared the surrounding land of scrub and lantana, and built an air-conditioned bunkhouse. Several veterans had moved their caravans to the property, and the DVA had funded a workshop where the men can maintain their bikes. Most of the construction was done by members, using donated materials, but they had to get help with the concreting because, said Tiny, 'There's a lot of bad backs.'

The members trickled in during the afternoon, every man in leather, denims and boots, all wearing their colours. Some had adopted the old-style biker rainforest-hair-and-lichen-beard look, but many still looked like the police officers, firemen and prison guards they had become when they left the military. They tended to be tanned, hefty, well-muscled men, gaining weight and losing hair in late middle-age. I asked Tiny how many of them had post-traumatic stress disorder (PTSD). 'I would say about 90 per cent,' he said. 'I could take you to some blokes who are as mad as snakes. Old Frankie used to be a painter all his life, and all of a sudden he painted the office and painted his boss.'

At the bike show, the VVMC mixed with hundreds of local people: revheads in Oakleys; young families; would-be tough guys hoping a bit of bloodstained glamour might rub off onto their Ned Kelly tattoos; friends and sympathisers; and a handful of camp followers who seemed to have turned up to meet a vet. While I was drinking with Skip, a genial storyteller with a calming, nasal lilt, a woman who had painted a younger face onto her own interrupted, 'I was just eavesdropping the conversation, and I just wanted to say ...'

'Go somewhere else,' said Skip.

Mutha served in signals in Vietnam. Skip was attached to a cavalry unit. Their comrade, Headhunter, was in the cavalry too. A huge, impressive, reflective man named Padre was also in signals. Kind-faced Huck was a tank commander. They came from wildly different backgrounds – Headhunter was a New Zealand-born Maori who served 20 years in the Australian Army; Huck was a South Australian primary school teacher drafted to fight in Vietnam – but, heard together, their voices told one story.

'When I joined, I didn't even know there was a Vietnam,' said Headhunter. 'They said, "You're going to Vietnam." I said, "What's that?" I went in 1969 and came home in 1972. You see a lot of atrocities. You can't get that out of your mind. I shot first and asked questions later. That was my mentality. You teach yourself to block out the bad things, but the bad things are still there while you sleep. The Vietcong, the Vietnamese, they all come back in dreams.'

'They flew us back in the middle of the night,' said Huck, 'so the demonstrators couldn't see us. There was no one there to welcome us, no counselling, no one to help us.'

'We were rejected and spat on,' said Headhunter, 'and a motherfucker poured a bucket of paint on me. It was our welcome home from the students.'

'Once I got out of the Army, my life turned to shit in a few weeks,' said Mutha. 'I was a piece of shit, as far as anyone was concerned and, even more so, I thought I was a piece of shit, and I treated everyone else around me like a piece of shit. That's how it went on for 35 to 40 years.'

'I started drinking really heavily,' said Huck. 'I was very abusive to my first wife and kids. I was very aggressive, and finally I got to the stage where I just didn't want to be here. I was suicidal.'

'I started really losing it in 1993,' said Padre. 'At night I'd hear noises outside, so I used to have a pick-handle under the bed and I'd sneak out to try to find the cause of the noise. Catch them!'

'I live down the border in the country,' said Huck, 'and, even now, I've been known to patrol the area at night, with a gun.'

'I was a drill sergeant for two-and-a-half years,' said Headhunter, 'and I tried to run my family like that.'

'I don't sit in a room unless I've got my back against something solid,' said Mutha. 'Even in a restaurant, I'll go and sit in the corner with my back always covered. I'm never in bed before 3 am, and I'm up again at seven. Most of us still get our night sweats. You'll hear the thump-thump noises, the choppers, guys yelling, guys talking. I have a radio going in the room, and it's set just off the channel a bit, making a hissing noise, because most of us have got tinnitus.'

'The Vietnam experience totally changed my life,' said Huck. 'I would've probably been a headmaster in South Australia. I still would've been happily married to my first wife. I would've had a cruisy life.'

The numbers that describe Australia's commitment to the Vietnam War have changed over the years. The total figure for the men (and the very small number of women) who served has ballooned – particularly with the addition of a large contingent of Royal Australian Navy (RAN), many of whom spent no more than one week on Vietnamese soil or in Vietnamese waters – while the number of national servicemen thought to have been posted to Vietnam has fallen by several thousand. The first Australian regular soldiers arrived in Vietnam in 1962, with what became the Australian Army Training Team Vietnam (AATTV). The first national servicemen came in 1966. Australia left Vietnam in 1972, but there were still a few soldiers in-country – almost all of them embassy guards – until the middle of 1973. According to the figures in the final volume of the *Official History of Australia's Involvement in Southeast Asian Conflicts 1948–1975*, about 60 000 Australians served in Vietnam, including about 41 957 army personnel. Of the army contingent, 15 381 were national servicemen. The DVA lists 521 fatal casualties, of whom 212 entered the Army as national servicemen.

Padre and Mutha believed that Australia was correct to go to Vietnam; Headhunter and Huck said the war was a mistake. But David Forbes, then clinical director of the Australian Centre for Posttraumatic Mental Health at the University of Melbourne, said it makes no difference to their chances of developing PTSD whether men think they were right or wrong to fight. PTSD, he said, has three groups of symptoms: re-experiencing, or 'flashbacks'; avoidance and numbing – feeling emotionally flat, finding it hard to love, and pushing traumatic memories out of the mind; and hyperarousal, which includes sleep disturbance, concentration problems, general irritability, an exaggerated startle, and the kind of hypervigilance that has some men patrolling their yards with pick-handles, and others only ever sitting with their backs to the wall.

The veterans had an angrily poetic understanding of their condition. 'A doctor told me once that there's a certain part in the brain of the male that doesn't mature until they're in their mid- to late-twenties,' said Mutha. 'All the young diggers over there were around 19 to 20 years of age. And that part of the brain, when it gets a massive rush of adrenaline from the fear of death, never ever develops. When you left Vietnam, what you left behind was your common sense and reason.'

Padre said he had heard that 'they believe now that if you ramp a guy up to hypervigilance for a hundred days, you can't turn him off. Once you've got him up there, that's basically it. We thought we were turned off, but 30 years afterwards you find yourself exhibiting a militaristic way of living, because when you're feeling anxious, this is how you stay in control.' Forbes agreed that 'when your traumatic experience is prolonged, and you're in a conflict zone where you're having to be hyperalert and hypervigilant for long periods, there is a significant risk that your whole arousal system gets recalibrated. You've been in high levels of vigilance or arousal for so long that that has become your new baseline.'

According to Forbes, one of the biggest factors affecting whether an ex-serviceman went on to develop PTSD was the amount of social support on which they could rely to help them process, digest and 'validate' their experience. 'An important factor for the Vietnam generation,' he said, 'was the level of conflict within civil society that they came back to – the degree to which many of them felt accused for having fought in Vietnam.'

When VVMC members were out on the road with their comrades, they said, they got an idea of how they thought things might have been if they had come home from a different war. 'When we ride, we've got our banner flying at the back, and however many of us on bikes,' said Headhunter. 'Two weeks ago, we went to the township of Woombye and we rode in as a troop. I was so proud, and the crowd there, they were cheering us, and when we got to the pub they all came to see us, and they enjoyed it. And they came back the next morning and invited us back. Every place we've gone to, we've been invited back. And you feel proud of that.'

'It's being with blokes you like,' said Skip. 'Standing out. Being admired again. On Anzac Day, we march as the VVMC. We don't march with the units we were in Vietnam with. This is now our unit. They stick us right down the arse end of the parade, which is fine. We get the biggest cheer coming around the corner.'

It was getting late, and I was fizzy with XXXX when the Vegetable Lady arrived with her zipper bag. I left before I could find out what was inside, but I filed a piece of reportage which, I felt, accurately reflected the stories told to me by the veterans, their partners and Dr Forbes. The accounts of the veterans seemed to me interchangeable, and I structured my article to reflect that. I repeated, faithfully and uncritically, that the men came back from Vietnam to face a national consensus that they were 'bludgers, baby killers, morons'. I did not think to check if this was really a widespread belief at the time. I did not question the story about the man who painted his boss, or ask to meet the painter, or even wonder how it might be possible to paint an adult human being who, presumably, was an unwilling participant in the process. I did not ask how or under what circumstances Headhunter had a bucket of paint poured over him, or how he knew the bucketeer was a student. I did not press him for a date, a location, or a newspaper report, because I believed it must be true. After all, everybody knew Vietnam veterans routinely had buckets of (red) paint poured over them by students. I repeated Huck's assertion that he had been flown home in the middle of the night to avoid demonstrators, because I understood that the Army would have been sufficiently fearful of student protesters to redesign its flight schedules around their plans to demonstrate – and, of course, I accepted that the protesters would want to meet the soldiers at the airport and douse them in spit and red paint, because the soldiers had been away in Vietnam committing atrocities, shooting first and then interrogating the (probably civilian) corpses.

Having spent almost six years studying the media of the period – first for a book, *The Nashos' War*, then for my doctoral thesis – I no longer believe a significant number of people in the 1960s and early 1970s regarded Vietnam veterans as baby-killers, bludgers or morons – although negative stereotypes of the returned men existed in some circles, and these stereotypes altered, mutated and probably intensified from the late 1970s through to the mid-1980s. I doubt Old Frankie painted his boss. I do not think Australian students poured paint over returning soldiers in Australia in 1972 – or that they held any protests against returning soldiers that year. I doubt that many – if any – Australian veterans were spat upon. I do not think many – if any – Australians committed large-scale atrocities. I know no serviceman was flown home in the middle of the night specifically to 'avoid protesters'. But I also know that I wrote my story in good faith. I believed what I was told, and I am certain the men who spoke to me felt they were telling the truth.

I also wrote, 'Queensland is the veterans' favourite state. The open spaces, clear skies and silence draw them in from all over the country. Men can disappear in Queensland, living in the bush in swags, dugouts or huts, or off the coast in fishing boats or yachts, still waiting for an enemy that never comes.'[2] I cannot remember why I felt Queensland might be home to more retired soldiers than, for example, superannuated journalists or zoo-keepers. Today, I have grave doubts that a significant number of veterans live in isolated camps in the bush – except for those who choose to spend time in dedicated therapeutic retreats – and even fewer expect an attack from the Vietcong (VC). To my embarrassment, my assertion about Queensland is quoted uncritically in the distinguished historian KS Inglis's magnificent history of Australian war memorials,[3] presumably because it sounds lyrical and romantic. But this serves as an example of a phenomenon that reoccurs throughout Australia's literature of Vietnam, in which an inaccurate, unconsidered statement of one sincere writer is picked up by a learned, earnest author, and quoted, footnoted and enshrined as fact.

There is more to any feature story than the words that end up on the page. While I was interviewing members of the VVMC, I was told in a whisper that Headhunter had spent his time in Vietnam carrying a bunch of Vietnamese heads in a bag. I believed it. I never stopped to consider the practicalities of soldiering through the jungle weighed down by a bag of heads. I concluded that there was so much more I was not being told – the stuff of dark allusion, and secrets taken to the grave – that I could never give my readers a true picture of the horror of Vietnam. Therefore, I can understand why someone who had heard or read the story of the beheadings, and knew he could not attribute it to the alleged decapitator, might decide to recount another story of a man who carried heads in a bag. Or he might simply make the broad claim that Australian soldiers in Vietnam walked around with heads in bags, and never reference his source. That person might believe that lending the anecdote to a fictitious character would be an act closer to telling the truth than ignoring the anecdote and pretending the atrocity had never happened. Similarly – almost identically – a soldier who claims to have had paint thrown over him but who did not, personally, have paint thrown over him, might believe the 'reality' that veterans had paint thrown over them would be ignored if other men did not tell their tale. Or he might be simply making the broad claim that anti-war protesters walked around with buckets of paint, throwing them over soldiers.

It can be difficult to feel sympathy for a man who murders

innocent people and takes their heads as trophies. It is only possible within a paradigm that embraces the soldier as a victim – a victim of impossible circumstances, political machinations and military brutalisation. And the victim paradigm is a favourite of right-thinking (that is, left-thinking) people like me. Sometimes, it seems it is the only way we can accommodate the veteran within our worldview. More surprisingly, the ideological right, historically more comfortable with the view of fighting men as heroes, has come to see Vietnam veterans as victims too – but as victims of a brutal and misguided, thoughtless and immature anti-war movement.

The thing that strikes me the most, as I read back through my story, is how little I learned about what the men really did, in the army or in Vietnam. Alessandro Portelli has written that the question 'Daddy, what did you do in the war?', posed in a 'naïve picture of the schoolchild interviewing a grandparent about World War I', has been often 'used to belittle the whole enterprise of oral history'.[4] My magazine feature, essentially a montage of oral history interviews, barely even sought to address the enquiry.

In 2011, before my Vietnam projects began, I was appointed editor of *The Penguin Book of Australian War Writing*, an anthology whose contents ranged from memoir of the 18th-century European invasion of Aboriginal Australia to reportage from 21st-century Afghanistan. I noticed there was little of aesthetic value in the non-official professionally published literature of Australia's Vietnam War and, with the exception of Barry Heard, author of *Well Done, Those Men*, few of the veterans had much range or ambition as writers. I was also surprised to discover there was no single-volume history of the 1964–72 national service scheme.

Since the book I wanted to read did not exist, I resolved to write it myself. The fruit of this rather rash decision was *The Nashos' War*, published in 2014 and based on archival research and about 160 semi-structured interviews with former national servicemen, the great majority of whom had served in Vietnam.

In February 2012, just before I began to write *The Nashos' War*, I was privileged to travel to Vietnam on a tour of Australian war sites which was co-led by Alexander 'Sandy' MacGregor MC, a retired colonel who had served in Vietnam as a captain with the Royal Australian Engineers (RAE) and is the co-author of *Tunnel Rats*, a lively journalistic history of combat engineers in Vietnam.

MacGregor was combative with our Vietnamese guides. He stiffened at suggestions the VC might have been patriots, or that their cause was just, and challenged any implication that the US and their allies might have been careless with Vietnamese lives. He repeatedly asked a guide if his former-VC relatives have changed their minds about communism. It seemed important to MacGregor that others might believe his war was justified, but he told me he did not care what they thought. 'I know that we did the right thing,' he said.

Later, he revealed that he had first returned to Vietnam in the mid-1990s because he had hoped to learn how the Vietnamese felt about Australians who had fought in the war and 'whether there was any forgiveness on their part'. He was pleased to discover there was no animosity.

Reconciliation had reached the heart of MacGregor's life in 1987, when three of his daughters and one of their friends were shot dead in Sydney by a mentally ill stalker named Richard Maddrell, who had chosen not to take his medication on the day of the killings. MacGregor turned to meditation and mind-control techniques to deal with his grief, and eventually visited Maddrell in jail and offered him a father's forgiveness. MacGregor said, 'I didn't do it for Maddrell. I did it for me. Forgiveness is for the forgiver, not for the forgiven. I think there were parallels between talking with the Vietcong and Maddrell. Forgiveness is a process of cleansing for yourself, so you can get on with your own life. I didn't want there to be bitterness and hatred with the Vietcong that would consume me, and I didn't want to be affected by bitterness between me and Maddrell.'[5]

Like many of my generation, my first conscious exposure to Vietnam veterans took place in a cinema, through the blustering cruelties of the 1982 US action movie *First Blood*, in which Sylvester Stallone stars as disturbed and expertly violent former Special Forces soldier and ex-POW John Rambo. The hero who responds to humiliation and harassment at the hands of a small-town police force by beating up the deputies, slaying the tracker dogs sent after him, and killing the deputy sheriff. After speaking to MacGregor, it struck me that there was some distance between the paths to closure chosen by the fictional US veteran in the movie and by a genuine Australian veteran in real life.

The year after I toured Vietnam, I interviewed John Stuart 'Charlie' Lynn, who was then a Liberal member of the NSW Legislative Council. Lynn is a one-time national serviceman who signed on as a regular soldier in 1967 to experience a year-long tour of duty in Vietnam, but ended up serving only five months in-country with 17th Construction Squadron – and retiring as a major in 1986. His daughter Sharon was raped in October 1986 by Peter Nightingale, a stranger who threatened to kill her if she resisted. Her attacker was identified the next day but was freed on bail for 21 months before he was finally convicted and sentenced to three years' imprisonment with an 18-month non-parole period.

Lynn was furious at the leniency of the sentence and swore he would force his daughter's rapist to pay for his crime. He told the press (perhaps apocryphally) that he had been contacted by an Army friend who had known Sharon since she was a baby – 'He stood on a mine in Vietnam,' said Lynn, 'and he now has only one leg, one arm, one finger and one thumb. He rang me and said, "Well, I can't do much but I can drive the getaway car."'[6] But instead of going after Nightingale, Lynn founded a community pressure group, Victims Against Crime and Corruption, to campaign for tougher sentencing and victims' rights. He told me he had decided that he could not act outside the system as he had defended that same system his whole life.[7]

From this admittedly small sample, it seemed to me that Vietnam veterans did not necessarily respond to extreme pressure with extreme violence. If anything, they appeared more rational and committed to the rule of law than non-veterans. In addition, Lynn's position as a member of parliament hardly matched the disturbed drifter Rambo image. Other Vietnam veterans to have sat in Australian parliaments include Tim Fischer, a national service officer with 1RAR who served in Vietnam from April 1968 to February 1969, was elected to the NSW state legislature in February 1971, and eventually became leader of the National Party and deputy prime minister of Australia; Ernest Ross Smith, a Regular Army officer who had been caught up in the famous 'water-torture' scandal in Vietnam and who sat as a Liberal in the Victorian parliament from 1985 to 2002; John Walter Bradford, a national service officer with the RAAOC who served in Vietnam from October 1969 to October 1970 and went on to represent the Queensland seat of McPherson as a Liberal Party/Christian Democratic Party member from March 1990 to October 1998; Frank Donovan, a regular soldier who toured Vietnam with

5RAR from May 1966 to May 1967 and sat as ALP member for Morley-Swan in the Legislative Assembly of WA from 1989 to 1991, then left the party to sit as an independent until 1993 (his dissatisfactions with the ALP included the party's decision to send service personnel to the Gulf War); Graham John Edwards, a regular soldier with 7RAR who lost both his legs to a landmine in Vietnam in May 1970 and held the Western Australian seat of Cowan for the ALP from October 1998 to October 2007; Greg Hall, a national service trooper with B Squadron, 3rd Cavalry Regiment in Vietnam from August 1969 to June 1970, who sat as an independent in the Tasmanian Legislative Council from 2001 to 2018; Kevin Newman, a Regular Army officer who commanded a company of 2RAR/NZ (ANZAC) from May 1967 to April 1968 and held the Tasmanian seat of Bass for the Liberal Party from June 1975 to October 1984; and James Pearce, a former national service corporal with the RAASC who served in Vietnam from July 1969 to June 1970 and sat in the Queensland Legislative Assembly as the ALP member for Mirani from January 2015 to November 2017.

Evidently, not all veterans were hiding out in humpies in the scrub, and the proportion of (Army) veterans who went on to become parliamentarians probably compares favourably with retired zookeepers, if not with former journalists. Equally clearly, the public opprobrium supposedly extended towards Vietnam veterans was of insufficient depth to thwart their popular election to parliaments throughout the country, as candidates for all three major parties, during the war or at any time since – even if, like Ross Smith, they had been present outside the tent at the alleged torture of a female prisoner.

In *The Nashos' War*, I hoped to fill in some of the particulars missing from my VVMC feature, build a picture of the daily lives of national servicemen in a war zone, and recount in more detail events that I believed had shattered the psyches of returned men. Like many writers before me, I was drawn to the stories of the protests that were thought to have met the troops at Sydney Airport. I was particularly interested in the narrative of 'Mike' from the pamphlet *Homecomings*, which was first published as part of the Vietnam Veterans Counselling Service or VVCS (now Open Arms – Veterans & Families Counselling) contribution to the 1987 Australian Vietnam Forces Welcome Home Parade and National Reunion. Ostensibly, Mike was a national serviceman who had served in the Royal Australian Artillery in Vietnam and come back to Sydney, relieved, in January 1970, when, he said, 'At Mascot, the relief turned to anger. We were pelted with tomatoes and spat on. But we got our satisfaction afterwards – 150 toey, angry lads from Vietnam versus 400 demonstrators – they didn't stand a chance. The cops were very good about it. They seemed to be otherwise occupied for a while ... It's something you never forget ... to be spat on and treated like shit.'[8]

I pursued this story because I hoped to flesh out 'Mike's' account with those of other men at the airport that evening and track down some of the protesters who were beaten by the soldiers. My only interest, at that stage, was to build a dramatic narrative, perhaps a set piece for the later pages of *The Nashos' War* that might demonstrate the depths of the divide that had opened in Australian society by 1970. After all, the battle at the airport would have been one of the largest outbreaks of mass political violence in 20th-century Australia. However, there *are* no other accounts of the event. It was not reported in any newspaper, in January 1970 or at any other time. It does not appear in the literature of the left, nor in the right-wing publications that keenly monitored the activities of the anti-war movement. Beyond Mike's pseudonymous testimony, there is no evidence that it ever happened.

I began to have doubts about many of the stories I was reading. While initially I had embraced the model of the veterans' experience as outlined in my VVMC feature, several of the narratives about soldiers being confronted and spat on by protesters seemed on closer examination to be apocryphal. Often, it was impossible to investigate them, as the details provided were so sparse, but when there was a date and location attached to the story, there was rarely even a hint of corroboration to be found. If these stories were untrue, then I began to wonder if the assumption on which they were founded – that there was widespread, violent hostility to the veterans upon their return from Vietnam – might also be mistaken.

It seems to me now that mythology dogs and distorts the Australian soldier's Vietnam experience, from its beginnings (for some) in the workings of the national servicemen's birthdate-lottery selection process – to its end, in the lost memories of 16 often enormous, enthusiastic wartime welcome home parades.

What do I mean by mythology? Until the 20th century, the term almost always referred to the Greek myths, although many writers about Vietnam appear to regard a myth as any idea with which they disagree. But myths are traditional stories that survive the passing of gods and demons because they are thought to contain some truth about the world. They are poetic conceptions of the past. Aristotle wrote that the true difference between the historian and the poet was 'one relates what has happened, the other what may happen ... how a person of a certain type will on occasion speak or act, according to the law of probability or necessity'.[9] Many of the stories recounted by veterans about protesters, for example, would seem to be told to demonstrate how such people – as conceived by the veteran – might be expected to act, rather than anything they did. Therefore, when I talk about some veterans' stories as mythological, I do not consider them to be mistaken or dishonest, but tales that are based on arche-types – the rejected returning serviceman; the soldier as a dupe of higher powers; the man-hating feminist; the fanatical agitator – and told to make sense of subsequent events. It has been said that 'what informants believe is indeed a historical fact (that is, the fact they believe it) as much as what really happened',[10] but people believe all kinds of things, for reasons that range across the whole breadth of human experience. The Vikings believed that the thunder god Thor fought a giant sea serpent but, as the earthy Australian historian Graham Wilson points out, 'No-one would offer the myth of the battles of the Norse gods as accept-able Scandinavian military history.'[11]

Initially, I had imagined that the national service experience was at the heart of almost every fabrication about Australia's Vietnam War, but it often makes little sense to separate the participation of national servicemen from regular soldiers. The myths explored in this book – that every Australian soldier sent to Vietnam was a volunteer; that, in the words of Headhunter, many Australian soldiers saw (or committed) 'lots of atrocities'; that there were no welcome home parades for the veterans; that returning men faced demonstrations at Sydney Airport; that women spat on them – congealed in the public mind through the agglutination of accumulated testimony of both conscripts and volunteers, accepted uncritically by well-meaning journalists and historians.

In parts, this book goes over similar ground to *The Nashos' War* and picks at some of the same scabs – to heal, I hope, rather than to scar. In *The Nashos' War*, I merely identified the myths.

Here, I try to explain what they mean and how they came to be. I lay out my data, show the workings behind my calculations, and hope against hope I will not be misunderstood.

Why is another book even necessary? The flow of misinformation continues despite *The Nashos' War*. I attended a conference where one of the speakers – who had clearly read *The Nashos' War* and seen the evidence I had laid out to the contrary – continued to claim no man had been sent to Vietnam against his will. The myth of the rigged ballot reappeared reinvigorated with the release of the Normie Rowe compilation album *Frenzy!* in 2015, when the long-discredited story of the supposed mystery behind the singer's conscription was raised once again – despite it having been repeatedly and comprehensively disproved – in *The Saturday Paper* and other credible (and credulous) media.[12] New lurid claims about the relationship between the anti-war movement and recently returned veterans continued to be made in biographies of men such as Frankie Hunt and Allan Aldenhoven. The circus carried on.

I hope this book might finally put some of the myths to the sword, but I do not believe it will. As the eminent Australian military historian Craig Stockings has written, myths appeal to sentiment more than reason and, 'Many of the misconceptions of Australian military history have survived the blows landed by academics and historians for decades. Each time an individual "story" might lurch or stumble for a short time, but then it seems to grow back undiminished.'[13]

Stockings calls them 'zombies'. I fear it would take more than mere books to slay them.

2

'I want 15,381 volunteers: you, you, you, you, you, you...' The myth of the volunteer in Vietnam

The national serviceman had to specifically volunteer for overseas service by signing a declaration during corps training, and thus all national servicemen who served in Vietnam volunteered to do so.

– *John Healy in* Duty First: The Royal Australian Regiment in war and peace, *1990*[1]

A national serviceman opposed to service in Vietnam has been sentenced to 28 days' confinement at Holsworthy Army camp near Sydney … An army spokesman said last night that Private Morse had been posted to Vietnam and was due to leave Australia soon.

– The Australian, *29 September 1966*

The whole point of Australia's Vietnam-era national service scheme was that conscripts could be compelled to fight overseas. The entire trajectory of Australian Army history through two world wars and beyond had led military planners to conclude that it was necessary for wartime commanders to be able to deploy every trained man. The unqualified acceptance of this contentious requirement was the only reason the Army ultimately accepted the return of national service in 1964, and the primary motivation for mainstream political hostility to the scheme.

The government did not try to hide the element of compulsion. The issue was widely debated in parliament and the press, and the government's position was advertised and unambiguous. On 31 March 1966, in the face of a challenge from the ALP's Jim Cairns, Attorney-General Billy Snedden said he would 'investigate whether legal doubts existed on troops serving overseas without their consent'[2] – since compulsory service overseas was government policy. In April 1966, Malcolm Fraser told journalists at Kingsford Smith Airport that national servicemen could not refuse service in Vietnam, since they 'were an integral part of the army and would not receive special treatment'.[3] *The Age* published a feature entitled 'National Servicemen and Vietnam: A case by the experts', in which the newspaper's correspondent, Hugh Armfield, presented the view conveyed by 'army sources' that, 'It was necessary for the army to know at any given time just how many men it had available to send overseas without juggling units. It was also felt that if a man had been given the opportunity to volunteer for service in Vietnam he may at a later stage, perhaps even while in the field, drop out. The army believes that if it did call for volunteers there would be a good response from the national servicemen. It is understood that surveys have been taken among some national service units which have shown that up to 70 per cent of national servicemen would volunteer for service overseas.'[4]

In the face of all this evidence – and much, much more – it seems extraordinary that there should have developed a broad official consensus that every national serviceman in Vietnam was a volunteer. The idea appears to have been published first in 1990, in *Duty First: The Royal Australian Regiment in war and peace*, an official regimental history edited by David Horner and Jean Bou. Former Director of Infantry John Healy, who served as a company commander during 1RAR's first tour of Vietnam (when the battalion included no national servicemen), wrote: 'The national serviceman had to specifically volunteer for overseas service by signing a declaration during corps training, and thus all national servicemen who served in Vietnam volunteered to do so.'[5] Seven years later, in her appendix to the Official History volume *A Nation at War*, Sue Langford wrote that 'the general impression given by serving Army officers at the time is that more national servicemen were keen to serve in Vietnam than were needed, and that those unwilling to serve there were transferred to units serving only in Australia'.[6]

Healy's more firm idea was endorsed by Jeffrey Grey in *The Australian Army: A history* in 2001,[7] but reached the peak of its stridency in Paul Ham's popular history *Vietnam: The Australian war*, when Ham wrote, 'The great myth about conscription was that national servicemen were forced to serve in Vietnam. In fact they were all given the chance not to go.'[8] Actually, the great myth about conscription is that national servicemen were all given the chance *not* to go. Ham uses the same wording as Healy, saying that the national serviceman 'had to specifically volunteer for overseas service by signing a declaration during corps training … all national servicemen who served in Vietnam volunteered to do so', but references it to an author-sighted letter from Brigadier Colin Khan to David Horner. Grey, in *The Australian Army*, references David Horner. It seems that each writer, beginning with Healy, probably took the statement from Colin Khan.

In order to understand why conscripts were compelled to fight the Vietnam War, it is necessary to go back to the First World War. By October 1916, the Australian Imperial Force (AIF) had suffered horrifying casualties in the corpse farms of the Somme and replacements were desperately needed to fill the trenches. The *Defence Act 1911* had mandated military service for all males between the ages of 12 and 25 years old, who would be junior cadets at age 12, senior cadets at 14, and obliged from 18 to enter the Citizen Military Forces (CMF), where they served the equivalent of 16 full days a year as partly trained part-time soldiers – who could not be drafted to fight overseas.

On 28 October 1916, the then-Labor prime minister Billy Hughes sparked a referendum which saw his proposal to conscript men of military age for overseas service defeated by a majority of 72 476 voters. As a direct consequence of this setback, Hughes left the ALP and formed a new 'National Labor' government with Liberal support. In January 1917, the new party merged with the Liberal Party to become the Nationalist Party. In November 1917, Hughes embarked on a second campaign to convince the public of the need to press men to fight. This time, he suggested a 'selective service' scheme, by which 7000 reinforcements a month would be chosen by ballot. The editor of the *Australian Worker* called this 'the Lottery of Death' (a sobriquet later revived to describe the Vietnam War–era ballot) and Hughes's second proposal was defeated by a larger majority of 166 588 voters.

No scheme of conscription for overseas service was ever implemented in Australia during the First World War, but even the debate drove an axe through the ALP and forced the party out of government until 1929, when it indignantly repealed the *Defence Act 1911*.

It is estimated that about 50 000 CMF men enlisted in the AIF during the course of the First World War. Among those who did not was future prime minister Robert Gordon Menzies. A student when war broke out in 1914, Robert Menzies held a commission in the Melbourne University Regiment (MUR) from 1915 but, despite his support for universal conscription, he never joined the AIF. Menzies always declined to give the reasons behind his decision.

In a biography of Menzies published during the Vietnam War, journalist Kevin Perkins wrote that Menzies' two elder brothers, Frank and Les, had volunteered to fight, and it was 'traditional at the time for one son to stay at home in a family of two or more'. However, even if only the bereaved are counted, more than 150 Australian families lost three sons on the battlefield between 1914 and 1918, and at least five families lost four. Famously, six of the seven sons of Frederick and Maggie Smith of the South Australian hamlet of Yongala were killed in action, but the surviving son also volunteered and fought overseas. And Robert was not even the youngest Menzies brother – Syd Menzies was of school age during the war and would have stayed at home anyway.

AW Martin, the author of Menzies' authorised biography, wrote that Frank and Les Menzies had enlisted with their parents' approval, but a 'family conference' – an apparently regular event in the Menzies household – had decided that Robert should stay at home.[9] With a tin ear for the language of Vietnam, a later Liberal prime minister, John Howard, credited Menzies' decision to stay out of the fighting to the 'lottery of birth'.[10] Martin argued that 'if conscription had come into force, Menzies would have been one of the first to be drafted – a fact which he must have known and which would have overridden (possibly to his relief?) whatever other loyalties or scruples were keeping him out of the AIF'.[11]

Menzies may not have been drafted at all under the selective service terms put to voters in the second conscription referendum, which would have drawn troops from a ballot of single men aged 18–44, and there is no logical reason to believe he would have been one of the first. However, it is worth noting that, in the form eventually taken by Menzies' Vietnam War–era national service scheme – by which the only way a man could be certain to escape overseas service was to remain in a CMF unit he had joined before his birthdate was pulled out of a barrel – the young Robert Menzies would definitely *not* have been conscripted.

By the time the Second World War erupted in September 1939, Robert Menzies had become leader of the United Australia Party and prime minister of Australia. His government quickly sent a first batch of 'universal trainees' – all of them unmarried men turning 21 – for three months' compulsory military training, with the guarantee they would be used only within the Commonwealth and its territories. Menzies said in November, 'There is no question of conscription for overseas service. We are definitely pledged against it.'[12] The Labor Party leader John Curtin replied the next day, 'There is no justification for compulsory military training. I see no necessity for it.'[13] Both men were to change their minds.

In October 1941, Labor came into power, this time under Curtin, who had been a dedicated and energetic campaigner for the 'no' vote in the First World War conscription referendums. In May 1942, after the Japanese invasion of New Guinea had been resisted by local militia, Curtin as a military planner – as opposed to a young idealist – declared he could see no logical reason that 'a man could be sent to Darwin, where he could be bombed, but not to Timor to save Darwin from being bombed'.[14]

Decades before Menzies was faced with similar accusations over Vietnam, Curtin was harangued by his own Minister for Labour and National Service, Eddie Ward: 'You're putting young men into the slaughterhouse ... although 30 years ago you would not go into it yourself.'[15]

The January 1943 Special Federal Labor Party Conference backed Curtin, and the subsequent Militia Act which allowed the CMF to be used as part of the Australian Military Forces in the South West Pacific. Curtin admitted he was 'very disappointed' in the limited scope of the changes, which would not enable the militia to join a MacArthur offensive in the Philippines.[16] While the Militia Act did not split the Labor Party as some had feared, it increased passionate and public enmity between Curtin's leadership and that part of the party represented by the anti-conscriptionist Arthur Calwell. In the end, the war was won with only the smallest contribution by conscripted Australians: militiamen were barely deployed beyond areas where they might have expected to find themselves before the Act was passed, although the 11th Brigade of the CMF served outside Australian territory in the Dutch East Indies in 1943–44.

In two great conflicts, two distinguished leaders had sullied their legacies by advocating for others a fate they had avoided themselves, and two very different governments had been unable to mobilise a maximum number of men of military age to fight overseas due to adherence (however reluctant or limited) to the principles of volunteerism.

Curtin died in the Lodge in July 1945. The ALP under Ben Chifley remained in power until the December 1949 election of a conservative Coalition government, once again headed by Robert Menzies. An important plank of the new government's platform was the establishment of a national service scheme, with the idea that young Australians would be taught basic military skills in peacetime, which they could use in wartime if they came forward to serve. National Service was held to be necessary because it was recognised that 'under the system in the past, there [had] not been anywhere near the required number of volunteers, either for the Regular Army or the CMF, to provide a trained force in the required time' to mobilise against an immediate threat.[17] It was not, however, envisaged as a substitute for volunteering, but rather a kind of pre-enlistment program for potential volunteers.

Training under the new scheme began in 1951, and it was initially promoted as universal.[18] The scheme would be administered by the Department of Labour and National Service (DLNS). Every 18-year-old male was required to register for 176 days' training with either the Army, the Navy or the Air Force. If they chose the Army, they served the first 98 days consecutively (77 days for students), with an additional 78 days of drills and camps with the CMF. There was no requirement for national servicemen to serve overseas unless they chose to join the Navy or the Air Force, where they were obliged to see out the full period in a single block and leave the country if necessary.

The sailors' and airmen's liability for overseas service was clearly spelled out to the public and publicised in the press, just as the soldiers' responsibilities were later made clear in the 1964 scheme: the *Argus* reported Navy and Air Force trainees would be required to fight 'in the event of the war at any time within five years of joining up'. DLNS officials said young sailors and airmen would be required to sign 'an instrument of volunteering' and 'if they did not sign they could not serve with the Air Force or the Navy, but must go to the Army'. Army trainees, meanwhile, could only be called on to serve in Australia and New Guinea (where some CMF units were based).[19]

It was hoped and assumed that a large number of men would volunteer to stay on with the CMF at the end of their period of compulsory service.[20] At this juncture in Australia's defence planning, it was projected that there would not be a third AIF – in the event of an expeditionary war, the CMF would make up the bulk of the field force. However, these plans were hamstrung by the existing Defence Act, which prevented the CMF from fighting overseas except under specific measures in the case of a world war.

The government used financial inducement to inspire men to make themselves available for war. CMF volunteers were already entitled to an 'efficiency grant' of £10 per annum if they attested they were willing to serve overseas. In February 1952, when the government agreed that equal conditions should exist between national servicemen and CMF volunteers, national servicemen became eligible for the grant too. In the eyes of the Military Board, which was responsible for the administration of all matters relating to military forces, the main task remaining was 'the encouragement of the National Serviceman ... to volunteer for service overseas'.[21]

The government had predicted it would have 30 000 CMF volunteers by 1953. In fact, the number was much smaller – closer to 15 000, or only 25 per cent of all national servicemen. The situation was made far worse by the fact that about 2000 willing soldiers had quit the CMF to join the Regular Army and fight in Korea. Since conscripts could only be sent overseas if they volunteered, and only one in four had volunteered, the regulations had created a curious situation in which volunteer officers and non-commissioned officers (NCOs) could be relied upon to go to war, but they would not necessarily have more than a quarter of their troops to command.

There was much debate over proposals to exempt from national service any youth who lived more than five miles from a CMF training establishment. This was an idea that proved popular with Country Party MPs, and several supported the proposal that, if the ideal of universal service was to be abandoned, those who served should be chosen by ballot.[22] It soon became clear that youths in remote areas had never been called up anyway. The universal scheme had not really been universal as 50 000 young men had never received their training. In addition, most CMF units were at full strength by 1953, although the CMF was not to reach its peak strength until 1955, when it could boast more than 85 000 active personnel.[23] The CMF could not feasibly grow much larger, but – due to immigration and a higher birthrate – there were many more 18-year-olds in Australia than the government had anticipated. The *Sydney Morning Herald* summarised the government's predicament: 'National Service intake has swollen to such dimensions – apparently, if inexplicably, unexpected by the Government – that an unduly high proportion of the Regular Army personnel has to be diverted from combatant units [to train the national servicemen]. The result has been the near paralysis of the A.R.A. as an effective fighting force – which means that Australia is in no shape to make an adequate contribution in any South-East Asian emergency.'[24]

Not only did the government have insufficient numbers of CMF men who were willing to fight overseas, professional soldiers were prevented from fighting because they were needed to train men who would never fight.

At the end of September 1954, the government announced that it would indeed defer all youths who lived more than five miles away from a military base ('out-of-radius personnel') and also every other rural worker. It was stressed that the deferment was in response to short-term needs and would not be indefinite – deferred men could remain liable for call-up until the age of 26 (which later became the standard cut-off for most men in the 1964 scheme). While the press – like its readers – had been vigorously supportive of national service in its early years, the Sydney *Daily Telegraph* admitted in 1955 that the training was of little real military benefit and the scheme had not only been 'a waste of defence funds, it has been a waste, too, of many trainees' time and industrial ability'.[25] The Navy and Air Force reduced the number of trainees' days to 154, further compromising their effectiveness.

A defence review in 1957 abolished universal service and replaced it with a system of selective conscription based on a birthdate ballot, which would train only 12 000 young men each year, all of whom would serve an initial 77 days' full-time training in the CMF and an additional 63 days' service over two years. The Navy and Air Force were excluded from the system altogether.

Under the reduced arrangement, the birthdates of potential Army national servicemen would be represented by marbles plucked from a barrel. The number of marbles drawn would be calculated with allowances made for similar percentages of defer-ments and unfit candidates to those in previous registrations. The Minister for Labour and National Service, Harold Holt, said the ballot had 'the great virtues of being simple, fair, easily understood and of not lending itself to any manipulation'.[26]

In 1958, the CMF Member of the Military Board, Major General Risson, said the government should make overseas service a compulsory component of national service. Back-benchers such as Liberal Party MP Sir Wilfrid Kent Hughes – a colourful figure who had fought in the First World War in the

Middle East; declared himself a fascist in 1933; fought in the Second World War in Malaya; been imprisoned by the Japanese and liberated by the Red Army – argued the selective scheme should run for 18 months or two years, and national servicemen should be sent overseas if necessary. In 1959, there was a reassessment of the principles on which Australian defence planning was based: the emphasis shifted to regular forces, partly because only 16 500 CMF men had volunteered for overseas service – but even they could not necessarily be ordered to fight. Transferred national service volunteers had to step out of the umbrella of the National Service Act entirely and volunteer for the CMF a second time before they could be sent to war![27]

As it turned out, no national serviceman saw combat during the 1950s scheme, which finally came to an end in November 1959, but it had been hugely popular throughout the 1950s, with the approval of 83–88 per cent of voters.[28] The last national serviceman who had been conscripted into the CMF was discharged on 30 June 1960.

There can be no doubt that one of the biggest problems with the 1950s national service scheme was that trainees had to volunteer for overseas service. This was a mistake that the government and the Army would not see repeated in 1964, when Menzies' last national service arrangement finally put an end to the voluntary principle.

Australia's Vietnam commitment began in 1962, when the government sent a team of 30 military advisers – eventually designated the Australian Army Training Team Vietnam (AATTV) – to help train the Army of the Republic of Vietnam (ARVN) to fight a communist–nationalist insurgency, partially maintained and ultimately directed by the government of North Vietnam, against the government of South Vietnam.

As the military situation in Vietnam turned more volatile, Menzies became concerned that the Australian Army might have to fight on three fronts – against Indonesia in the newly independent Malaysia; against Indonesian 'subversion' in Papua New Guinea; and perhaps also in support of the US and the ARVN in South Vietnam. Menzies was convinced the Army would have to expand to meet these potential challenges, and the impetus for a new national service scheme came not from the military but from the Menzies government. It was Army Minister Jim Forbes who concluded in early 1963 that national service was the 'only solution' to the Army's post-war recruiting problems, but Forbes found it difficult to persuade the Chief of General Staff, General John Wilton, who feared a repeat of the 1950s fiasco. It took more than a year for Wilton to come around to the idea that national service was inevitable, and even then the general would only countenance a 'highly selective scheme' with a small annual intake committed to compulsory overseas service.

Wilton would not have agreed to another national service proposal where Army manpower was determined by the caprice of individual soldiers. He would not countenance a situation whereby men were given the option of volunteering to fight. Once Wilton had acquiesced to a limited, compulsory proposal, the potential hazards of the arrangement were canvassed in depth. The DLNS gave the view that the precedent of the 1950s scheme did not 'provide a warrant' for the new proposal and that 'in administration and in public reaction the two schemes would be vastly different'. The proposed scheme would be 'at least twelve times as selective' as its predecessor, and last 'more than five times as long': 'And – an immense difference from national service – it is proposed they should be liable to be sent overseas.'

The department pointed out 'it is one thing to favour compulsory service in the abstract, it is quite another to face this prospect for oneself or one's son, and especially when oneself or one's son is at worst 1 in 100 or at best one of 6 in 100'.[29] However, with Wilton's late acquiescence, Menzies was keen to push forward.

On 10 November 1964, the government announced that selective national service training had become 'inescapable'.[30] Once again, it was a tremendously popular idea: a Gallup poll reported that 71 per cent of Australians were in favour of conscription.[31] Arrangements began to be put in place for the new scheme.

On 14 December 1964, the US president Lyndon Johnson wrote to Menzies canvassing the possibility that Australia might send 200 additional military advisers to Vietnam. He specifically excluded ground forces from his bid but asked for medical and naval support that was beyond Australia's capabilities. On 17 December, the Foreign Affairs and Defence Committee of Cabinet met to discuss a response. The historian Garry Woodard describes the meeting as 'lacking in rigour and surprisingly brief'. The Australian Chiefs of Staff had recommended Australia might offer a battalion instead, and Menzies favoured this solution. (Woodard calls this 'foisting the battalion on Johnson'.[32]) The Official Historian Peter Edwards wrote, 'The new national service system meant that Australia would find it easier to send a battalion (of about 800 troops) than the 200 advisers, who would have been drawn from precisely the army ranks required to train the conscripts.'[33] In other words, Australia could not supply particular Regular Army volunteers for Vietnam as they would be needed to train general national servicemen who might eventually be sent to Vietnam. If these national servicemen were subsequently given the option to opt out of (or into) the deployment, the entire arrangement would become farcical. In April 1965, in reply to a formal US request that Australia and New Zealand field about 150 instructors to Vietnam, Cabinet instead offered the battalion, along with an SAS squadron and logistical support troops.[34] Australia's infantry build-up in Vietnam had commenced.

The first intake of national servicemen marched into recruit training battalions (RTBs) in June 1965. Each man was issued with an *Information Booklet for National Servicemen*, which clearly stated, 'When a unit is required for overseas service, National Servicemen serving in it will normally accompany the unit overseas for the remaining period of their service ... In this connection, units of the Australian Army are at present serving overseas in Malaya, Singapore, Borneo, New Guinea and South Vietnam.'[35]

By May 1966, however, it became apparent some mysterious person or persons in the Army had been circulating forms asking for volunteers for overseas service. When the matter was raised in parliament, Fraser admitted 'some units' of the Army had prepared questionnaires asking national servicemen what kind of corps training they preferred and in 'one or two' of these there was a reference to overseas service. These questionnaires were 'not issued by the Government or the Army as such, and questions about overseas service had been withdrawn to prevent misunderstanding', said Fraser.[36] In June 1966, Fraser wrote a newspaper piece in which he said that 'under a system of calling for volunteers from National Servicemen military planners would never know how many volunteers might come forward'.[37]

In September 1966 a national serviceman who refused to go to Vietnam was sentenced to 28 days' confinement at Holsworthy. A 'Private J Morse, 20, of Randwick' was court-martialled at Victoria Barracks and sentenced on two counts of having refused to obey lawful commands when ordered to pick up his equipment and board an army vehicle. An army spokesman said that 'Private Morse had been posted to Vietnam and was due to leave Australia soon ... Private Morse was alleged to have said on several occasions that he would not serve in Vietnam'.[38]

Many Vietnam veterans believe they recall an informal, voluntary selection process for overseas service. Mike Towers, a former national serviceman who went to Vietnam with 1 Australian Reinforcement Unit then served with 4RAR, and who insists he was sent to Vietnam against his will, writes that volunteers were solicited and 'those who did not want to serve in Vietnam were ordered to take a pace forward ... Peer group pressure and this contemptible reversal of normal volunteering procedure ensured that many unconvinced and frightened men did "volunteer".'[39]

Towers was sent to Vietnam anyway, and his picture of military volunteering is barely contested. When veterans suggest every man was a volunteer, they tend to agree every man went through a similar process to that outlined by Towers. Those who claim that all national servicemen volunteered accept that they were subjected to pressure from both their mates and their officers – and a service culture based on hierarchy and obedience – and chose to go along with the majority. In this version of events, the men may have chosen out of expedience rather than conviction, but they made a choice nonetheless. However, it is far from clear that even these remembered opting-out parades are anything more than myth.

I had hoped to lay the volunteer question to rest in *The Nashos' War*, in which I presented evidence that one man, Corporal David Wittner of the Royal Australian Army Medical Corps, had, on 11 July 1970, upon learning that he had been scheduled to attend the battle efficiency course prior to embarkation for

South Vietnam, written to the Minister for the Army, Andrew Peacock. Wittner told Peacock he had informed his commanding officer in writing that, although he was prepared to serve anywhere in Australia, he definitely did not want to go to South Vietnam. Wittner said he was soon to be married, did not believe in Australia's commitment to the war, and was prepared to go absent without leave rather than accept an overseas posting. The reply he received from Peacock read, 'While the Army endeavours to employ every soldier in a location of his choice, this is not always possible and when the requirements of the Army and the soldier are at variance, the needs of the Service must take precedence ... Careful consideration has been given to your case but it does not appear that the circumstances are such as to warrant your retention in Australia on compassionate grounds ... retention may only be granted for the most pressing reasons. I am, therefore, unable to accede to your request.'[40]

In other words, Wittner was a radiographer, the Army needed radiographers in South Vietnam, Wittner was in the Army and he was therefore going to South Vietnam. Wittner eventually served in South Vietnam with 1 Australian Field Hospital from September 1970 to September 1971.

The evidence here does not come from Wittner's memory – both sides of the correspondence remain in Wittner's Army service record and are reproduced in this book as Appendix I. As a radiographer, Wittner was a highly trained specialist who would be far more difficult to replace than an ordinary infantryman or clerk, and it's not unreasonable to suggest that men in similar positions might have been the only soldiers compelled to serve in South Vietnam. However, immediately upon publication of *The Nashos' War*, I received correspondence from Patrick Davoren of Brisbane, who served as a corporal in South Vietnam with

2 Advanced Ordnance Depot (2AOD) of the Royal Australian Army Ordnance Corps (RAAOC) in the period December 1970 – October 1971. Davoren, too, had done all he could to avoid being sent overseas. On 25 November 1970, he had refused to take his pre-embarkation leave, as he was not willing to embark for South Vietnam. His refusal was recorded by his adjutant on a witnessed document which was appended with a note written the next day stating that Davoren had been informed of the contents of Section 51 of the National Service Act.[41] On 1 December, Davoren refused to attend his pre-embarkation medical and was charged with disobeying a lawful command when ordered by a sergeant to report to the Regimental Aid Post. Both the adjutant's note and the charge sheet are part of Davoren's service record, as is a report from 2AOD in South Vietnam stating 'soldier is not happy about being in SVN – but making the most of his lot'.

Some long-held convictions seem impervious to evidence. When I spoke publicly about Wittner's and Davoren's cases, I was accused, slightly bafflingly, of working from a sample that was 'too large'.[42] This appeared to be a variation on the idea that in an infinite universe there are infinite possibilities: that is, if I were to interview every one of the 15 381 national servicemen who were sent to South Vietnam, I would eventually hear every variation on the conscripts' story. In some ways, this was the point I was trying to make – just because a thousand men might have been given the chance to volunteer, it does not mean that every man was afforded that privilege. By the same token, the opposite is true – just because one man was not given the choice, it does not mean a thousand others were compelled to obey. There is solid documentary evidence that Wittner and Davoren were sent to Vietnam against their will, therefore the statements made by Paul Ham and John Healy, that no man was compelled to serve, are not true. This does not mean, however, that only two men were compelled.

The bulk of the volunteering debate has occurred decades after the fact, but it's perhaps worthy of note that, while the war was still being fought, one of the few national servicemen who publicly identified himself as having been sent to South Vietnam under duress was Rodney Power. He wrote to the *Sunday Australian* in 1971 to say, 'I was a nasho and did not volunteer for service there. When ordered to go, I made known my objections to my commanding officer, but to no avail.'[43] Power, like Davoren, was an RAAOC soldier (albeit a private) at 2AOD. Power left 2AOD the month before Davoren arrived. This suggests there may have been a policy within the RAAOC of overriding objections, at least during the period 1969–71.

Many other men recall signing a form volunteering for overseas service, an idea that probably has its roots in the documents circulated in 1966 and denounced by Malcolm Fraser. However, as former Regular Army officer and Vietnam veteran Ernest Benjamin Morris wrote, 'This "volunteering form" has not been found in any national serviceman's personal file that I have encountered in the course of this research. After my Vietnam service I served in the Third Training Battalion preparing men for Vietnam and I never saw the form under discussion. The register of Government forms contains no such form. The National Service Bill presented to Parliament and passed into legislation did not set out a procedure for volunteering.'[44]

I, too, examined a large number of national servicemen's service records when researching *The Nashos' War*. I did not find a copy of this form. However, many service records include a form in which the national serviceman is asked to give his first and second preference for corps; give his preference for unit;

express his attitude to the corps to which he is allocated; give up to six preferences for his posting; and express his attitude to the unit to which he is allocated. This form seems to have been designed to be issued both to all men at the end of basic training and to infantrymen at the end of corps training (its heading is 'PLATOON SUMMARY OF PERFORMANCE IN BASIC/INF CORPS TRAINING TRG.' and either 'BASIC' or 'INF CORPS' has to be struck out). Most – if not all – of these forms that I have personally sighted have been filled out only partially or not at all, and many are unsigned. There is no reference to overseas service.

The Army was driven by the imperative not to fill its ranks with unwilling, unco-operative soldiers who might be a danger to their comrades, but the Army itself was endangered if it appeared that the views of individual soldiers counted for more than their orders. Men could not be seen to get away with disobeying an order to go overseas. Some units seem to have adopted informal procedures to identify reluctant soldiers, but others – such as 2AOD – apparently did not.

When I was working on my doctoral thesis, I was extremely lucky to be given access to an archive created by 7RAR veteran and military historian Michael O'Brien: a collection of more than 200 completed questionnaires circulated among former members of 7RAR who took part in one or both of the battalion's tours of South Vietnam (1967–68 and 1970–71). O'Brien passed the questionnaires on to me to finish the work he had begun: while anecdotes extracted from some of these questionnaires had informed his 1995 study, *Conscripts and Regulars: With the Seventh Battalion in Vietnam*, and he had drawn certain broad conclusions from the mass of responses, he had not completed a statistical analysis of his results. O'Brien's data is immensely valuable as it offers a portrait of the infantryman's war that is all but free of folklore and mythology. The respondents are not veterans bragging – or weeping – to a journalist or a naïve historian, they are men remembering their service to their battalion's intelligence officer.

Most of my work with the 7RAR Survey is not included in this book but is published online with my thesis.[45] However, the survey included a yes/no question for national servicemen only: 'If NS did you volunteer for overseas service?' Of the first-tour veterans thus surveyed, 59 per cent of national servicemen in the ranks reported that they had not volunteered for overseas service. The single national service officer reported that he had not volunteered either. Thirty-five per cent of men said they had volunteered, and 5 per cent did not answer the question.

The most striking difference between the statistics as they relate to 7RAR's first and second tours is the much larger percentage of second-tour national servicemen who reported having volunteered for Vietnam. Only 24 per cent of national servicemen in the ranks responded that they had not volunteered for overseas service. A full 71 per cent of men said they had volunteered. The two national service officers were split: one said he had volunteered, one said he had not. Five per cent of men did not answer the question. The fact that more than twice the number of second-tour national servicemen than first-tour national servicemen reported having volunteered for overseas service suggests the existence of different circumstances in the second tour.

However, 7RAR second-tour veteran/author Bob Whittaker, whose *Jellybeans in the Jungle* is one of the more accomplished self-published Vietnam memoirs, does not recall attending anything resembling a volunteering parade. A former school principal and energetic researcher, Whittaker took umbrage at the contention on an Anzac Day commemoration website that if a soldier's unit was scheduled for Vietnam, he was 'generally given the chance' to transfer. He shared with me his email to the Anzac Day Commemoration Committee in Queensland, in which he wrote: 'I have searched infantry battalion records held on-line at the AWM. Every parade, including those held prior to embarkation, was recorded for every infantry unit ... Nowhere is there a record of such a parade. I gave up after looking through the parade records of four of the nine battalions in existence at the time. It was an entirely fruitless search ... This is hardly surprising. If these parades had been held, the Commanding Officer of the unit in question would have been in breach of the National Service Act ... Perhaps there were "unofficial" parades mounted by some units – but to say that the soldiers were "generally" given the chance to avoid service in Vietnam is at least misleading, and at most a lie.'[46] The committee promptly removed the claim from its website.

Although I have spoken to many infantry veterans who recall being given the option to refuse service in Vietnam, these were all men who elected to take the posting. I have not yet come across an account of an infantryman who was explicitly and publicly offered the chance to stay at home and took it (although Special Air Service veteran Rolf Kling described in *The Nashos' War* his public apostasy at an SAS assembly).[47] I did, however, interview infantrymen who privately made their objections to Vietnam clear and were permitted to remain in Australia. Among these men was Gus Howard, a cinematographer and national serviceman who marched into the Army in 1969. I was unable to use Howard's story in *The Nashos' War*, but he told me that, during his infantry corps training at Singleton, he approached his sergeant and said, '"I can't do this. I'm not going to be part of a war that I don't believe in. I'm the wrong kind of guy to put into a platoon on active service. I don't feel like risking my own life, I don't want to risk the lives of others."

'I had to go and stand up and explain to a whole bunch of people why I didn't want to do it,' he said, 'and that was accepted and there was comment on it. I thought I was going to get the shit kicked out of me, frankly. But I didn't. I said it as formally as I possibly could and stood at attention while I did it. There was no hint of physical rebellion about it. So they bought it. And they said, "We're gonna send you to Townsville."' Howard was told he would be posted to a battalion that had recently returned from Vietnam and would not, therefore, immediately be redeployed. Instead, he was ordered to go to Sydney, where he might continue his training and await a position as a one-off replacement for a man returning from Vietnam – 'which was, like, the complete opposite of what I needed to happen', said Howard.

'So then I just went, "I can't do that. I'll do the courses, but I'm not going to sit there waiting to replace some guy that's been killed." And they kind of went, "Well, I'm sorry, but that's the way it's got to go. But don't worry about it, it doesn't mean a thing, you could just spend the rest of your life there."

'They kept us busy,' said Howard. 'And I think I was on a firing range in Singleton and this old sergeant walked up to me. They had looked at my record and saw "cinematographer", and a movie projector is called a "cinematograph"; if you're a cinematograph operator, it means you're a projectionist. They had a full-on movie theatre at this base in Singleton with a big screen, big speakers, thirty-five mil projectors, and they used to run movies twice a week, a double-bill. And the sergeant said, "We've got a job. Do you want to come and work for me as a projectionist?" So I said, "Okay," and I took it. And so I spent the rest of my time working as a projectionist in this theatre and it was, in its way, fantastic.'

Neither Davoren nor Howard were entirely negative about the Army. Davoren told me he was an RAAF kid and a geology graduate who had grown up on military bases. The Army was of no interest to him. 'For me, one of the great things in my life was not living on an RAAF base,' he said. However, he found recruit training 'pretty good' – which, it is fair to say, was not the consensus among the national servicemen I interviewed, many of whom seemed to have not yet recovered from the shock of their introduction to the Army.

'I quite liked our staff,' said Davoren, 'Our platoon sergeant was a good bloke and we had a pretty reasonable time of it. Corps training was rather good: we had excellent instructors who were decent people. There was one guy who was in our class who was a non-combatant. I think he was a schoolteacher, but he'd had some incident in his past involving a weapon. One of our sergeants handled it beautifully. He came into our class and said, "You'll notice Private Macmillan isn't carrying a rifle. He won't be carrying a rifle. If what had happened to him had happened to you, you wouldn't want a bloody rifle either." And that was the last that was said about it.'

Even Vietnam was not a wholly negative experience for Davoren. Once he was in-country, he didn't bother sparring with the Army. 'You were just inconveniencing people who were involved in some very serious matters,' he said. 'I had a reasonably interesting job to do. I was kept very busy, and there was a fairly good spirit amongst the guys there.'

It was simply that Davoren believed the Vietnam war was 'a disgrace'.

'I thought it was a tragedy,' he said. 'I thought it was a waste of lives. It was very depressing in our unit: we were right next to the hospital, where you'd hear the sirens go when a medevac was on. It used to be a conversation stopper in our unit – the choppers went right over the top of us. We were constantly aware of that. We thought it was all for nothing.'

Gus Howard appreciated his infantry corps training at Singleton. 'You couldn't really fault the operational standards of the place,' he said. 'They trained you, and you were taught a lot of stuff. It was reasonably physically tough, but there was a fantastic sense of professionalism about the whole thing, and we were treated well. We were treated like individuals and taught how to be an individual within a group, which is the Australian Army way of doing things. And they're very good at it. So it was really hard to remain angry about much at all, because everything was done so well.'

Although he shared his radical peers' perspective on the war, Howard came to a different opinion of the Army. At Singleton, he said, 'There were people around the place who had been to Vietnam, seen a lot of action, and were burned by it. A part of my demeanour the whole time I was there had to be driven by the awareness of being in the presence of people like that, at a kind of one-to-one level of respect and understanding. I had a huge amount of empathy for them.

'When I was at home for leave periods,' he said, 'you're sitting there with a silly short haircut in a day when everyone in my peer group looked like they were in a band, and I *was* in a band. And me, with no attitude – I'm still saying the same things, still thinking the same things – I'm getting all this shit from my friends, this wall of sarcasm and cynicism directed at me. I'd just go, "Yeah, yeah, yeah." Already I was thinking, "They misunderstand the human side of this so deeply that it's not even worth talking about."'

A point that struck me over and again during my research was that everything was more nuanced than I had first believed; that every generalisation I had heard or made was, in some part, false; that every man's army experience was vastly more complicated than I had understood when I first came away from the VVMC.

The myth of the volunteer was too clear-cut to ever be true, but it is worth considering the meaning behind the mythology, and why the idea continues to animate veterans.

Ernest Benjamin Morris asked why so many veterans prefer to think of themselves as volunteers, and wrote, 'One possible reason is that it increases the prestige of Vietnam veterans if they can claim that they were volunteers just like those who went to all the heroic, nation-building battles of World War One. It is much more heroic to have chosen to become a warrior.'[48]

However, the clearest function of the volunteer myth is that it absolves the government of blame: if a man knows nothing else about the army, he knows never to volunteer for anything. And, if every man in Vietnam chose to fight, then none were compelled to die. It is a way of blaming the soldiers, if not for the war, then at least for their own fate: the dead were all willing fighters; they knew the risks.

The idea of the national serviceman as a volunteer for Vietnam is a post-war construction. However, during the war itself, all men of military age were given the chance to sidestep the draft by joining the CMF. Men who chose the CMF option were expected to perform six years' effective service in the Citizens'

Forces. Students could join their university regiment and train in the vacation. If a man failed to fulfil his CMF obligations, he was notionally liable to be drummed into national service, but it's unclear if this ever happened. It seems unlikely the Army would be inclined to accept as a full-time soldier a recruit incapable of performing the often less-than-arduous part-time duties expected in the CMF. The government and its supporters sometimes argued that a man's decision not to choose the 'CMF option' was the equivalent of volunteering for overseas service. The CMF option allowed that if a man joined the part-time CMF *before* his birthdate went into the ballot, he would not be considered for national service and could not be sent overseas. This was not a choice that could be made retrospectively. In his authorised biography, *The Boy from Boree Creek*, Tim Fischer recalls that, once his birthdate had come out of the barrel, he considered the CMF option but decided to serve full-time instead.[49] This is not possible. The law was clear that the commitment had to be made prior to the draw.

A 1966 Liberal Party document contended: 'No Australian youth has to go to Vietnam. He has to make a decision on whether he will do part-time National Service in Australia as a member of the Citizen Military Forces or not. If not he takes the risk that he might be called up to serve two years as a National Serviceman and go to Vietnam for 12 months' service as part of an integrated unit of regular troops and National Servicemen. In other words there is no compulsion upon the youth to serve in Vietnam.'[50] This was the Liberal argument at the beginning of the war, and it remained the Liberal position in October 1971, when Senator John Carrick told the Senate, 'Every person who has gone to Vietnam has elected to do so by leaving himself in the ballot and not opting for service in the Citizen Military Forces or registering as a conscientious objector. They have all opted, by elective choice, so to do.'[51]

Bizarrely, in recent years, a third notion has come to exist, somewhere between the ideas that every man volunteered and every man was compelled. It was said in 1983 that service in Vietnam was 'the subject of a second ballot because of those who went into national service under a contract to serve two years training, there was for them a second ballot for service in Vietnam'.[52] No such second ballot ever existed, nor was it ever claimed to have existed until 1983. It is emblematic of the level of confusion about the workings of the national service scheme that the man who made the statement was Sir Allen Fairhall, Minister for Defence 1966–69, whose own son (also called Allen) was conscripted in 1966 and served in Vietnam in 1967.

Even more recently, a fourth idea emerged – that men who volunteered for CMF service had actually volunteered for Vietnam! Queensland politician Bob Katter Jnr, the leader of Katter's Australian Party and son of Queensland National Party politician Bob Katter Snr, enlisted in the CMF on 3 March 1965, a week before the first ballot, at the age of 19 and nine months, thus ensuring he could not be sent overseas if his birthdate was drawn from the barrel (which it was). Katter Jnr later remembered this another way: in 2015, he told *The Australian*: 'As a young man of 18, I was handed an SLR rifle and had to give two next of kin phone numbers. I was in the 49th Battalion and we were on a full war footing with Indonesia.'[53] In fact, Katter was almost 20 and a member of the Queensland University Regiment, which was not on a 'full war footing' with anywhere.[54] However, for some time he had held the belief that he could be sent to war at an age younger than anyone else in Australia. In 2011, he had told parliament, 'When I was 17 years of age ... I was handed a rifle and had to give three telephone numbers to my commanding officer. I was on 24-hour call-up to go and fight a war to secure our supply line of oil.'[55] Once again, neither the QUR or any other CMF unit was on '24-hour call-up' to go anywhere overseas. And in the 1960s, even an application form for the Regular Army asked for the name and address of only one next of kin, with one phone number ('if applicable').[56]

Long after the Indonesian Confrontation was over, Katter Jnr did indeed transfer to 49th Battalion, another CMF formation with no chance of being sent overseas. However, in 2006 he had told parliament, 'I was on 24-hour call-up to go to Indonesia and then Vietnam. I was a trained platoon commander and I had done the course to go to Indonesia and to Vietnam.'[57] It seems that in the years since the 1960s, Katter Jnr had genuinely come to believe he had volunteered for Vietnam – on the mytho-archetypal grounds that it was the type of thing men like him would do. However, if he had nursed any doubts about his availability for overseas service in the Vietnam years, he would have been well advised to consult his father, Bob Katter Snr, who was Minister for Army during the twilight years of the national service scheme, March 1971 – December 1972, including Katter Jnr's last months in the CMF.

3

'And the winner is…'
The myth of the
rigged ballot

*[Normie Rowe] long believed his birthdate, February 1,
1947, was never drawn in the conscription ballots … [but]
all ballots except the first in 1965, were accompanied by a
supplementary ballot … In the sixth ballot, the dates for the
second group included February 1.*

– Sunday Herald Sun *(editor, Alan Howe), 30 January 1994*

*It can now be revealed that pop idol Normie Rowe was falsely
drafted into the army and should never have been sent to war.
The Department of Veterans' Affairs has this week confirmed
that Rowe's birth date – February 1, 1947 – was never
raised in the controversial ballot of dates that selected which
20-year-old men would be called up to serve.*

– Alan Howe, Herald Sun, *15 May 2008*

*The War Memorial … said: 'Well Normie's date actually
did come up, it came up in the small supplementary ballot
in September 1967' and I was surprised to hear that.*

– Alan Howe on 2UE, 23 May 2008 [1]

In 2015, eight months after the publication of *The Nashos' War*, I was invited to a conference, entitled 'The Great Debate: Conscription and National Service 1912–1971'. The keynote speaker was Tim Fischer. He called his presentation 'It should never be selective National Service ever again: Either all in or none in!'

In his youth, Fischer had been a political prodigy. A likeable man who speaks with a curious mixture of humility and bombast, he was wounded at the Battle of Coral but has never made political capital out of his military service. However, it is clear from his authorised biography that he had a limited understanding of the mechanics of the national service scheme, and it seems to have become further clouded over the years. At the conference, Fischer talked about his own experience with the call-up. He said, 'At the time I thought the same number of balls or marbles marked with a particular date for the six monthly ballots were placed in the barrel for each day of the relevant six month period. I no longer think this is the case. It appears that after the Department of Labour and National Service and the Army reviewed the trades and experience and education of each registrant, some dates were then overloaded with marbles to ensure the right talent mix was called up.'[2]

In a 2014 letter to the *Canberra Times*, Fischer had called for a comprehensive 'Statement of Facts' associated with the ballot, which would answer questions such as, 'Was there more than one marble or ball for particular days?'[3] A reader responded that even the idea that birthdate marbles were ever pulled out of a barrel at the Department of Labour and National Service in Swanston Street, Melbourne, was 'purely fictitious', as his former colleagues at the former Department of Civil Aviation had 'reliably' informed him the ballot was actually conducted on their department's computer system in Henty House on Little Collins Street. This was done, apparently, because Civil Aviation had a very big computer, and the building was easily secured, being 'one of the few Commonwealth-owned properties in Australia that was bounded by four laneways'.[4] Another correspondent, perhaps more appositely, wrote of being 'intrigued and puzzled by Tim Fischer's suggestion that the national service ballot was skewed to select birth dates which yield particular skills' and asked, 'Are we to believe that the Australian army includes astrology in its tactical armoury, or is it Tim who is losing his marbles?'[5]

Undeterred, Fischer continued to press his point at the conference. He had been sent a document by the Australian War Memorial (AWM) that had originally formed a part of Sue Langford's appendix to Peter Edwards' splendid Official History of the 'homefront' during Vietnam, *A Nation at War*, and is freely available on the AWM's website.[6] The document includes a list of every birthdate drawn in every ballot, and the total number of marbles pulled out of the barrel in each draw. Fischer's study of the charts led him to realise 'not all registrants whose birth dates were drawn were called up in the twice yearly ballots (even allowing for health and other declared non call up or exempt categories)'. Therefore, he concluded, 'It appears some person within the system played God big time. Further, note 1 Jan to 30 Jun 1946 births, the month of May saw 13 days drawn out including mine but only 4 for albeit the short month of Feb.'

He pronounced this as 'almost beyond random possibilities' – which it is not. But on he thundered: 'Let those who played God in the national-service ballot of fifty years ago – you know who you are; you're out there in the retired ranks of the Department of Labour and National Service, the retired ranks of the army, somewhere around Canberra and Melbourne – please step up and explain how you decided those that went in and those that went out ... we're entitled to know who played God and how, and what reason, and what methodology they used. It does go to the core fabric of our great nation of Australia.'[7]

It was an extraordinary oration, full of sound and fury, but it was hard to understand what it was supposed to signify. How could there possibly have been a date on which, for example, an appreciably greater number of engineers were born? More importantly, how could this confusion continue to exist, 50 years after the first ballot was drawn, even in the mind of a man such as Fischer, who subsequently served in government with some of the architects of the national service scheme? And why did Fischer choose to identify his faceless targets, his guilty men, as retired civil servants and army officers, but not as members of the Menzies, Holt, Gorton or McMahon Coalition administrations that oversaw national service? It was as though the Army and the public service had somehow devised and executed this scheme independent of the legislature.

I gave my presentation to the conference some hours after Fischer had left and I tried to explain the way the ballot had actually worked – that is, fairly, inside its own parameters, with no intent to include or exclude any particular group or individual within its legal remit, apart from a secret proscription of young delinquents and potential security risks.

At the end of my talk, there was a comment from the floor from another speaker at the conference, Rafe Champion, who told the story of 'a Tasmanian cricketer' who was exempted from national service because he had flat feet. Champion's point was that people in the public eye could use their influence to evade national service. Ironically, however, he appears to have mis-remembered a story told by Doug Walters, a hugely promising

Tasmanian cricketer who became a symbol of patriotic acquiescence to national service when he marched uncomplaining into the Army in 1966. Walters used to say he had believed he would be rejected by the Army because he had 'the flattest feet you've ever seen'.[8]

The public confusion around national service seems interminable. The idea that the ballot was fixed appears irrepressible. The concept that an entity other than the government might have been responsible is as enduring as it seemed to me incomprehensible.

The workings of the national service scheme were quite straightforward. Each year, there were two main ballots – in March and September – and four intakes to the Army. Alongside every draw from the second ballot onwards, a supplementary ballot was held, to draw birthdates for those men who had been out of the country during their registration period. The number of birthdates chosen varied with each draw, determined by factors including the number of deferments that had expired.

Initially, the government aimed to use the scheme to quickly increase the size of the Army by calling up 4200 youths in the second half of 1965, and 6900 every subsequent year (although from 1966, the number of conscripts called into the Army each year was raised to 8400, with the goal of increasing the force's strength to 40000). The arrangements were rushed in. Registration opened on 25 January 1965 and continued until 8 February. Every male British subject was obliged to register for national service when he turned 20 years old, with the exception of diplomats; 'full-blooded aboriginal natives, and persons who have an admixture of aboriginal blood and live as aboriginal natives or amongst aborigines'; members of the permanent armed forces; and resident 'aliens' (non-British subjects). Compliance was close to universal: a total of 40 989 men registered, and the secretary of the DLNS Sir Henry Bland wrote, 'a much higher percentage of our estimated number of registrants had registered on 8th February than was our experience under the earlier Scheme'[9] – although the 'much higher percentage' was itself relative to a very large percentage, as 95 per cent of those liable for national service had registered for the first call-up in 1951.[10]

Since the number of registrations in 1964 was almost ten times greater than the Army's manpower requirements, the pool of potential recruits had to be narrowed by birthdate ballot. A former Tattersall's barrel, last employed in the final years of the 1950s scheme, was wheeled out in the Melbourne offices of the DLNS in March 1965. At the first draw, the barrel contained 181 marbles, each bearing a number corresponding to a date between 1 January and 30 June 1945, and 96 were selected. Men whose birthdays fell on the dates matched by the marbles had to either make themselves available for two years' national service in the Army or give a valid reason why they should defer. Those in full-time study or working to complete an apprenticeship could defer until they had completed their qualification. Cases of exceptional hardship could also apply for deferral but, like students and apprentices, they remained liable for call-up until the age of 26, or in some cases – such as men completing medical or law degrees with a further professional training requirement – the age of 30. Men who married before their ballot were initially deferred indefinitely but, once an early loophole was closed, men who married after their birthdate had been drawn were required to serve if selected.

At the same time, men were encouraged to join the CMF, and CMF men were not to be sent overseas. Those who opted to enlist in the CMF in advance of the draw were, subject to conditions, relieved of their national service obligations – but a man could not join the CMF as an alternative to the Regular Army after he had been balloted in to national service.

The history of the national service scheme is intertwined with the rise and decline of Australia's Vietnam commitment. The first battalion of Australian infantry sent to Vietnam was 1RAR, a formation made up entirely of regular soldiers, which left Australia in May–June 1965, before the first national servicemen marched into their recruit training battalions on 30 June. From the beginning, the conscripts were met at their local Army depots (but not the RTBs themselves) by generally silent and always peaceful pickets from the Save Our Sons (SOS) movement – a group of women opposed to conscription – offering them support if they chose not to enlist.[11]

In January 1966, Menzies resigned and was replaced by Harold Holt as prime minister of Australia. Meanwhile, the first national servicemen had completed three months' specialist training with their allotted corps, including the infantry battalions. Then 5RAR, the first battalion to comprise a mixture of national servicemen and regulars, was readied for the notoriously tough three-week battle efficiency course at the Jungle Warfare Training Centre, Canungra, which future troops would recognise as a sign they had been chosen for Vietnam.

On 8 March, Holt announced that the Australian commitment in Vietnam would be drastically increased, with the establishment of an independent task force comprising two infantry battalions and numerous support forces and including 'more than 500 national servicemen'. The next day, it became apparent that 'more than 500' meant 1400.[12] 5RAR received official notice that it would be deployed to Vietnam in three months.

It would be followed swiftly by 6RAR, and these battalions would be the first to leave Australia with a national service component. The two incoming battalions formed the 1st Australian Task Force (1ATF) with its base at Nui Dat in Phuoc Tuy province. The Task Force was supported by the construction, medical, transport and repair units of the 1st Australian Logistic Support Group (1ALSG), which had its base in Vung Tau.

On 26 November 1966, a federal election was fought partly on issues of conscription and the Vietnam War, and Harold Holt's Coalition won the largest parliamentary majority since Federation, a massive public endorsement of the Vietnam commitment. Arthur Calwell resigned as Labor Party leader and was replaced by Gough Whitlam, whose opposition to both conscription and the Vietnam War had always seemed less spirited and less essential than Calwell's impassioned commitment.

In January 1967, the government began to call up non-British subjects who had been resident in Australia for more than two years. They were called up at the age of 21, rather than 20, and permitted to leave the country rather than go in the ballot. Exemptions applied to citizens of countries such as Morocco, Peru and Denmark, which, in their turn, agreed not to conscript resident Australian citizens into their armies.

Harold Holt disappeared in the sea off Cheviot Beach Victoria in December 1967. That same month a third battalion, 3RAR, joined 1ATF. Holt was eventually replaced as prime minister by John Gorton, under whom the army in Vietnam reached its peak strength of 6917 in May 1969. Gorton narrowly won the 1969 general election and the results of the national service ballot were publicly announced for the first time by the Gorton government in September 1970. Minister for Labour and National Service Billy Snedden said they had not been published previously because publication had been thought to be contrary to the interests of the men concerned, but he did not explain how either government thinking or the men's interests might have changed in the interim.[13] 1ATF reverted to two battalions towards the end of 1970. William McMahon became prime minister in March 1971, and – in response to a massive US drawdown – his government decided that the remaining battalions would not be replaced at the end of their foreshortened tours. Minister for the Army Andrew Peacock announced that national servicemen would no longer be compelled to go to Vietnam with their unit – a compromise the government had always denounced as unworkable and the Army had previously fiercely opposed.

In October 1971, the required term of full-time service for conscripts was reduced from two years to 18 months. It was thought that the Army would be able to maintain its nine battalions under the new 18-month national service period, although up to seven of the battalions would be well below full strength. However, the government believed there were sufficient men in national service training to build up the battalions if necessary.[14] The implications for overseas service were unclear: with only 18 months in the Army, it seemed a man would have to be dispatched on a year-long overseas deployment immediately after he had completed his corps training – and before he had gone through jungle training at Canungra – then demobilised the day he arrived back in Australia. Practically speaking, the 18-month period probably meant an end to overseas service, but if this was intended, it was not made explicit.

In April 1972, when only a few hundred Australian troops remained in Vietnam, a Gallup poll asked whether or not respondents supported the idea of compulsory military training. Those questioned were offered a range of options, from universal service for three months to selective service for 18 months. A full 74 per cent favoured some kind of compulsory military training, with the most popular option being universal service for six months.[15] The same question was asked six months later with similar results.[16]

In December 1972, Gough Whitlam's Labor Party won the federal election, and immediately abolished national service. During the period of the scheme's operation, 804 286 men had registered for national service and 63 740 men had served in the Army, of whom 15 381 went to Vietnam. Only 1242 men had their conscientious objections upheld, and only 14 were imprisoned for refusal to obey a call-up notice. However, a further 3890 men were under investigation for suspected breaches of the National Service Act.[17] The level of compliance with the national service scheme was high, and the level of public support was also high. Even in March 1973, when Australia's Vietnam commitment was over, 78 per cent of respondents to a Gallup poll supported the proposal that all young men should go to military camp for several months.[18]

During the life of the national service scheme, there were two men who came to be seen as symbols of stoic, dutiful, patriotic conformity: the musician Normie Rowe and the cricketer Doug Walters. Rowe and Walters were held up by the media as role models for Australian youth. They had so much to lose. They were already hugely successful at the age of 20, and only better things could follow. Nonetheless, when their birthdate came out of the barrel, they obeyed the law, insisting only that they receive no special treatment.

Walters voiced no complaints about the ballot – but a few about the Army – in a ghostwritten autobiography published in

1981. However, in the second authorised iteration of Walters' life story, written by his sometime teammate Ashley Mallett and published in 2008, Mallett and Walters together develop an impenetrable conspiracy theory about the ballot which, Mallett writes, caught up Bill Hayden and 'prominent sailor and wine baron' Sir James Hardie, even though Hayden was born in 1933 and Hardie in 1932 (presumably both men served their time under the universal obligation of the 1950s scheme). By 2008, Walters had concluded that 'supposedly it was a ballot system but I doubt very much whoever introduced that ballot system got it right. If you went up to the boozer with a thousand guys, which there invariably was ... there should have been heaps of guys celebrating a birthday every night in the pub. Now there was never any more than the usual average of two or three guys celebrating a birthday on any given day.' Walters himself was born on 21 December 1945. 'I never struck anyone else in my time in the Army who did Nashos with me and shared that birth date with me,' he said. Mallett confidently pronounced that 'we may never discover the truth about how many young men whose birth date matched the drawn marbles were actually called up'.

In fact, a perusal of the Nominal Roll of Vietnam Veterans reveals that 28 national servicemen who served in Vietnam alone had the birthdate 21 December 1945. As those who served in Vietnam made up only about a quarter of the national service cohort – since most, like Walters, never left Australia – it is reasonable to assume that about 110 men who shared Walters' birthday were called up and performed their national service at about the same time as Walters. Walters' grievance ultimately rests on the idea that he was 'drummed into the Army as part of a government "plan" of targeting certain people'.[19] Just as Tim Fischer apparently believes he may have been chosen for the military utility of the occupation he briefly pursued between school and national service – that is, farming – Walters is convinced he was conscripted because he was a cricketer, to set an example, and show that nobody was exempt.

In the same year that Mallett's biography of Walters was published, Normie Rowe, who had gone to Vietnam as a national serviceman with the 3rd Cavalry Regiment in 1969, appeared in the media with claims of his own. Rowe said he had been booked for speeding by a police officer who shared his birthday, 1 February 1947, but the officer told him he hadn't been called up for national service. The press 'investigated' and a spokesperson for the DVA confirmed Rowe's birthdate had not been drawn in the ballot. Rowe was resigned to the fact he'd been manipulated, and he too blamed a conspiracy of the faceless, rather than the government of the day. 'I could spend a lot of time and energy pursuing the truth,' said Rowe in an interview in 2008. 'Would the people responsible ever be held to account? Probably not.'[20]

Within a couple of months, however, the truth 'came out', even though it had been in the public domain for more than a decade since the results of the supplementary ballots had been published in the official history in 1997 – and even the Sunday *Herald Sun* (which led the 2008 investigation) had already printed an explanation of the supplementary process from official historian Peter Edwards the last time the matter was aired in 1994. Rowe had been out of the country when the ballot for January–June 1947 birthdates had been drawn in March 1967, so he had gone into the next supplementary ballot, in September 1967. The date 1 February 1947 was drawn in this ballot and the Nominal Roll reveals three national servicemen with that birthdate ended up in Vietnam – which is not at all statistically unlikely, given the small number of young men who would have been absent. The story was later further complicated when it transpired that Grant Coulthart-Smith, a Vietnam veteran and former regular soldier, claimed to have heard a deathbed confession from his father, Lieutenant Colonel Beverly Smith, that he had come up with the idea of drafting Rowe as a publicity stunt, following the example of Elvis Presley – whom he believed had been drafted into the US Army on his birthday on the suggestion of his manager, Colonel Tom Parker. Coulthart-Smith said Smith had asked him to apologise to Rowe – but not, presumably, to Glenn Barry Curtis or John William Meredith, the other two national servicemen with Rowe's birthdate who served in Vietnam. Upon receiving this information, the Melbourne *Herald Sun* pronounced 'the final piece of the jigsaw that saw singer Normie Rowe drafted to serve in Vietnam may have fallen in place'.[21]

I liked and admired Normie Rowe when I met him at Revesby Heights Ex-Servicemen's Club in the south-western suburbs of Sydney in 2012, a couple of hours before he was due to go on stage. He was warm, intelligent, thoughtful and sincere, thankful for his extraordinary years as Australia's 'King of Pop' and philosophical about a commercial downfall he had come to believe was inevitable. He also seemed hurt – not wounded, or even wronged, but somehow misunderstood. He was a good man who tried to do good things with his life – he had even gone to the war with the intention of hurting no-one – but in some way, for some people, that had not been enough.

We did not discuss his call-up in anything but general terms and Rowe did not mention any concerns he might once have held about the validity of his conscription, but the 'mystery' of Normie Rowe – which does not contain a single mysterious element – lives on today, and was vigorously aired in the press in 2015, when several Australian newspapers carried stories about the release of a Normie Rowe retrospective CD and repeated the old allegations. No matter how often it is conclusively proved that Normie Rowe's birthdate was drawn in a national service ballot, there is always a journalist to be found who will say it was not.

Some of the rigged-ballot stories are difficult to understand. In his oral history *Ashes of Vietnam*, author Stuart Rintoul introduces 36-year-old 'Wayne', a former national serviceman who registered for national service in Hurstville, NSW, in January 1969.[22] Wayne expresses scepticism about the ballot as he believes his birthday came up every year from 1965 to 1971. In fact, no birthdate came up every year from 1965 to 1971. He says there were 28 boys in his class at Kingsgrove High School and all 28 were called up. It is not clear what inference Wayne draws from this incredibly unlikely proposition. It is possible he is suggesting national service was universal in working-class areas or that, for murky and incomprehensible reasons, the odds were stacked against Wayne personally – or conceivably, he is implying that both propositions are true, since everyone with his birthdate and everyone in his class at school was, for some reason, targeted by the government for military service.

Depressingly, Wayne's unproven and almost impossible story is reprinted in the high school history textbook *Australia in the Twentieth Century: Working historically*, coupled with questions such as 'How were people selected for national service?' and 'When was Wayne called up?'[23]

If Wayne's point is a little obscure, a more recognisable undertone lies beneath Hector Munro 'Tub' Matheson's assertion, in Roger Donnelly's *The Scheyville Experience*, that his initial thoughts upon learning he had been drafted were, 'The bastards! Why me? What about my Melbourne High School Jewish mates?' Donnelly explains (with no apparent evidence) that 'between

15 and 20 per cent of the sixth form were Jewish, but not one of them was drafted'.[24] Even if this were true, it would have been impossible for Matheson to know. Matheson would have opened his letter of notification at the age of 20, when he was no longer at Melbourne High or even in Victoria. According to an oral history interview he gave in 1994, he was working as a pilot in Wyndham, WA, one of the furthest towns from Melbourne in Australia.[25]

I first heard Tim Fischer's unique theory of the rigged ballot when I interviewed him for *The Nashos' War*. Fischer told me, 'It's only just become aware to me [sic] that the ballots for national service were stacked. You had to register and register your occupation. The Army then presented [a] list that it wanted from the intake, and that then led to the Department of Labour and National Service putting more marbles in for particular days of the six-month period to ensure broadly a result in line with the occupation requirements that the Army was seeking at that time. I was not fully aware of that when I was deputy prime minister. I would've asked for a full explanation of that. I began thinking about it. I asked then federal minister Ian Sinclair and he confirmed it.'[26]

However, when I emailed Ian Sinclair for clarification, Sinclair replied, 'I have no recollection of the reported question from Tim nor does my suggested response to him match the advice I recall being given the Foreign Affairs and Defence Committee of Cabinet on which I served in the late 1960s that "there was no prior distortion in any form in the conduct of the National Service ballot". The subject was politically sensitive and I doubt misleading responses would have been given to that Committee.'[27]

Fischer's idea that certain occupational groups appeared in greater numbers in certain ballots is probably based on the fact that certain occupational groups did indeed appear in greater numbers in certain ballots – although not because the Army needed their special skills at that specific time. As the deferment of men who were balloted in expired, the senior end of each national service cohort became a little older and better qualified. Men who had completed their apprenticeships were followed into the Army by men who had completed their undergraduate degrees, who were, in turn, followed by men who had completed their post-graduate degrees. The first cohort of doctors – who had been in the early stages of their medical degree when they registered for national service in 1965 – did not enter the Army until September 1969, and most of those posted to Vietnam probably did not arrive until late 1970, when the commitment had begun to wind down. As a consequence of the comparatively short life of both the national service scheme and Australia's peak commitment in Vietnam, it seems likely that the best-educated Australians – who were also, in many cases, the most affluent – were never represented in Vietnam in proportion to their numbers in society. This may be the point 'Wayne' was trying to make in *Ashes of Vietnam*.

The 7RAR Survey offers an interesting insight into occupational differences both between national servicemen and regular soldiers and the men of the battalion's first and second tours – data that helps explain the impression that similar people were drafted simultaneously.

The pre-Army occupations of the 'other ranks' (those who were not commissioned officers) in 7RAR's first tour were classified according to the Australian Board of Statistics' Classification of Occupations criteria. The largest number (31 per cent) were labourers, then tradesmen (18 per cent); machine operators (16 per cent); sales workers (10 per cent); clerical (8 per cent, of which public servants made up 3 per cent); and apprentices (5 per cent). The regulars were overwhelmingly working-class men in manual occupations.

Among national servicemen, the largest occupational category was clerical (32 per cent, of which bank clerks made up 12 per cent). This is a similar percentage as that of labourers among regulars. The next largest categories were labourers (23 per cent); tradesmen (19 per cent); machine operators (8 per cent); and sales workers (6 per cent). Since only 8 per cent of regular infantrymen had come from clerical jobs, it seems clerical work was an unlikely background for an infantryman – although it was the background of almost one in three first-tour national servicemen. There was a similar number of tradesmen among both national servicemen and the regulars, a ratio that was to change significantly.

By 7RAR's second tour, the largest number of regular soldiers in the ranks were, once again, formerly labourers (34 per cent); followed by clerical workers (17 per cent, of which public servants made up 9 per cent) and students (also 17 per cent, likely to be mostly school leavers); tradesmen (11 per cent); and community workers (6 per cent).

The largest numbers of national servicemen on 7RAR's second tour were tradesmen (27 per cent) and clerical workers (24 per cent, of which men who explicitly identified themselves as bank clerks made up only 5 per cent). The percentage shift away from clerical workers and towards tradesmen is probably a result of more skilled men entering the Army after the expiration of their trades deferments. The remainder of the national service cohort was made up of labourers (22 per cent); machine operators (10 per cent); and students (5 per cent).

With this data in hand, it is easy to see how an observer might note that a large number of national servicemen from a popular trade – engineering, for example – might have been drafted together, and conclude this was because the Army particularly needed engineers. But this would no more be true than an assumption that the Army might have suddenly required a large number of doctors in 1969. It was simply that the men were available.

So I dismissed Tim Fischer's doubts until I found a newspaper clipping from April 1966, reporting that Gough Whitlam had said, 'There has never been an adequate explanation of the figures for the first conscription ballot,' and demanded of Leslie Bury, 'Can the Minister for Labour and National Service say how those balloted in were subsequently administered out?'

Whitlam believed Bury's department had hand-picked the men it thought should go forward to the medical examination. 'On what basis was this hand-picking done?' he thundered. 'Who was favoured and who was penalised?' A departmental spokesman explained, 'Eventually all youths selected by ballot were medically examined. Those left over from one intake and those whose deferment expired joined a pool from which draftees considered for the next intake were drawn. Of the 8000 from last year's first ballot, 5000 had been medically examined for the second intake in September. Generally speaking there was no handpicking of draftees. If only a specific number of youths from each ballot came up for medical examination, how were they chosen? – "Two principles apply – those who express a desire to go in first, and then in order of age."'[28]

Astonishingly for me, the statement would seem to prove one of Tim Fischer's assertions: as Fischer had suggested to the conference in Victoria, somebody at the DLNS was involved in selecting an unspecified number of men at the margins of the ballot. If they had too many people, they chose first the most willing and then the oldest. This was the biggest surprise of my doctoral research, and I owe an apology to the always gracious Fischer. However, it is difficult to imagine this 'tinkering' had much effect on the final results of the ballot – and especially not on Fischer, who had been willing to serve and, with a birthday in early May, was one of the younger men in his ballot.

It does not take much insight to divine the message behind the myth of the rigged ballot. Many veterans believed, and continue to believe, that national service should have been a universal obligation. They considered themselves unfairly singled out, because they felt it was unjust that such a small group of some-times reluctant young men should have been forced to shoulder Australia's burden in Vietnam. In reality, it was just bad luck, but to attribute misfortune to a conspiracy gives it meaning. And that meaning carries a certain truth – there were forces working against certain individuals, powerful currents they could not oppose. These were, for the most part, nothing more than the dynamics of chance, but to give them a face – even a 'faceless' one – allows the story to be told the way they felt it.

It is just that is not the way it happened.

4

'Like thieves in the night…' The myth of no welcome home parades

None of them were welcomed – the official 'welcome home' parade for Vietnam veterans was not held until 1987.
– Sydney Morning Herald, *25 April 2013*

300 000 Sydney people came to watch and welcome them home, with cheering, handclapping, torn-up telephone books and office stationery.
– Sydney Morning Herald, *9 June 1966*

The 5th Battalion came home from the war yesterday and the people of Sydney came into the streets to do them honour. Hundreds of thousands of people packed the pavements.
– Sydney Morning Herald, *13 May 1967*

Sydney yesterday gave Australia's newest Anzacs warm welcome. It was a magnificent military parade.
– Sydney Morning Herald, *27 April 1968*

Sydney yesterday gave its by now traditional welcome to homecoming troops from Vietnam – claps, cheers, confetti and ticker tape.
– Sydney Morning Herald, *1 March 1969*

Streamers and ticker-tape showered over 1100 Vietnam veterans who marched through the city yesterday to the cheers of tens of thousands of onlookers.
– Sydney Morning Herald, *11 March 1970*

A four-deep crowd and a 20-minute barrage of ticker-tape marked Sydney's reception yesterday to the 7th Battalion, Royal Australian Regiment, on its return from Vietnam.
– Sydney Morning Herald, *3 November 1971*

The Army, Navy and Air Force marched through a storm of streamers and torn paper in Sydney yesterday to the final welcome this city will give to veterans of Vietnam.
– Sydney Morning Herald, *19 November 1971*

Today it is widely believed that Australian troops returning from Vietnam were either afforded no welcome home parade until 1987, or that their parades were disrupted by protesters. Sometimes, the two ideas seem to be held simultaneously. On 3 October 1987, 14 years after the last Australian soldier had returned from Vietnam, a massive Australian Vietnam Forces Welcome Home Parade and National Reunion was held in the centre of Sydney. About 100 000 people packed the streets from the Domain to Town Hall to cheer on 22 000 marching Vietnam veterans, many of whom were stunned by the massive and unexpected display of public support, as they had turned up simply hoping for a reunion with their mates. Old soldiers smiled with tears in their eyes as women rushed out of the crowd, kissed them and handed them flowers. At a concert in the Domain, the veterans and their supporters were entertained by artists including Normie Rowe, although the star turn was the folk-rock band Redgum performing 'I Was Only 19' with wounded veteran Frankie Hunt on stage in a wheelchair by the side of singer John Schumann.

The parade was organised out of pride. Its ACT co-ordinator, Geoff McGibbon, had said it would be more of a reunion than a welcome home. 'Although we didn't have in Australia the same kind of animosity that was often shown to Vietnam veterans in the United States,' he said, 'many veterans still feel a little uncomfortable about their past and many people who objected to Australia's involvement in the war still cannot understand what happened over there.'[1]

On the day, the Sydney press found unhappy veterans such as Peter Kilby, a former regular soldier who had served with the cavalry from September 1965 to September 1966, and who said he had never spoken about his service until the previous year; one of the 'bastards' at the RSL had told him he was not wanted in the club because he had not fought in a real war; and the last time he had marched through the streets of Sydney somebody had thrown pig's blood at him.[2]

An editorial in the *Canberra Times* said the veterans were entitled to be feted as 'they had endured a horrible war, but their return to Australia was very different from that given the troops who returned from the World Wars of 1914–18 and 1939–45 ... The Australian soldiers did not, like previous veterans, return to a heroes' welcome but to a nation almost embarrassed by its involvement in Vietnam and wanting to forget.'[3]

And yet, the idea that all returning servicemen expect a welcome home parade appears to have been retrospectively grafted on to the Vietnam experience. There was no single huge government parade – either national, state or city-based – for every serviceman who returned from either of the world wars. Nor is there much basis for the popular belief that the earlier diggers were invariably feted and admired.

Most of those who served in the 1st AIF did not come home with their mates – even in those cases where their mates were still alive. The First World War ended suddenly in November 1918, and the demobilisation of the AIF was a complex and laborious process. Men were repatriated as individuals, and not on a unit-by-unit basis. The weeks after the Armistice ground into months for many of the troops in Europe as their families waited for them in Australia. Some soldiers began job training in England, France or Belgium. Others took actual jobs. There were still 10 000 members of the AIF in Britain in August 1919, eight months after the Armistice. While huge outpourings of public welcome, relief and congratulation greeted the first men home, by 1919, 'one or two inches of column space announced the return of men, and their welcomes were restricted to relatives and "Red Cross kitsch and teas of ham, eggs, jellies, cakes and scones",' wrote the historian Stephen Garton in 1996. 'Tasmanian officials complained that they were misinformed about the arrival of ships, with the result that men arrived to no public welcome whatsoever.'[4] Nor were the first Anzacs always received with generosity. As Garton wrote of a digger who returned home with wounds sustained on the Western Front, 'he encountered lingering bitterness from the anti-conscription campaigns and, worse still, jealousy of soldier repatriation benefits. He and his comrades "were ashamed and afraid" to wear their [active service] badges ... Newspapers reported that men were removing their badges to avoid getting "a tough time" and were being jeered for having been "fool enough" to fight.'

The situation in the Second World War was similarly complicated. There were several parades for units that returned during the war. For example, almost half the population of Sydney – 500 000 people – lined the streets to honour the 18th Brigade's arrival from the Middle East in September 1942. The 7th Division marched through Melbourne on 19 April 1944, and men on leave in Wollongong, NSW, were offered a welcome home banquet at an Anzac Eve Smoko entertained by local acts including a whistling postman and bird mimic. But the war ended in August 1945 not with a burst of martial pride, but with enormous civilian relief. According to Paul Hasluck's volume of the Official Histories of the Second World War, published in 1970, 'The old pictures of victory with a fanfare had already been lost ... In August 1945 people did not celebrate a great and final victory. There was no crowning feat of glory. They rejoiced because the war was over.'[5]

The repatriation system virtually assured that, once again, a huge number of men could not return with comrades from their units, and it was a long time before the last serviceperson came home. Locally organised welcome home ceremonies, banquets, marches, parades and balls were held in cities and towns well into 1947. Even the Communist Party staged a parade through Sydney – followed by a welcome home ball at the Town Hall – for about 400 party members returned from the services, but the great parades for a conquering army did not happen.

Some troops home from Australia's smaller wars did receive official welcomes. When 3RAR returned on MV *New Australia* from Korea in October 1954, the battalion was given three welcome home parades, first in its home base of Brisbane and later in Sydney and Melbourne.[6] There was at least one huge parade for some of the troops who had been fighting in the Malayan Emergency: the *Sydney Morning Herald* reported that on 31 October 1957 more than 100 000 spectators turned up in Sydney to give a 'ticker-tape' reception to 1000 returned men from 2RAR, 105 Field Battery and 4 Field Troop. The men had sailed home on MV *New Australia*, which had berthed that morning.[7]

There is little evidence that the first large body of Australian troops to come back from Vietnam had any interest in a welcome home parade. In April 1966, the Australian journalist Wallace Crouch, reporting from South Vietnam, wrote, 'Over the next couple of months, in dribs and drabs, mostly by jet, the men of 1st Bn. Royal Australian Regiment, will go home from Vietnam – neither expecting nor wanting a welcome of brass bands and cheering crowds.'[8]

The first returned contingent of 1RAR arrived at Sydney Airport on 2 June 1966. The *Sydney Morning Herald* reported, 'Several troops said they were annoyed at having to march through the streets of Sydney next Wednesday.'[9] In fact, the men had to be ordered to attend their welcome home parade; many would have preferred to be with their families. Soldiers were warned they would be charged as absent without leave if they failed to turn up for the parade – and, if they used their single allocated return rail ticket to go home between their disembarkation and the parade, they would have to pay their own way home for their annual leave.

On 8 June, a crowd estimated at about 300 000 people gave the soldiers what *The Australian* called a 'Mardi Gras' welcome home: 'In Martin Place office girls tore up telephone directories and office paper to shower the troops with confetti. One elderly woman dashed into the marching ranks and began kissing the cheeks of the soldiers. Young girls repeatedly ran up to the soldiers and threw streamers into their ranks. PMG employees in Martin place sent down a thick hail of ticker tape.'[10] As *The Age* reported, 'City employers had obviously responded to the appeal by the Premier (Mr. Askin) to let staff off to see the march.'[11] There were isolated dissenters among the spectators: 'An elderly man laid about them with a metal crutch, sweeping placards into the gutter and knocking one long-haired protester almost senseless. A woman with an umbrella beat two demonstrators over the head. One youth who broke towards the saluting dais clutching a placard was knocked flying by a detective. [But] barristers in Macquarie Street, splendid in their gowns and wigs, lined the footpath to applaud [and] building labourers perched on scaffolding opposite the town hall to join in the welcome. "It was a very inspiring reception, we hadn't expected anything like this," said Major [Brian] Harper, leader of the troops for half the march.'[12]

Later, as 1RAR CO Lieutenant Colonel Alexander Preece approached the saluting dais outside Sydney Town Hall, Nadine Jensen ran at him and threw her arms around him, smearing him with red paint, kerosene and turpentine – 'symbolic', she later said, 'of the blood being shed in Vietnam'.[13] Preece shrugged her off and kept his eyes fixed on the dais, as she moved on to the next man in the parade, Private Don Aylett, and smeared his neck and face. (Aylett later undertook a second tour of South Vietnam, with 7RAR, and was killed in Phuoc Tuy on 6 August 1967.) Police pulled Jensen out of the way, dragged her off and took her to hospital 'for a clean up' before charging her with offensive behaviour. Jensen said she would plead guilty, with an explanation: 'I wanted to make the politicians realise that some people in Australia are opposed to our sending the troops to fight in Vietnam.'[14]

The next day in court, she waived her right to a first offender's closed hearing and was fined $6 and given a $100 good behaviour bond for a year. She said she'd felt it was her personal responsibility to do something about Vietnam and that the protest had been her own idea – she didn't belong to any party or organisation – and her actions were not directed against the soldiers, whom she called 'the instrument of high authority', but against the authority itself. She apologised for taking up the court's time and said, 'My actions were wrong, I know, but there are moral issues at stake.'[15]

The idea that returning soldiers in Australia had blood – or, indeed, anything – thrown over them dates back to this single incident. Jensen was a lone actor, not part of an organised movement, and her actions at the time were accorded little significance. She remains a mysterious figure: having written her paragraph in history, she disappeared from Australian public life, if not from the memory of Vietnam veterans. Jensen assumed a greater prominence after 1987 than she ever had in 1972. Even those veterans and journalists who believe returned men from Vietnam had no welcome home parades remember Nadine Jensen.

The second welcome home parade to march through the streets of Australia – and the first to include national servicemen – marked 5RAR's return to its home city of Sydney on 12 May 1967. It involved 550 'just returned' men from 5RAR, 130 'other' 5RAR troops, 200 men from other 1ATF units and 100 RAAF personnel. The 5RAR contingent included some 300 national servicemen. The *Sydney Morning Herald* reported, 'Hundreds of thousands of people packed the pavements along the three-mile route of the battalion's march from Garden Island through the city. This was one of Sydney's truly splendid occasions. And it was made all the greater because it was spontaneous, impulsive.

The arrival of the 5th Battalion after a year's fighting in the jungles and paddy fields of Vietnam touched the heart of this city ... the bands played and Sydney gave its heart to the men ... From the high buildings came showers of floating streamers. The coloured paper caught and twisted in the hats and the rifles of the troops. They marched on, trailing it with them as they passed. In the crowds, pressing hard on to the road, some women wept.'[16] The Sydney *Daily Telegraph* estimated 250 000 people turned out to greet the marchers.[17]

In Queensland, Enoggera-based 6RAR was the first battalion to march through the streets of Brisbane on its welcome home parade. The infantrymen were joined by members of 101 Field Battery and 161 Reconnaissance Flight, and the governor of Queensland, Alan Mansfield, took the salute from former Task Force commander Brigadier OD Jackson in front of City Hall. There seems never to have been any suggestion that 6RAR's ticker-tape parade was anything other than wildly enthusiastic. The homecoming of 6RAR is recorded by Charles Mollison, who came back to Queensland with his men on HMAS *Sydney*, and remembered, 'Brisbane people gave us a tremendous welcome. There were none of the "Murderer" placards or the red paint or the spitting experienced by 1 RAR and other units that arrived in Sydney on later occasions. Our hearts filled with pride as we marched past the saluting base, listen to the applause of the crowd and witness the frantic waving flags and screams of recognition for individuals as we passed.'[18] Phrased like this, even a clear recollection of a triumphant and jubilant welcome home parade serves to reinforce the broader impression of generalised spitting and paint-throwing at unit marches.

7RAR's welcome home parade in Sydney on 26 April 1968 was the largest of the war. According to the *Canberra Times*,

'More than 500 000 people lined main city streets ... and gave 1300 Vietnam veterans a spectacular homecoming with showers of ticker tape and confetti ... The march caused traffic chaos in the inner city and for an hour afterwards George Street was still blocked with cars.'[19] The *Sydney Morning Herald* called the returned men 'Australia's newest Anzacs'. Outside the Town Hall, reported the newspaper, the veterans were treated to 'What was, in one way, an unusual Sydney welcome – they cheered. Seldom do Sydney crowds cheer, except at football matches. They always applaud and they applauded the troops yesterday – long, loud and enthusiastically.'[20] The salute was taken by the prime minister, John Gorton.

However, the homecoming of 7RAR had its own unique font of bitterness. The battalion left Vung Tau on 9 April 1968 and, as Michael O'Brien notes, many of the troops erroneously believed their return was deliberately delayed by one day so as to keep them from marching in the Sydney Anzac Day parade on 25 April.[21] In fact, the *Sydney* had to sail home via Thailand to pick up a signals squadron that had been taking part in a SEATO exercise, then a soldier contracted peritonitis and had to be flown to hospital in Singapore, so the ship could not reach Sydney until the morning of 26 April. However, the author Gerard Windsor has written that the *Sydney* was due to dock on the morning of 25 April, which would mean that the troops would march with other veterans on Anzac Day, 'but the RSL didn't want that'.

'The charitable interpretation of the request/order was that the Vietnam veterans deserved their own individual march,' wrote Windsor. 'The more common belief was that the RSL didn't regard them as having fought in a real war and therefore they were not eligible for the Anzac Day March. The latter is the more likely interpretation.'[22]

Windsor does not offer a source for his assertion that the *Sydney* should have docked on the morning of 25 April. The *Sydney*'s recent previous trips back to Sydney from Vung Tau had lasted 12 days (June 1966) and 13 days (February 1968), which would have had the men home on 21 or 22 April respectively.[23] Nor does Windsor suggest how, or at what level, the RSL might have been able to make an 'order/request' to the Australian Army and the Royal Australian Navy (RAN), and why the military would agree to a petty, insulting entreaty that would, in effect, cost thousands of dollars in wasted sea time and lost shore time. The idea seems to be that the late arrival was accomplished by deception, which directly impugns the integrity of the captain of the *Sydney*, Captain DAH Clarke MVO, DSC.

It is myth-making to suggest the RSL had some kind of official policy that Vietnam was 'not a real war' or that Vietnam veterans were not 'eligible' for the Anzac Day march in Sydney. On Anzac Day in 1967 members of 5RAR's advance party, who had returned by air before the majority of the battalion came home by sea, marched in Sydney, and veterans marched in Melbourne, too. The *Sydney Morning Herald* headlined its front-page Anzac Day report, 'Vietnam gives new meaning to Anzac'. The report continued, 'A wave of applause ran along the streets of Sydney in tribute to young veterans of Vietnam [who] looked tanned and tough, big youngsters in their prime. They were a small contingent ... but they drew the loudest recognition. It came from youth [whose] strongest acknowledgement was for their own generation – the young Regulars and National Servicemen.'[24] The NSW RSL state secretary, WG Osmond, said it was one of the biggest marches he had ever seen and attributed its size to 'public concern about Australians serving in Vietnam'.

It is a myth that the RSL was institutionally opposed to Vietnam veterans.[25] The RSL, locally and nationally, was vigorously supportive of Australian troops throughout the conflict. This is not to say that individual veterans did not hold justifiable grievances against individual members of individual RSL clubs. However, it is worth remembering that the only RSL members who were publicly reported as being expelled or suspended from the league during the Vietnam years were Second World War veterans such as Les Waddington, whose Ex-Services Human Rights Association of Australia was opposed to the Vietnam War. 'RSL members disloyal to Australia's defence policy should be very careful what they said,' warned NSW RSL state president William Yeo, after Waddington's expulsion in May 1967, as the league was '100% behind the Commonwealth on its Vietnam commitment and also believed in compulsory national service'.[26]

In 1968, 100 000 people watched the Anzac Day parade in Sydney. Once again, the *Sydney Morning Herald* noted that the young cheered the most 'particularly for those nearest their own age group – the recently returned Vietnam veterans ... As the young Vietnam veterans came along, near the end of the parade, they [were joined] behind the barriers, by other excited young people – girlfriends, brothers, sisters, even a few of the younger Mums – in a way never before seen at an Anzac march.'[27]

For her doctoral thesis, the academic Janine Hiddlestone interviewed a former soldier who remembered a march through Sydney in 1968 in which 'we were booed. We were spat on. We had condoms full of water thrown at us. Lunch is thrown at us as we march through the city. And then back at the Domain with blokes with tears in their eyes, ripping parts of the uniform off'.[28] All the veterans in Hiddlestone's study are anonymous. This particular quote is attributed to 'Vietnam Veteran Interview #27', who could be anybody, but the march to which he refers can only be 7RAR's unprecedently huge and enthusiastic parade.

The testimony of Vietnam Veteran 27 illustrates the biggest problem with the secondary literature of Australia's Vietnam War: the most outlandish stories are told by anonymous or pseudonymous sources, and there appears to have been no attempt made by the interviewer to verify them. There was only one welcome home parade in Sydney in 1968. It was widely reported. Spectators threw nothing but ticker tape and confetti.

Later in 1968, 2RAR received an enthusiastic welcome on the streets of Brisbane with 'thousands of people' cheering the troops as they marched two miles through the city. As usual, 'office workers released clouds of ticker tape and streamers from upper floor windows. Welcoming banners and flags were strung across buildings and crowds surging behind the soldiers blocked streets for up to 40 minutes'. One national serviceman received a welcome all of his own. 'Australian Mutual Provident Society staff stretched a 30ft banner across their Queen Street office entrance, saying "welcome home, Bob Campbell" to a former staff mate.'[29]

In December 1967, a third battalion, 3RAR, joined 1ATF in Phuoc Tuy. While 3RAR was away, the first rowdy demonstrations against the war startled Australia. On 4 July 1968, the US Consulate in Melbourne was besieged by about 2000 protesters who smashed every window in the building and fought with smoke bombs and fire crackers against mounted police. About 54 demonstrators were arrested and police seized petrol that was allegedly going to be used to burn down the consulate; 500 protesters tried to storm the police headquarters in Russell Street and free their arrested comrades. More large protests followed. In December 1968, a Gallup poll asked Australians, 'Do you think we should continue to fight in Vietnam or bring our forces back to Australia?' Forty-nine per cent of respondents said Australia should stay in Vietnam and 37 per cent said the troops should come home. The number of Australians in favour of remaining in Vietnam had dropped below 50 per cent for the first time, but they still comfortably outnumbered the respondents in favour of withdrawal, and the number of undecided had risen by six percentage points since a previous poll in September.[30]

Against this background, 3RAR came home to Adelaide on 2 December 1968 to a 'hearty welcome', marred not by protest but by bad weather. The *Advertiser* reported, 'Despite steady rain thousands of people lined King William Street at lunchtime to cheer and clap a welcome as the soldiers marched past [in] the first time since World War II that a body of troops had returned direct to Adelaide from a war zone. Three hours earlier at Outer Harbor, more than 300 wives, girlfriends and relatives, waited patiently in the rain as the huge grey troopship HMAS *Sydney*, carrying the men, moved slowly to her berth. Later there were hundreds of excited reunions on the wharf.'[31]

On 1 March 1969, 1RAR marched for a second time in a welcome home parade through the streets of Sydney. According to the *Daily Telegraph*, 'Police officers estimated that more than 300 000 people crammed the pavement to cheer the troops, and that almost another 100 000 crowded office windows along the route ... The crowd, in places 10 deep on each side of the route, generously applauded the marchers.'[32] However, the *Sydney Morning Herald* took a different view of the reception. Its reporter felt the city 'gave its by now traditional welcome to our home-coming troops from Vietnam – claps, cheers, confetti and ticker tape, but in a more restrained way than in the past'. Tellingly, none of the newspapers mentioned Nadine Jensen's

1966 protest and, in fact, the reason the newspaperman felt the reception was more muted than in previous times was because veterans of both parades told him so. 'The city's welcome was nothing like that accorded the battalion on its first return from South Vietnam in 1966, according to men who marched then,' he wrote.[33] In 1969, three years after the Jensen incident, Jensen was forgotten and 1RAR's first welcome home parade was seen as an episode in a golden age to be recalled with nostalgia. It is difficult to pinpoint exactly when this impression changed.

When 4RAR came home to Brisbane on 30 May 1969, a puzzling news story in the *Courier-Mail* recorded its return: 'Anti-Vietnam protesters called off plans to demonstrate against the return of 550 troops of the 4th Battalion, Royal Australian Regiment, who marched in triumph in Brisbane yesterday. Protest leaders decided not to proceed with any demonstration because Brisbane gave the troops one of the warmest welcomes since World War II. The troops ... were clapped and cheered throughout in a most spectacular "ticker tape" reception. The commanding officer of the returning battalion, Lieutenant Colonel Lee Greville said: "It was a most wonderful welcome. I must admit I got all emotional." ... At the corner of Queen and George streets the air exploded with confetti, streamers and cheers ... Offices and shops emptied and work virtually came to a standstill as crowds packed up to six-deep along city streets.'[34]

It was not clear how would-be protest organisers could have gleaned before the fact that the city was poised to offer such an enthusiastic welcome, nor at what point their plans were called off – nor, in fact, if such plans had ever existed. But there were no protesters at 4RAR's march, nor apparently were there any substantial Vietnam street protests in Brisbane between January 1967 and May 1970.[35]

The only time an appreciable number of demonstrators turned up at a welcome home parade was during 9RAR's march through Adelaide on 9 December 1969. When the battalion returned to South Australia, the men were met by cheering young women tossing rice as confetti. As the troops reached the town hall, however, they passed 20 silent demonstrators wearing black armbands and carrying banners reading 'Withdraw Them All Now' and 'Peace Now' (in contrast to the folkloric 'Baby killers!'). As 9RAR marched past the banners, the demonstrators formed two columns and joined the end of the parade. Inevitably, the protesters were attacked, initially by 'an elderly man', who ran up and tried to grab the banners. According to the Adelaide *Advertiser*, 'One of the men exclaimed: "We can't let you scruffy lot of b———s spoil Adelaide's honoring fine lads back from Vietnam." A large crowd shouting "Pigs", "Dogs," "Why aren't you over there?" and "Why don't you get your hair cut?" then surrounded the demonstrators.'

The newspaper noted 'elbows were used freely in the melee'. The demonstrators, who were identified as anarchists along with members of the Women's International League for Peace and Freedom, included politics lecturer Brian Abbey and draft resister Bob Hall. Regular demonstrators were familiar faces to both police and press and, had they turned up anywhere, they would have been easily identified. Their banners were confiscated, although Hall said they had chosen the 'least emotional' slogans they could find, and only at the last moment decided to fall in behind the march.[36]

The march is sometimes remembered differently to the way it was reported and photographed. Some soldiers, showered with rice by well-wishers, recalled instead being pelted with vegetables by demonstrators. The silence of the protesters became a cacophony of abuse. The troops' supporters melted into insignificance. One 9RAR national serviceman recounted only 'boos, taunts ... vegetables, abuse, name calling, it was so humiliating ... so embarrassing ... so disgusting. We thought we would've been welcomed home and we were rejected by our own Australians'.[37]

A curious account of the parade and its aftermath was given to the Adelaide *Advertiser* many years later by 9RAR veteran Geoff Williams, who, according to the newspaper, was a patient at 'the psychiatric unit at the Daws Road Repatriation General Hospital, where he and other veterans are being treated for post-traumatic stress disorder': 'It was the quickest march I have ever seen ... It was clear that we just were not welcome. We were branded as baby killers, all sorts of terrible lies ... On one early day back, I was wearing my uniform, just so proudly. Then people started waving red flags in my face, shouting abuse, spitting on my country's uniform. A bloke turned around and hit me with a pole. He had ribbons on from World War II but his son had been killed in 'Nam. He was having a go at me personally. He was so angry but I couldn't understand it.'[38]

Presumably, when Williams talks of being attacked by spitting people waving red flags, he is referring to a demonstration, of which there were none of any significance in Adelaide in the four months following Williams' return – and there are no contemporary accounts of demonstrators in Adelaide attacking soldiers ever. This does not mean Williams' story should be dismissed as fantasy, only that it should be accepted as myth.

On 30 May 1968, national serviceman Dal Abbott of 1RAR was killed in action, and his family instructed the Army to bury the body of their son overseas. 'My son's death in Vietnam was a form of legalised murder by the Federal Government,' said Dal's father, Trevor Abbott, a former sergeant in the AIF. 'They grab someone off the streets, train him in a sort of a way, and send him off to Vietnam. What else can you call it but murder? This is a local political war and our boys should not be there. This war is not worth one Australian life – my son's or anyone else's.'[39] The attacker in Geoff Williams' story can only have been Trevor Abbott. The likelihood of the grieving ex-serviceman carrying a red flag and using it to assault a soldier – and the press ignoring the whole drama – is extraordinarily slim. Williams is telling the story that a veteran of the Second World War blamed the government and the Army for the loss of his son in the Vietnam War – but that story has no emotional power without a personal link to Williams. Therefore, he has that veteran hit him with a pole. Perhaps Trevor Abbott's attitude, signifying that even earlier veterans could not comprehend the meaning behind the sacrifices made in Vietnam, felt to Williams like being hit with a pole – although maybe that is taking the argument a step too far.

The Adelaide parade produced a particularly wild and bizarre mythology. The book *Veldt to Vietnam: Haleians at war*, published in 1994, included the first – and, to date, only – account of a Vietnam veteran apparently murdered for his service. The author, WJ Edgar, claimed that when 9RAR marched through Adelaide in December 1969, 'the commanding officer had red paint thrown at him by anti-war protestors' and 'that night, one of the 9th RAR soldiers, still in uniform, was accosted and knifed to death in the street'.[40] Nothing like this ever happened. The CO did not have red paint thrown on him and nobody was 'knifed to death' in the street in Adelaide in December 1969. The Hale School old boy who provided the information to Edgar, 9RAR national serviceman David Guthrie, was not at the march anyway, as he told Edgar he had returned to his home city of Perth earlier in the month.

When 5RAR returned to Sydney in March 1967, the *Sydney Morning Herald* reported crowds up to 14 deep, as 'streamers and ticker tape showered over 1100 Vietnam veterans who marched through the city ... to the cheers of tens of thousands of onlookers'. The salute was taken by the Minister for the Army, Andrew Peacock. A police spokesperson said 'no incidents occurred during the march'.[41]

The only infantry battalion not to receive a welcome home parade during the war years was 6RAR, whose main body returned to Australia piecemeal by air, rather than together by ship, as HMAS *Sydney* was in docks for a refit. This must have been particularly galling for the men, who had lost 13 of their comrades in Vietnam, as their arrival coincided with the first large Moratorium demonstrations with their scattered NLF (National Liberation Front) flags and banners referencing My Lai. The Moratorium marches of May 1970 saw crowds of 70 000–100 000 in the streets of Melbourne; 25 000 in Sydney; 8000 in Brisbane; 6000 in Adelaide; 3000 in Perth; and 2000–3000 in Hobart. These demonstrations must have seemed like the battalion's true welcome home.

However, while the Moratoriums are generally remembered as having been huge, successful, spectacular, unprecedented, and unopposed, it is worth looking back at the way the Sydney march was reported at the time. At Fairfax, which had never had much patience with demonstrators, the *Sun-Herald* described a crowd of 'about 10,000' walking from Hyde Park to Rushcutters Bay: 'Carrying candles and chanting peace slogans that were, at times, obscene, the marchers were heckled sporadically. In William Street, police held back anti-protest sailors who threatened to start an anti-moratorium demonstration. Earlier moratorium demonstrations planned for over a dozen suburbs proved to be mini-protests that almost fizzled ... Before the rally, a group of half a dozen men in military-type uniforms, and wearing swastika armbands, shouted pro-war slogans outside the stadium ... Strong squads of police, posted throughout the metropolitan area, had little difficulty in controlling small crowds. Senior police officers said yesterday was little different from a normal Saturday.'[42]

The latter years

In the latter years [ticker-tape parades] tended to be sombre affairs ... The men felt like curiosities, slightly freakish emblems of a grave mistake. Their photos show ranks of unsmiling eyes that seem to bore into the back of the men in front, as if afraid to make eye contact with the crowd. No young women ran up to kiss them.
– Paul Ham, 2007 [43]

It was streamers, tickertape, applause, cheers, and tears of joy all the way as Brisbane 'turned on' yesterday to give its Vietnam veterans, the men of 8th Battalion, a tremendous welcome home. Tens of thousands of people lined the inner-city march route. People frequently left the main body of the spectators to kiss the marchers.
– Courier-Mail, 1970[44]

A more sophisticated variation on the refrain that Vietnam veterans received no welcome home parades was expressed by a Major John Bridley in 2003. 'There may have been a welcome home,' said Bridley, who was not a Vietnam veteran, 'but there was no welcome.'[45] However, after a year of the largest anti-war demonstrations Australia had ever seen, 8RAR returned to its home city of Brisbane in December 1970 to a rapturous reception from patriotic, horse-racing, speedway-watching, beer-drinking, conservative Queenslanders. The story told in the Brisbane *Courier-Mail*'s front-page report is worth quoting in detail, to get a feeling for the sheer breadth and depth of support for the troops in Premier Joh Bjelke-Petersen's Queensland towards the end of Australia's war: 'Many of the watchers wept openly with joy and pride ... They pressed forward onto the streets and in places the 8th Battalion had just enough room to march through. The men were obviously impressed by the reception. They grinned broadly. But they marched on, stepping out with traditional digger precision ... From the crowd on the Bellevue Hotel corner came a cry, "Good on you, boys!", a phrase which was to be shouted again and again ... "Welcome Home Men" read a placard prepared by Bill Johns, of Salisbury, who held it aloft as he and his workmates hung from the windows of the State Government Printing Office in George Street ... Police officers who patrolled the march route said there were no incidents. One officer said: "The ratbags wouldn't have been game to try anything today." ... Hundreds of 8th Battalion soldiers will have a free day at the Queensland Cup race meeting at Eagle Farm tomorrow. The Queensland Turf Club is offering free invitations to each soldier and his guest. The Paddock Bookmakers' Association members are giving $5 betting vouchers, and the Eagle Farm caterer (Mr. E. Stewart) will offer free afternoon tea to the Diggers. Promoters of the Exhibition Speedway yesterday announced a free night for the troops at Saturday's record 30-event meeting. Invitations also have been issued to 250 soldiers to attend the Toowoomba Beer and Barley Festival.'[46]

The march marked the beginning of the end. 8RAR was not replaced at 1ATF. The Australian withdrawal had begun.

It is difficult to understand how and why conservative Australia has been written out of – and allowed itself to be expunged from – the social history of the Vietnam War. The welcome home parades, enormous and heartfelt outpourings of patriotic joy, were no less an expression of public feeling than the smaller Moratorium marches. Many of the good things organised for the soldiers seem to have been forgotten or replaced in the memory of veterans with insults that may never have been thrown. The banners that met returned men said 'Welcome Home Men' not 'Baby Killers!' Women ran out of the crowds to kiss soldiers, not to spit on them.

7RAR marched through Sydney for the second time on 10 March 1971. Michael O'Brien wrote, 'In direct contrast to the reception afforded to smaller groups returning by air, the march was very well received by the people of Sydney, with large, cheering crowds. There were no visible protest groups.'[47] It appears there actually was a tiny protest, but it was so minor and abortive that even 7RAR's diligent historian remained unaware of it. The *Sydney Morning Herald* reported, 'About 700 members of the battalion marched through city streets, accompanied by about 300 other men recently returned from Vietnam ... They were clapped and cheered along the way ... There was a small group of anti-Vietnam protesters outside the Town Hall, but they were discouraged after police confiscated some of their placards.'[48]

There does not appear to be any pictures of the incident. Assuming it actually happened, it was the last recorded protest at a welcome home parade in Australia.

On 30 March, Prime Minister William McMahon announced that a further 1000 Australian servicepeople would be withdrawn from Vietnam, including RAN and RAAF personnel. On 31 March 1971 at United States Army Base Fort Benning, Georgia, Lieutenant William Calley was convicted of the murder of 11 Vietnamese civilians at My Lai. The killers at My Lai had the sympathy of the majority of Australians. In March–April 1971, 59 per cent of people surveyed in Sydney believed the My Lai soldiers should not be punished, and 30 per cent said they themselves would have followed orders and killed civilians. Only 27 per cent of all the survey respondents – and only 31 per cent of ALP supporters – thought the soldiers should be punished if they had been following orders.[49] Paul Ham writes that the Australian response to My Lai 'demonstrated Australia's immersion in the American experience of Vietnam and underscored our ignorance of, or indifference to, the Australian soldiers' predicament'.[50] However, far from blaming ordinary Australian troops for the war crimes of Americans, the majority of Australians did not even blame the Americans who had committed those crimes. Among those proponents of the war whose commitment remained undiminished by evidence of gang rape and mass murder was future prime minister John Howard, who argued for the war and conscription at St Felix Hall, Bankstown in April 1970.[51]

This is not to say that reports of Calley's trial did not help build and solidify opposition to the war – simply that their effect does not seem to have been as dramatic as it is now remembered, nor to have assumed the form that it is now sometimes supposed to have taken.

Back in Queensland, 2RAR was the first Townsville-based battalion to both leave from and return to Lavarack Barracks, and it arrived on HMAS *Sydney* on 1 June 1971. The battalion had been away for a year and lost eight men dead. The *Townsville Daily Bulletin* wrote that 'streamers, confetti and loud applause greeted the troops, as they marched ... There were no anti-war demonstrations – the only signs had "Welcome" written on them'.[52]

Another perspective on 2RAR's homecoming was given in the self-published memoir, *Too Young to Vote but Old Enough to Kill*, by DF Ryschka, a regular soldier with 2RAR who came back on the *Sydney*. Ryschka's is an enormous work, with 545 closely set pages of detailed reminiscence. When they arrive in Townsville, Ryschka and his mates spot 'a couple of the barmaids from the Sun Hotel. The Barmaids say, "Hey, fellas, welcome home and here, have a cold XXXX." Taking the beers from them, as we're digging into our pockets to pay a barmaid says, "No-no, it's on the Sun."' The episode continues: 'Ah, the good old uni students not out in mass, but there are a few representatives scattered throughout the crowd and along the route. Bringing a smile to my face are their tried and proven old clichés – baby killers, murderers and a few more choice muffled and inaudible words: what, no spitting, fuck, they're definitely losing their touch.'[53]

As we shall see, spitting on soldiers played no part in the behaviour expected from anti-war demonstrators in 1971 but the myth's peculiar ubiquity is established here by a comment noting its absence. The *Townsville Daily Bulletin* saw no cat-callers in the crowd but Ryschka, writing in 2012, remembers himself as a world-weary youth, already inured to the tiresome taunts of 'baby killer' and 'murderer', even though there is no evidence these epithets were hurled regularly at soldiers during the Vietnam years, and even though he does not claim to have witnessed any other demonstration, and even though there was virtually no anti-war movement in Townsville. Once again, one of Hiddlestone's anonymous veterans also offers a bitter perspective. Veteran 34, who marched in Townsville, remembers being welcomed but then hustled away 'quite quick before the university students came out'.[54]

Who exactly were these reviled 'university students'? In July 1969, *The Bulletin* had published a six-page feature entitled 'The trouble with students: An Australia-wide survey'. According to the magazine, it was 'impossible to detect anything remotely resembling political activity at the Townsville University College (700 full- and part-time students)'. There was not even a political club.[55]

On 18 August 1971, McMahon announced the majority of Australian combat troops would be withdrawn from Vietnam by Christmas. He portrayed this as something close to a victory. 'The enemy has largely lost the initiative,' he said, although he conceded they were 'still there'.[56] When 3RAR came back from 1ATF, it was not to be replaced. The men arrived home in Adelaide on Sunday 16 October. The *Advertiser* reported, 'After reuniting with their families and friends they will have another "welcome home" when they march through Adelaide 2½ hours later with the advance and rear parties of the battalion ... The Lieutenant-Governor (Sir Mellis Napier) will take the salute as the march passes the Town Hall. The Central Command Band and the 3 Bn. Pipe Band will march with the veterans, and the SA Police Band will play them past the saluting base. Channel 7 will show a 15-minute film report at 11.15 a.m. of the battalion's arrival at Outer Harbor, followed by a direct telecast of the march.'[57]

The *Sunday Mail* wrote, 'Hundreds of welcomers gathered at the wharf gates early this morning long before the troopship berthed. [They] crammed on the wharf behind closed gates and jumped, shouted, and waved with excitement as the ship made fast ... The soldiers hurried off the Sydney clutching rifles and kitbags. They assembled briefly in a cargo shed before being "let loose" among the crowd. Then for 10 minutes it was bedlam – kissing, hugging, back-slapping and hand-pumping, tearful reunions by the score … At 10 a.m., the soldiers boarded buses and trucks for the trip into the city and the home-coming march. They were joined in the city by 200 more of their number, the advance and rear parties of the battalion who had flown home earlier.'[58]

On Monday, the *Advertiser* reported the men had marched to 'claps, cheers and streamers thrown by the large crowd lining the route'.[59] However, according to Hiddlestone, 'Four veterans spoke of a march in Adelaide in 1971 where they were … targeted by groups.'[60] This time the attribution is to Vietnam Veterans 11, 12, 25 and 26.

There was only one parade through Adelaide in 1971. While it is conceivable, given the level of hostility between troops and protesters in Adelaide (see Chapter 7 for more details), that protesters would turn up at the parade, it is inconceivable, bearing in mind the history of this enmity and the amount of coverage it was given in the *Advertiser*, that the newspapers would not have reported the story. And, of course, it would have been recorded on Channel 7's direct telecast.

The 1ATF base at Nui Dat was handed over to South Vietnam on 16 October and most remaining Australian troops in the country withdrew to 1ALSG in Vung Tau. Many soldiers returned to Sydney on HMAS *Sydney* on 18 November 1971 and paraded through the city. The *Sydney Morning Herald* reported, 'The Army, Navy and Air Force marched through a storm of streamers and torn paper in Sydney yesterday to the final welcome the city will give to veterans of Vietnam. And if it was not exactly a victory parade, it was at least a warm homecoming. Thousands of people in the streets paused to wave and applaud as the sailors, soldiers and airmen swung past … The band of the Eastern Command, playing "Waltzing Matilda", took them past the Town Hall, where the Minister for the Army, Mr Peacock, reviewed the parade. A blizzard of paper poured down on the marching men from office windows above. It was a moving moment.'[61]

This final march through Sydney was smaller and quieter than the previous and better attended parades, but all the regular features of the welcome home were present and correct, from the streamers and the applause to the Minister for the Army. It was small news, however, relegated to page nine of the paper. On the day the troops arrived, their upcoming parade had been flagged by a small item on the front page, a news story dwarfed in the shadow of a much longer piece about the appearance of draft evader Michael Matteson on ABC TV two days earlier.

The welcome given to 4RAR in Townsville was more traditionally enthusiastic. The battalion marched through its home city on 17 December 1971 with 104 Field Battery and 9 Squadron RAAF and, according to the *Townsville Daily Bulletin*, 'For 360 Army veterans, seven months in the war-torn jungles of Vietnam must have all seemed worthwhile ... As the dark green ranks of servicemen marched through city streets, thousands of Townsville people turned on a rousing heroes' welcome. Cheering drowned the sound of marching feet for three city blocks as Townsville made the most of the last major parade by troops from Vietnam. The marchers were swamped with streamers and ticker-tape thrown from balconies and road-side vantage points. The crowd which packed the Flinders Street footpaths to capacity has been described as the largest ever to turn out and welcome troops returning from the war zone.'[62]

The salute was taken by Defence Minister David Fairbairn, and the parade was observed by Army Minister Andrew Peacock, opposition leader Gough Whitlam, Queensland Premier Joh

Bjelke-Petersen, and Chief of the General Staff Lieutenant General MF Brogan.

The last men of 4RAR to leave South Vietnam were the diggers of D Company, who had remained behind in Vung Tau to provide security during the last days of 1ALSG. The veteran/historian Gary McKay has written: 'No one in Delta Four on board the *Sydney* expected to be given a hero's welcome because they had seen the increase in the anti-war movement protests and demonstrations, and some had even had their mail stopped because the postal workers union members had refused to deliver mail to soldiers serving overseas in Vietnam.'[63]

In fact, the anti-war movement – if not the anti-conscription movement – had more or less burned itself out by the time of 4RAR's eight-month tour, postal union workers had never refused to deliver mail to soldiers serving in South Vietnam, and even the furphy of the mail boycott far preceded the arrival of 4RAR. D Company returned to Townsville on the *Sydney* on 9 March, with several hundred other servicepeople, but only about 20 men disembarked in the battalion's home city. There was no welcome home parade for the last large contingent of Australian troops to leave Vietnam. Instead, the new Minister for the Army Bob Katter boarded the vessel to congratulate them.

The root of at least some of the stories about demonstrators would seem to lie in New Zealand, where, on 12 May 1971, returned men genuinely faced a theatre piece of fake blood, and drove down the streets of Auckland towards banners branding them as mercenaries and murderers.

Like Australia, New Zealand had a mixed record on welcome-home parades. During the First World War, 'public enthusiasm for particular arrivals varied, and government policies first encouraged, then discouraged, public receptions'.[64] Paul

Diamond has written that, in the Second World War, 'only one unit, the Maori Battalion, had a formal welcome home. There were also no formal welcomes for New Zealand veterans on their return from Korea and Malaysia, [and during] the Second World War, soldiers returning from overseas were held up when the wharfies refused to work on a public holiday, and when they finally landed, the soldiers threw eggs at waiting politicians.'[65]

New Zealand had sent conscripts to both wars, and in a 1949 referendum a huge majority (77.9 per cent) of voters who responded to the question voted to reintroduce compulsory military training (known as CMT) in the post-war years. New Zealand adopted a scheme similar to Australia's 1950s arrangement, in which most young men had to train for 14 weeks with one arm of the military, then serve for three years in the reserves. A Labour government discontinued the universal scheme in 1959, but in 1961 the National government introduced a birthdate ballot to select 2000 20-year-olds each year for a very similar program. New Zealand national servicemen were not fully trained soldiers and were not expected to fight overseas. New Zealand had troops in Vietnam from June 1964 to December 1972, but they were all regular, professional, full-time soldiers. Many served alongside Australian infantry in ANZAC battalions; there was an artillery battery in country from July 1965 to May 1971; and a New Zealand SAS troop was attached to the Australian SAS Squadron from 1968 to 1972.

There were two immediate welcome home parades: the Auckland march that was disrupted by demonstrators, and another which took place in relative obscurity in the small beach-side town of Raglan. At the Auckland welcome home parade for the artillerymen of 161 Battery and the SAS, reported the *New Zealand Herald*, 'about 150 anti-war demonstrators, some smeared with paint to look like blood, greeted the returning soldiers with placards and shouted slogans. The chanting by the protesters was at first partly drowned by the Army band leading the parade, then by equally loud shouting by other people in support of the battery. Red paint "bombs" and firecrackers were thrown on the road as the troops neared the saluting base. Three people were arrested.'

As was the practice at the fearsomely methodical *New Zealand Herald*, the report then plunged into the incident in ever greater detail: 'Liberally daubed with red paint and writhing in simulated agony, the demonstrators caused only a momentary disruption of the parade. The band altered course likely to avoid them and the protesters were removed by the police ... Protesters around the Town Hall carried about 20 placards bearing such slogans as ... "We Only Went For the Money," "N.Z. Troops Are Murdering In Our Name" ... Placards carried by rival factions read "Well Done, Kiwis," and "Nothing Is Too Good For Our Boys".'[66]

After the parade, according to NZ SAS trooper George Babbington, the veterans went to look for the protesters who, supposedly, were drinking in an (unnamed) student pub, where 'There was one humongous scrap ... there was this young female about 19, in my face screaming obscenities decrying our role in the war ... I grabbed her by her hair and smashed her face against the door. When it was all over, surprisingly, no one was ever charged. The police never came. We learned later they were told to stay away.'[67]

Whatever the police made of Babbington's supposed revenge, it was not reported in the media or remembered by the left. While the attack may or may not have occurred, the protest did. As with the majority of dramatic events staged in public spaces in modern times, it was recorded by press and television cameras. The banners can be clearly read and the protesters could be identified.[68]

The reception granted the returned men in Auckland was incomparably more hostile than any event in the war years in Australia. This raises the question: would the Australian anti-war movement have been more militant and, perhaps, larger, in the absence of a national service obligation for overseas service? It is a counterintuitive and hypothetical proposition but that does not necessarily mean it should be dismissed outright. European nations such as England, France and the Netherlands, which sent no troops to South Vietnam, suffered larger and more violent demonstrations against the war than any that occurred in Australia. The possibility is that national service actually served to maintain a level of social cohesion and emasculate the bitterest criticism of the troops as, after 1966, at least some of them were unwilling conscripts.

In the aftermath of the Auckland parade, the soldier who led 161 Battery on the march, Major John Masters, was taken to court by the protesters for offensive and disorderly behaviour (in prosecuting the war in Vietnam). The charge was dismissed, but it would be difficult to imagine a more naked attempt to hold the soldiers responsible for the war: if this had happened in Australia, that is the physical form it could have taken.[69]

New Zealand's Vietnam forces were given a symbolic home-coming on 30 May 1998 as Parade 98, and the veterans eventually reached a settlement with the government. Its terms included the commissioning of the oral history project that resulted in the publication of some of the questionable claims in the book *No Front Line*, which I examine in Chapter 5.

There is something about parading facts that is incomparably more dreary than parading soldiers, but it is impossible for a serious observer to escape the conclusion that welcome home parades for Australian Vietnam veterans were regular, colourful, jubilant events throughout the war years. The largest of the welcome home parades attracted crowds of hundreds of thousands – far more people than ever demonstrated against the war in one single place, or even on one single day, throughout the country.

Gerard Windsor, in his generous review of *The Nashos' War*, called me a 'zealot intent on making one point' for my insistence on cataloguing the welcome home parades. Furthermore, 'There are some issues he doesn't discuss,' wrote Windsor [although I did]. 'Welcome home parades were held, but many nashos didn't march because they had not sailed home on HMAS *Sydney*. Instead, when their two-year service was up they had been flown to Sydney, told to make their way home on rail tickets, and then simply let go.'[70] However, the idea that there were no welcome home parades is only loosely connected with the number of welcome home parades that demonstrably took place, and it is an idea that can remain entirely robust in the face of detailed explanations as to why individuals might have missed out on their particular march. The veterans' issue with welcome home parades is not – as Windsor seems to imply – some kind of administrative grievance. Their complaint is not that the welcome home parades were difficult to attend, and the significance of the no-welcome-home-parades story is unconnected with logistics.

When men say they were not given a welcome home parade, they mean they did not feel welcome when they came home. It is difficult to communicate an abstract idea of social alienation, easier to weave a story around a sentiment, to provide the material answer to the question that even the most sympathetic listener silently demands – *what happened to you that made you feel that way?* There is also a deeper undercurrent to the no-wel-come-home stories: that troops were smuggled back either to protect them from hostile demonstrators, or because the government – and even the Army – was ashamed of them. The idea that veterans were not offered an 'official' reception serves to illustrate a feeling that the veterans – and the cause for which they fought – received no ongoing support from the government once the men were back in Australia. The feelings are real – at least today – even if the stories are not.

Windsor is only half-correct in his contention that 'many nashos' were 'simply let go' on their return to Australia. This was true right at the end of Australia's commitment, once the term of national service had been reduced to 18 months in late 1971, but until that time the overwhelming majority of national servicemen still had three-to-six months (minus leave time) left to serve in the Army. They came back from Vietnam, went home, then returned to their unit's base and performed often dispiriting duties until their two years was up. I cannot remember speaking to a man who enjoyed or valued this time – nonetheless, few were thrown back onto the street in the manner that Windsor suggests, although the idea that this often happened performs a clear function in myth, in which the damaged, un-decompressed veteran returns to civilian life with a fearsome, anomic jolt.

The men who marched in the welcome home parades are sometimes regarded as fortunate on two counts: firstly, of course, they experienced a welcome home parade; secondly, they had a long, slow sea voyage back from Vietnam to mark their passage from a war zone, generally in the company of men they had fought alongside. The main body of every battalion but 6RAR came home by ship but, for a variety of reasons, a large number of men who served with the battalion returned earlier or later. For example, the advance party would arrive beforehand by air and many members might leave before the end the battalion's tour, by air. Replacements might join the battalion at any point during its tour and have to remain in Vietnam until their 12 months was up. Michael O'Brien writes of the end of 7RAR's second tour, 'A small Rear Party, commanded by Captain Peter Leeson, remained in Nui Dat after the Main Body left. It assisted 3 RAR as best it could in settling in. They then flew from Luscombe Field to Saigon and on to Sydney. Few were there to greet them. [The main body returned by ship and] marched through Sydney, accompanied by a 200 man naval contingent from HMAS *Sydney* and HMAS *Perth* and a small RAAF group ... The march through the city was an important ceremony for many soldiers, particularly those being discharged from the Army soon afterwards ... Many felt that this ceremony indicated the community's approval for their job done in Vietnam. It was a great pity that only a small proportion of the National Servicemen who served on the tour of duty took part in the march. Many had already been discharged and were not recalled for the march. Others had been transferred to 3RAR to complete their twelve month tour. Soldiers who missed marching with the battalion resented it and felt much less appreciated by the community than those who did.'[71]

A table detailing the dates of the parades, the units that marched and the sizes of the crowds that greeted them appears in this book as Appendix II. From this information, we can reach tentative conclusions about the percentage of men – and national servicemen – who took part in welcome home parades. When the reported numbers of soldiers who marched is added together (after RAAF and RAN personnel are removed from the total figure) the total number of marchers is 11 800. If we remove 1RAR's welcome home parade, where 500 regular soldiers marched, and assume the other parades were split 50:50 between national servicemen and regulars (which is probably broadly true), then the total number of national servicemen who marched in welcome home parades could have been about 5650, or 37 per cent of the 15 381 who served in Vietnam. The percentage figure for the whole of the regular cohort is much lower (24 per cent), since many more regulars than national servicemen served in Vietnam. However, the great majority of soldiers who marched were infantrymen. There seems to be no publicly available figure for the exact numbers of national servicemen and regulars who served in the infantry in Vietnam (aside from the widely accepted idea of an approximate 50:50 split, perhaps weighted lightly towards national servicemen), but the percentage of national service infantrymen who marched would have to be greater than the figure for all veterans.

In the absence of a more rigorous analysis of the statistics, it seems likely that a counterintuitive proposition is true, and national servicemen were, percentage-wise, more likely to march in a welcome home parade than regular soldiers. It would take another four-year study to calculate how these figures compare with the experiences of veterans of the First and Second World Wars. Some Vietnam veterans seem to have nurtured an exaggerated idea of the extent of the welcome home from earlier wars. This is understandable. They are not military historians. They are not obliged to check their facts when they are writing about how they feel. However, when Windsor wrote, 'men returning from the two victorious world wars might have experienced the same military and public indifference, but we might have hoped human science and compassion had moved on by 1970',[72] he was asking from history something that history cannot give and wishing the 1970s into the 1990s. The British historian

EP Thompson famously warned against those who read history 'in the light of subsequent preoccupations, and not as in fact it occurred'.[73]

There remains, however, one glaring fact that I have not remarked upon but that is difficult to escape. There is one very large group of Vietnam veterans of which the huge majority did not receive any kind of welcome home parade until several years after the war had ended – American Vietnam veterans, who were replaced on an individual basis and appear to have received only one largely symbolic parade, in New York, at the end of America's part in the war.

Time and again, it is their experience that Australian veterans seem to have borrowed.

5
Looking for atrocities in all the wrong places
The myth of Australia's My Lai

The crimes [Australians] committed in Phuoc Tuy were in no way less ferocious than those of the US and puppet troops. Savage beatings, rapes, arbitrary arrests, beheadings, the plucking out of people's livers …

– Colonel Tran Quoc Trung, PAVN, in War: Australia and Vietnam, edited by Ken Maddock and Barry Wright, 1987

One adviser told me that the Cambodians used to eat Vietnamese livers after battle … This ritual cannibalism, as anthropologists would call it, is apparently not practised by Vietnamese. I suggest that indulgence in it by Cambodians fighting alongside Australians is the likely basis of Colonel Trung's startling claim.

Ken Maddock, 1991[1]

Fraudulent literature and suspect claims of atrocities on all sides have clouded Australian understanding of the Vietnam War since the beginning. They play to the idea of South Vietnam as an amorphous, anarchic hellhole, where the sadistic fantasies of half-mad heroin-crazed combatants could be acted out with impunity on the mute and helpless civilian population. It is a picture painted in the blood of the hundreds of innocents murdered by US troops at My Lai but it is, to say the least, a highly questionable portrait of the Australian area of operation in Phuoc Tuy province.

The first allegations of war crimes against US troops to be widely circulated in Australia appeared in 1966, when the pamphlet *American Atrocities in Vietnam* by US journalist Eric Norden was reprinted in Sydney. This closely typeset 16-page A4 booklet was published by the Vietnam Action Committee (VAC, from 1967 the Vietnam Action Campaign), a small group founded in 1965 by Trotskyists including Bob Gould, Rod Webb and John Percy. Its contents comprised a long article reprinted from the February 1966 issue of the US pacifist magazine *Liberation*, retelling a series of stories largely written by named individuals about specific acts of torture and killing perpetrated in South Vietnam by the US and its local allies. Norden conceded that 'of course' the Vietcong used terror too, but, he argued, 'Theirs is of a more selective nature, if only to avoid estranging the peasants and villagers on whom they depend for food and shelter. They will kill and mutilate the body of a government official but they generally pick an unpopular and corrupt victim whose death is welcomed by the peasants.' The US troops, in Norden's view, rarely knew whether the people around them were Vietcong or government sympathisers, and consequently often captured or killed innocent civilians.

Most of the accusations collected by Norden have not since been seriously questioned or refuted. They included *Newsweek*'s Saigon correspondent William Tuohy's assertion that ARVN units and their US advisers routinely tortured prisoners in the field; and press agency AP's Pulitzer-winning correspondent Malcolm Browne's observation that both male and female prisoners of the South Vietnamese were interrogated by the 'ding-a-ling' method of attaching electrodes to their body parts – in the case of female prisoners, the nipples – and sending an electric current through them. Other passages in *American Atrocities in Vietnam* included excerpts from *The Furtive War* by Australian communist journalist (and probable communist agent) Wilfred Burchett about Tran Thi Nham, a young woman from the village of Dien Hong who had delivered a petition for free elections to the Tourane offices of the International Control Commission (ICC), an agency established to oversee the implementation of the Geneva Accords. According to Tran Thi Nham's story, which was eventually substantiated by the ICC, she was imprisoned in the town of Faifo where the various tortures inflicted upon her body included 'soapy water and urine forced down the mouth and nostrils; electricity applied to vagina and breast nipples; flesh torn from the breasts, thighs, and shoulders by red hot pincers; a ruler thrust into the vagina. These were interspersed with beatings, starvation.' She was eventually left for dead and, although she survived, wrote Burchett, her reproductive organs were 'wrecked for all time'.[2]

The inclusion in the pamphlet of the story of Tran Thi Nham was arguably deceptive, as the events recounted occurred between 1956 and 1958 and the only explicit connection with the US was the allegation that she was driven to prison in an 'American police van'. Undated in the pamphlet and flanked by more recent reportage, the story was allowed to be perceived as if it had occurred in the 1960s.

On 1 September, copies of *American Atrocities in Vietnam* were seized from the International Bookshop in Elizabeth Street,

Melbourne, by the Victorian Vice Squad, whose chief said that 'charges, by summons, would be made over the pamphlet within 14 days'.[3] The squad had obtained a ruling from a stipendiary magistrate, a Mr McConville, that the pamphlet was obscene as it contained 'illustrations of gross cruelty'. On 19 September, the police action was abandoned.[4]

An apparently semi-official response to *American Atrocities in Vietnam* was *The Truth of Viet Cong Terror*, a pamphlet published by the Ministry of Information and Chieu Hoi of the Republic of Vietnam. Its authorship was credited to an Australian: Dr Robert Gurner Wyllie, a Melbourne physician and pathologist with the Alfred Hospital surgical team, a group of civilian medical staff working in a civilian hospital in Vietnam.

The text of the pamphlet had originally appeared in the Sydney *Daily Telegraph* on 24 November 1966, purporting to have been written 'in the form of a letter to a colleague'. The slightly defensive introduction provided by the newspaper insisted 'this horrifying exposure of the kind of atrocities carried out by the Vietcong on the peaceful peasants of South Vietnam comes from no professional propagandist' but an Australian doctor who 'worked there for six months'. Wyllie's letter is dated November 1966, and addressed to an unnamed colleague in Australia who has ostensibly sent Wyllie 'clippings from the local papers about the war in this unlucky country' including the pamphlet *American Atrocities in Vietnam* which, Wyllie noted – in a rather strange aside in a personal letter – 'was banned for a time in Victoria'.

'News is always welcome,' wrote Wyllie. 'We live surrounded by the war, frequently within sound of gun fire, and yet often not knowing what is happening.'[5] This is curious, since Wyllie was, at the time, almost certainly living in Melbourne. He does not seem to have been in Vietnam either when *American Atrocities in Vietnam* was seized in Australia in September, or when his letter to a colleague was written in November. Like the *Daily Telegraph*, the cover of Wyllie's pamphlet states that Wyllie worked in the country for six months. According to the 1966 annual report of the Baker Institute of Alfred Hospital, Wyllie 'spent the first half of the year on a tour of duty in South Vietnam'.[6] The 1966 *Ormond Chronicle* specified that Thwaites Fellow Dr RG Wyllie 'spent the first six months of this year with the Alfred Hospital medical team in Vietnam, then visited centres in South-East Asia with his wife, prior to returning to Melbourne in September'.[7]

At least some of the episodes described by Wyllie did not occur while he was in Vietnam. He wrote, rather buoyantly, about the consequences of an accidental bombing by US planes of a South Vietnamese village, in which both the local school and market place were hit and 'a number of people killed'. The next morning, he said, a team of US Army engineers began to rebuild the village and re-establish its water supply and drainage 'on a sounder basis'. A day later, the first reparation payments were made, and a Vietnamese friend subsequently told Dr Wyllie that 'allowing for the deaths and suffering caused, the village was now better off than it had been before'.[8] The village was described as being 'across the river, not far from the town'.[9] Dr Wyllie appears to be referring to one or both of the two villages Truong Trung and Truong Tay, attacked in error by the US, leaving 63 people dead and 100 injured. The bombing occurred on 9 August 1966, by which time, it would appear, Dr Wyllie was no longer in Vietnam. It defies belief that any sane person could have described an area that had lost its children and sustained 163 casualties in a single evening as having become, on balance, a better place due to improvements to its drainage system.

But Dr Wyllie was very much a glass-half-full kind of commentator. His assessment of the state of health care in South Vietnam was also extraordinarily upbeat. While he admitted to 'a deceptive appearance of uncleanliness' in the wards, he said they were nonetheless 'cheerful places that bubble with life and conversation'. A newspaper correspondent may not have noticed this, however, since the conversation 'stops immediately as strangers enter'.[10]

However, the primary purpose of Wyllie's pamphlet was not to defend the Saigon government's notoriously poor hospital system but to relate stories of Vietcong atrocities featuring victims such as the pregnant wife of a murdered hamlet chief, who had been forced to watch guerrillas strangle her husband before she was machine-gunned along with her three-year-old child. According to Wyllie, she lost her legs, her three-year-old and her unborn child. It could be that this – or something like it – did happen. It loosely fits the modus operandi of the Vietcong in the villages. But Wyllie may not be a credible witness. It is difficult to escape the conclusion that his 'letter' was, in part at least, the work of a 'professional propagandist', produced as a direct response to the 'unbanning' of Norden's pamphlet, and structured to offer examples of VC atrocities to be weighed against Norden's accusations against the US. Some of Wyllie's claims were repeated as facts in Paul Ham's popular history, *Vietnam: The Australian war*,[11] and so continue to form part of our picture of Australia's Vietnam.

The book with the greatest impact on the image of Australian soldiers in Vietnam was published not in Australia but the US. *Happy Hunting Ground*, by former US Marine Martin Russ, was the memoir of a war veteran hungry to find a new war zone and apparently eager to impress his readers with the dangers and hardships he ostensibly faced while wandering around South

Vietnam as a journalist, meeting with US, Australian and South Vietnamese soldiers. Russ, who lent pseudonyms to the soldiers he met, wrote that he was sorry to have missed an incident in 1966 in which Australian troops had taken a female VC prisoner and interrogated her by 'forcing water into her until she talked freely'.[12] The prisoner was To Thi Nau, who had been captured in October 1966, 18 months prior to the publication of Russ's book. Photographic evidence emerged of To Thi Nau being led in and out of her place of interrogation, and an unpleasant public debate began about how much water forced into a female prisoner – who was restrained by much larger and stronger, armed men – actually constituted torture. The ensuing 'water-torture' scandal was exhaustively reported in the Australian press. It seemed unlikely that the only torture at Nui Dat should have occurred while journalists were around to take pictures, and the water-torture revelations undoubtedly coloured the public perception of Australia's war. Three Australians present during the interrogation testified that Thi Nau swallowed 'less than a cup' of water from the three or four pannikins forced upon her. Her interrogator, WO Kenneth Borland, claimed that when he returned to the prisoner for the third time, carrying a 4-gallon jerrycan of water, it was entirely 'for theatrical effect'.[13]

While I was researching *The Nashos' War*, Brian Timberlake, a national serviceman who was involved in 'Code of Conduct' counter-interrogation training with the Australian Army Intelligence Corps in 1967, gave me a photograph of a trainee handcuffed to a brick wall while an interrogator forced the contents of a teapot down his throat – so the idea of water torture obviously was not unheard of in the Australian Army. He said his commanding officer was 'aghast' at the picture ('He said, "We can't let that be seen! Handcuffs!"').[14]

Walter Beattie, another national serviceman who worked in Intelligence, told me, 'We weren't allowed to torture anybody but the Vietnamese were, so we'd tell them what we were looking for … We'd also have South Koreans seconded to us, who also were very good at extracting information from people. We weren't allowed to be anywhere near.'[15]

This, in essence, was the underlying argument of the 1968 publication *Australian Atrocities in Vietnam*, a pamphlet by Alex Carey that sought to emulate the earlier success of *American Atrocities in Vietnam*. Although the cover showed two frightened-looking Australian provosts manhandling a blind-folded Vietnamese prisoner, the pamphlet did not present much evidence that Australians had committed what might generally be regarded as atrocities – with the exception of the display of the bodies of dead VC in the village of Hoa Long on 16 February 1968, apparently in repetition of a 'mistake' made one year earlier.[16] Carey relied more heavily on the idea that Vietnam was an atrocious and unjust war and the way Australians might initially treat their prisoners was all but irrelevant since captured VC were quickly handed over to the South Vietnamese, who tortured and killed them. All of Carey's accounts of the worst conduct of US and Allied troops concerned American and South Korean soldiers, and the most confronting photographs in the pamphlet (none of which were captioned) actually showed US troops in action. Yet Carey wrote there was 'no doubt at all that Australian troops are committing atrocities in Vietnam and that they will – and increasingly – continue to do so'.

But he did not blame the troops. In fact, Carey asked, 'Who is to blame for this? Surely not, or not principally, the soldiers themselves; pitched without choice at 20 years of age into the midst of a hopeless, immoral war? … the situation of these young

Australians must evoke our anger and our compassion, however much we may deplore the behaviour to which it drives them. Surely the principal, if not the entire, responsibility for every barbarity, every atrocity to which our troops are driven rests in one quarter only – with those political leaders who through lies, ignorance or folly have misled us into involvement in a war which so shamefully affronts every tradition of honour and humanity that our history lays claim to?'[17]

The year after Carey's pamphlet was published, the My Lai trials began in the US. The impact of the My Lai massacre in Australia is so comprehensively misrepresented that it merits a book of its own. The ACTU became a little more militantly opposed to the war and national service. The Waterside Workers Federation refused to load the HMAS *Jeparit* with supplies for Vietnam. A large group of left-wing 'rebel union' officials in Victoria issued a statement calling for calling for national servicemen to 'lay down their arms in mutiny'. National servicemen did no such thing.

In 2018, we know that between 347 and 504 Vietnamese civilians – old men, women and children – were slaughtered by US troops at the hamlets of Son My and My Khe in South Vietnam on 16 March 1968. Women were gang-raped and tortured, their bodies mutilated and their babies killed. This was not the picture most Australians had of the massacre during the Vietnam War – or for many years afterwards. Although the tabloid *Sun-Herald* published a special supplement relating to the massacre, the sexual violence seems to have attracted only cursory coverage in the Australian broadsheet metropolitan press. While the court was in session, the *Sydney Morning Herald*, for example, faithfully printed US press agency reports of the proceedings, but they never dwelt on the carnal details, and both the readers and writers of the newspaper continued to make excuses for the Americans, or sneer at naïve and unkempt anti-war protesters. The Reverend AL Davidson, General Secretary of the Worldwide Evangelical Crusade (Australia), wrote that while 'deploring' the massacre, he felt the 'silent majority' was 'thoroughly sickened' by 'the opinions, and often demonstrations of the loud-mouthed (and, in many cases, long-haired) minority'.[18] The consensus of respectable opinion seemed to be that soldiers were trained to follow orders and, anyway, the Vietcong did worse.

Only one person, Lt William Calley, was ever convicted of the murders at My Lai – nobody was ever found guilty of the gang rapes – and Calley served only three-and-a-half years under house arrest before being pardoned by President Nixon. Seventy-nine per cent of the American people disagreed with Calley's guilty verdict. A recording of a ballad that praised the killer as a hero, 'The Battle Hymn of Lt Calley', sold nearly two million copies. Even after Calley was found guilty, the *Sydney Morning Herald* reported that two office girls from Gordon had written to Nixon asking him to grant clemency to Calley but gas Charles Manson.[19]

The extent to which ordinary educated Australians were aware of the breadth and depth of the horrors at My Lai is perhaps illustrated in a news story in *The Age* in August 1976, which explained parenthetically that 'twenty-two unarmed Vietnamese died in the My Lai massacre'. The newspaper published this information in a story reporting that former anti-war movement leader and one-time deputy prime minister Jim Cairns had been told by an old man in Hoa Long that Australian troops had massacred 27 Vietnamese civilians, including women and children, as local peasants returned from their work in the rice fields in July 1970. Much confused and confusing journalism followed, with intimations that there might have been a military cover-up of Australia's own My Lai massacre. These implications did not come from Cairns, who specifically said, 'This incident occurred in difficult and dark circumstances. My Lai was deliberate and in the light of day.'[20]

Eventually, the focus shifted from 1970 to 1967, and the incident under investigation came to be the 'Bamboo Pickers' ambush of 23 October 1967, in which Australian troops accidentally killed six Vietnamese civilians. Members of the 2RAR ambush platoon, which had been led by Ernest Benjamin Morris, were prepared to come forward and admit that civilians had been killed, a process later described in Morris's own detailed study of the incident and its aftermath.

There had been no cover-up and no My Lai. Morris had recorded the incident clearly and honestly in an after-action report filed in the 2RAR Commander's Diary: 'The patrol had laid an ambush on a track when noise and talking were heard. Subsequently a group of 16 people walked into the ambush. The leading Vietnamese saw the machine gunner and pointed at him with his shoulder carrying stick. The machine gunner took the stick to be a weapon and opened fire. The remainder of the platoon then opened fire, catching most of the group as they ran back south. After 2–3 minutes firing, I ordered cease-fire when I heard a woman cry out. I moved forward and found what we thought to be weapons were in fact shoulder carrying sticks.' The report describes the party as 'civilians' and the 'lessons learned' from the action as the 'great difficulty identifying civilians from VC in close country'.[21]

The ambush seems to have taken place in the exclusion zone around 1ATF – although, as Morris willingly concedes, this has been disputed – in which case the troops were acting within their rules of engagement. Whatever the location of the incident, there is no evidence that it was anything other than a tragedy.

'I recall running towards the victims once I had called ceasefire,' wrote Morris, many years later. 'The moment between the machine gun firing on the civilians and hearing the whimpering of children caught in the gunfire was very short but still remains with me. I knew instantly on hearing the cries for help that something was very wrong. I ordered the platoon to ceasefire and ran towards the killing ground to assess the carnage I realised had taken place. I was confronted with a scene that will haunt me forever. As I moved forward I think I was inwardly hoping that the residual firing would kill me.'[22]

In the wake of what was to become the Bamboo Picker ambush allegations, other accusations – or, rather, 'admissions' – of Australian war crimes came to light on the ABC TV show *This Day Tonight* in August 1976. The first incident came via a psychiatrist (who did not appear on the program) who had treated a former soldier (who did not appear on the program) who had complained of anxiety and told him 'under ether' that in Vietnam he had 'raped women, and shot unarmed women and children'. He did not detail how many civilians he had abused, how, where, when or with whom. The second confession came from an RAAF officer who said that in 1967, while flying west of Nui Dat, he had obeyed an order to fire on a column of male and female Vietnamese civilians.[23]

In March 1980, the ABC show *PM* aired allegations that the Battle of Binh Ba had included a massacre of civilians. Binh Ba had been the scene of a heavily documented seven-and-a-half hours of bloody fighting after the village was 'over-run' by enemy soldiers in June 1969. There was a film crew present throughout the engagement. There is no doubt that civilians were among those killed – AAP had immediately reported the deaths of village children[24] – but ample evidence that the Australian Army had attempted to evacuate them. This is not to deny that something horrible happened in Binh Ba to an unknown number of Vietnamese civilians – only that killing the villagers was not the purpose of the operation, and it was not done for entertainment. In June 1980, former Trooper Tony Chaunavel told the ABC's *Nationwide* that he had seen the corpses of women and children when the fighting was over and 'many bodies were so badly mutilated that it was difficult to count, let alone ascertain if they were women, children, or North Vietnamese Army. The highest figure I was able to get for NVA was 30, leaving some 70 bodies which could only have been civilians.'[25] The Department of Defence scoffed at Chaunavel's figures. The day after Chaunavel's allegations were reported in the newspaper, another (anonymous) veteran came forward and told the *Canberra Times* that he had been at the battle and in the aftermath he 'saw a lot of bodies which were NVA or VC and a lot of weapons but there were certainly no women and no children'.[26]

When I was researching *The Nashos' War*, I interviewed a man who claimed to have been the source for the *Canberra Times*'s rebuttal of Chaunavel. He told me Chaunavel's account of the dead had been more honest than his own. I had turned off my recorder, so I did not use his retraction in the book.

I did not ask any of the veterans I interviewed if they had ever tortured a prisoner, shot a civilian or burned down a village with the people inside. Perhaps if I had, I would have heard some terrible stories. One or two men, unprompted, raised issues about the killing of enemy POWs; one man talked of souveniring an enemy skull from the battlefield; and one man said a member of his battalion had murdered an elderly woman. But I was taken aback when 7RAR veteran and accomplished author Barry Heard told me his unit would strip the bodies of the people they killed but he had never heard of anyone 'screw a dead human or something'.[27]

This is an extraordinary statement, and difficult to imagine coming from the mouth of a veteran of any other war. Why should Australian soldiers returned from Vietnam feel bound to defend themselves against unspoken accusations of necrophilia? The answer lies in the literature.

The first book I ever read about the Vietnam War was Mark Baker's dramatic oral history *Nam*. Some of Baker's sources admit to terrible pornographic war crimes in sickeningly forensic detail – the only facts missing from the stories are the names of the soldiers or their units or their comrades, and the dates and locations of the events, and anything else that would allow anybody to verify anything they said. There are similar problems with certain Australian books about the war, which perpetuate a minor tradition of unsubstantiated – and often unsubstantiable – accusations against both Anzac troops and the Vietcong, sometimes in the same publication.

Books published around the October 1987 Welcome Home Parade and National Reunion of Australian Vietnam Forces included the first oral history of Australia's war, Stuart Rintoul's *Ashes of Vietnam*. Many of the men interviewed for *Ashes of Vietnam* are quoted extensively under their full names. The years in which they served in Vietnam are given, and some pointer to their unit is usually provided. On the rare occasion when Rintoul gives only a first name for his subject, the interviewee often goes on to describe an atrocity of some kind. Early in the book, Rintoul introduces 36-year-old 'Wayne' – the same man who claims his birthday came up in every single national service ballot – who is interviewed in the ward of a repatriation hospital while a pianist, somewhat fortuitously, plays 'Pack Up Your Troubles in Your Old Kitbag'. Wayne arrives in Vietnam by plane on 21 January 1971,[28] a Thursday, although it does not seem flights from Sydney arrived in Vietnam on Thursdays.[29] We learn that he is a 'non-combatant' posted to Vung Tau.[30] He appears to be a medic. Wayne is sympathetic to the local population and regularly smuggles medical supplies to a 'small orphanage in a village just out of Vung Tau' where part-Vietnamese children (the offspring of foreign soldiers) are cared for by French nuns. One day he arrives to find the VC have attacked the orphanage, raped the French nuns, beheaded the village chief, and massacred ten orphans aged between 18 months and five years old. Four girls have been cut from their vaginas to their throats and six boys have been castrated and disembowelled. The Mother Superior warns him to leave straight away as there are still VC in the village, and Wayne never tells anyone about the atrocity as he should not have been out delivering medical supplies.

This is an incredible story, a terrible atrocity committed by the VC in 1971, involving not only the sadistic murder of orphaned children but the rape of foreign nationals, and it takes place within a short distance of the Australian base at Vung Tau. If such an event had occurred, it is implausible that it should not be more widely known or have stimulated wild outrage in metropolitan France. It would have been seized upon by the Catholic Church and the South Vietnamese government as irrefutable proof of the depravity of the enemy. It would also have represented an inexplicable change of tactics for the guerrillas, who were not well known as rapists,[31] and had not previously been inclined to murder mixed-race orphans. The barbarism seems motivated by little more than base evil, and its consequence would surely have been to turn some local villagers away from the sexually depraved savages of the VC and into the arms of the government.

The story seems to be based on an actual occurrence on 21 June 1966, which involved neither orphans, rape, nor nuns. Australian medical civil action (medcap) teams had being providing medical aid to civilians in Phuoc Tuy province in a bid to win local hearts and minds. A medcap team was requested at the hamlet of Hoa Long, where an 11-year-old girl was reported as having cut herself. When the team arrived, they found the girl had been disembowelled by the VC. The girl's father was an Army of the Republic of Vietnam (ARVN) soldier, and she had been murdered as bait to draw the medcap team into an ambush, but the guerrillas had attacked instead a Provost Land Rover and killed Provost Corporal Ian Jones. In the true story, there is no sexual element and a defined tactical purpose to the child's murder, which is chronicled in the Australian Official History.[32] The fantastical version is a senseless carnal atrocity that escaped the attention of the world.

There is no question that the VC regularly decapitated village headmen and murdered their families, and additional elements of Wayne's story seem to have come from the pamphlet *The Viet-Cong Strategy of Terror*, which describes the shooting of a local nun from the Vietnamese Sisters of Providence in Tay Ninh Province on 15 May 1961, and perhaps from a proximate paragraph in the same pamphlet in which the VC attack a truck carrying 20 unescorted girls between Saigon and Vung Tau, killing two and wounding ten on 22 March 1961.[33]

The worst war crime committed by Australian troops themselves in *Ashes of Vietnam* is remembered by 'Michael', apparently a volunteer national serviceman who went to Vietnam with an infantry battalion in 1971. Michael describes a village around which the Australians always seemed to be running into enemy fire. In order to teach the villagers a lesson, two platoons of troops (a total of 'maybe twenty blokes' – which would have made them the two smallest platoons in Vietnam) rounded up more than a dozen villagers, including children as young as ten, and murdered them. In Michael's words: 'The women were raped. It's a bit hard to pass up a bit of pussy like that, isn't it, although it might be hard to believe in a situation like that ... it's just a bit of the animal comes out. About half the blokes were involved in it. I didn't participate in that ... I thought there was a fair chance they would have the jack. I had my fun later with the machine-gun. One bloke in the platoon screwed one who was already dead.'[34]

This account, I think, was what Barry Heard had in mind when he told me he had never known of a man who screwed a dead human – along, perhaps, with another passage in Rintoul where an identified New Zealand soldier, Ray Caldwell, who appears on his country's nominal roll of Vietnam veterans, claims that in 1968 he saw another (unidentified) New Zealander machine-gun a female VC then strip her to try to have sex with her 'before she went cold'. He was, apparently, ordered to stop by his lieutenant.

To return to Michael's story, Michael claims the Australians destroyed the bodies with grenades, and the remaining villagers did not report the incident because nobody would have believed them. This is an extraordinary conception of daily life in the Australian area of operation. To imagine that local people would not complain of a massacre because they might be disbelieved belies the large number of claims related to vastly more trivial matters that were presented to Australian forces regularly by Vietnamese civilians. While researching *The Nashos' War*, I spoke with Ross McKeand, a former national serviceman with the Australian Army Legal Corps (AALC) who had been posted as legal officer to 1ATF in Vung Tau. McKeand told me, 'They used to put in compensation claims for any damage done by Australian forces, and we often had to review them. I did an investigation into the destruction of a Buddhist temple. Armed with a jeep and a soldier with a rifle, we went around seeing where an APC had allegedly knocked down a Buddhist temple, which turned out to be one of these little things you see by the side of the road, almost like a little drinks stand, where they do a little bit of praying with incense etcetera. And, from what I could tell, there were huge exaggerations as to the damage done and the person who was injured. It was worth nothing and you couldn't believe a word you were being told.'

While claims arising from combat were supposed to be referred to the government of South Vietnam, a history of the Legal Corps offers many other examples of civil claims brought against the Australian military. With an understanding of the relentlessly prosaic nature of the complaints, and the efforts sometimes made to satisfy the claimants, it becomes clear that an orgy of gang rape and mass murder was unlikely to have passed without protest. For example, in a case where an Australian soldier had damaged the contents of a Vietnamese house, 'An officer from the unit, the soldier himself, the provost who had first viewed the damage, the legal officer (Major Carter) and an interpreter, took an entire day to assess the damage and to haggle with the family, which resulted in a reduction of the claim from 25,000 to 8,000 piastres.'[35] In another case, an officer was sent to determine the loss caused by Australian soldiers in a bar room brawl. A provost explained to him that the usual method for settling the claim was to count the bottle tops left on the floor to calculate how many bottles had been broken in the fighting. When the officer paid up and tried to take away the bottle tops, he was told to leave them at the bar – from which he concluded they probably would be re-used in a subsequent claim.[36] The conclusion of the story has an apocryphal ring, of course, but the fact that Australians and Vietnamese haggled over bottle tops suggests they might have become even more agitated about raped, murdered then raped-again corpses.

Furthermore, the victims' home village should be easily identifiable, as there were a limited number of villages – if any – in Phuoc Tuy province that might 'regularly' be the base of 'hostile fire' towards Australian troops in 1971. In addition, a two-platoon operation would have involved two junior officers as platoon commanders. At any given time, there were about 16 junior officers with rifle platoons in each battalion in Vietnam. 7RAR left Vietnam in February 1971, replaced by 3RAR. Concurrently, 2RAR was in Vietnam until May 1971, when it was relieved by 4RAR/NZ. Therefore, the two platoons of murderers and rapists (each comprising a maximum strength of 34 men) must have been part of 3RAR, 2RAR or 4RAR/NZ. Even if each of these battalions had experienced a 50 per cent turnover among their junior officers, there would be a pool of fewer than 100 men who could possibly have led the worst massacre in the history of Australia's involvement in Vietnam. The culprits would be easy to find, for any journalist or historian. However, it appears that nobody has investigated the atrocity, as it is barely mentioned in any of the subsequent literature. The story might be based on well-known accounts of gang rape in Baker's *Nam*[37] and it is followed in Rintoul's book by Michael's assertion that he wore the ears of dead enemy around his neck.[38]

Specific accusations of atrocities by Australian troops were extremely rare during the war and only slightly more common afterwards. Another book published in 1987, Kenneth Maddock and Barry Wright's anthology *War: Australia and Vietnam*, includes a chapter by a colonel in the People's Army of Vietnam who accuses Australian forces of committing atrocities such as 'savage beatings, rapes, arbitrary arrests, beheadings' and 'the plucking out of people's livers' as well as the proven 'exposure of corpses for deterrent purposes'. The only named victim is a 'Mrs Bay Cong from Long Hoi' who was crippled after being beaten by Australian soldiers for 'taking to the fields a meal they considered too large for her needs alone'.[39]

These allegations were challenged in a footnote to the essay in which editor Barry Wright noted that during his service in Vietnam 'and in the Australian Army throughout the full period of the Vietnam War [he] never heard or saw anything which could be considered ill treatment of Vietnamese prisoners by civilian troops'. However, it is unclear how Wright might have had any form of contact with any prisoner at all since, according to the Nominal Roll, he was only posted to Vietnam for six months in 1970–71, as a captain in the Education Corps at Headquarters Australian Force Vietnam in Saigon.

In 1991, Maddock published the results of his investigation into the allegations raised in his anthology of 1987, and concluded it was probably Cambodians rather than Australians who cut out the livers of the Vietnamese, and broadly – although with qualifications – exonerated the Australian Task Force of most of the more colourful claims made against it. As an anthropologist, Maddock went to admirable length to explain why the Vietnamese were worried about their livers; how the Cambodians had a history of relieving their enemies of their livers; and how

Australians might be indirectly implicated in the removal and consumption of Vietnamese livers by Cambodian mercenaries (who, apparently, enjoyed them best either raw or cut into thin slices and added to vegetable soup)'.[40]

At least one further atrocity claim was made in the wake of the first airing of the liver-eating story: Vietnam veteran Don Tate said he was on patrol north of Nui Dat with three armoured personnel carriers when the lead driver said 'target practice' and 'bang bang bang', shot dead a woman and her child then drove his APC over their bodies. The woman was carrying a bundle that turned out to be a baby that had been alive before it was crushed under the wheels of the vehicle.[41]

In 2008, Tate published *The War Within*, which drew fresh attention to an incident in May 1969 in which a group of Vietcong were ambushed and killed outside the abandoned village of Thau Tich. Apparently at the request of the district chief, the bodies of dead guerrillas were taken to the village of Xuyen Moc and displayed in the marketplace for 'propaganda reasons'. There exists a photograph, which had already been reprinted across two pages of the Time-Life coffee-table book *Vietnam: The Australian experience*,[42] showing the sickened, horrified and tearful reaction of ragged local children watching as the VC corpses are dragged along behind an Australian APC. 'Two of them were headless,' wrote Tate. 'They'd been banging around in the back of the APC until they fell off.'[43] Tate also described the practice of the 'sappers' burial', by which bodies were disposed of by blowing them to pieces.

Claire Hall's *No Front Line*, published in New Zealand in 2014 and based on a government oral history project, fills out the skeleton of the academic narrative of New Zealand's Official History with various kinds of meat, some of it rotten. Ray

Caldwell surfaces again, described here as a 'rifleman' (although he was an engineer). Here, Caldwell claims he used to go to help out at a convent on his days off, and he brought to a nun a perfumed letter which the nun told him was written by a soldier in North Vietnam who wanted to split up with his 'wife or partner'. Caldwell's company had suspicions that their interpreter was 'playing both sides' so they gave him the letter to read. When the interpreter said it was from a soldier in North Vietnam who loved his wife, 'This was the complete opposite of what the nun had told us,' said Caldwell. 'So one of the boys just picked up a gun and blew the interpreter's brains out.'[44] This seems like slight evidence on which to murder a man – and does not explain why the letter should be perfumed – but it is not the only revelation of a previously unreported extrajudicial killing in *No Front Line*. While Hall herself writes that there were no local civilian workers at Nui Dat,[45] she nonetheless includes a rifleman's story about the execution of a civilian worker at Nui Dat: 'The barber shop got closed down because the [Vietnamese] barber was a communist. He was killed. He must've got a lot of intelligence out of that place.'[46]

Treacherous locals are something of a theme in *No Front Line*. Another man tells a story of an Australian soldier who had a regular Vietnamese girlfriend and who stripped the bodies of VC after a contact only to find his own girlfriend among the bodies.[47] This appears to mirror a scene from the TV miniseries *Vietnam*. The function of these myths is clear – they tell the familiar story that foreign soldiers in Vietnam could not distinguish friend from foe.

While there never was an Australian My Lai, not all of the alleged war crimes attributed to Australian and New Zealand forces in Vietnam are mythological – Xuyen Moc, for example, indubitably occurred. But the myths of Anzac atrocities perform several functions. The stories of treacherous locals getting their just deserts illustrate the feeling that friendly faces hid hostile hearts and the VC were everywhere. Attempts to uncover an 'Australian My Lai' are guided by the idea that Australian troops shared the guilt of US forces by dint of their involvement in the same war.

An Australian soldier might argue that by similar standards British troops in the Second World War might be held partially responsible for Soviet atrocities in occupied Germany. It seems unlikely many British veterans of the 1945 Battle of Hamburg felt particularly guilty about the rape of Berlin, but when I first spoke with Sandy MacGregor on our tour of the war sites of Vietnam, it was clear that he felt accused by association of American war crimes. But the Vietnamese no longer have an interest in remembering (or inventing) grievances against Australian forces.

While I was working on my doctorate, I took a 'holiday' to Vietnam, to visit the site of the My Lai massacre. What remains of the village of Son My is a horrible place. While other war remnants, such as the tunnels at Cu Chi, have been turned into theme-park rides, the only commercialisation of the massacre site is in the form of backpackers' day tours, tastelessly driven in army jeeps from the brash and unlovely city of Da Nang. I chose instead to approach from the ancient town Hoi An, with an independent guide, Than, whose father had been forced into fighting for the Vietcong but had escaped the guerrillas to hide in the hills.

As Than and I drove three-and-a-half hours north, the towering stupas of imposing new war memorials loomed bleakly over the rice fields. Each one remembers thousands of local dead. Than said, it is the fashion to raise these brutalist ossuaries, as it allows local bureaucrats to skim money off the cost of their construction. Many of the families of fallen Vietcong did not want the remains of their relatives moved from public cemeteries, where their plots had been bought and tended with love through the years.

Than told me that Vietnamese children learn about My Lai in school, where the war is still known as the American War. Among educated younger people, however, the conflict is spoken of as the Vietnamese Civil War. School students are not taught about Australia's part in the fighting and most Vietnamese have no idea that Australia was involved. But, he said, most of the travellers he takes to Son My are Australians. I assumed he was telling me this because he thought it was what I wanted to hear, but the guide at the site told me the same: more Australians visit My Lai than any other foreign nationality. The next largest groups are Dutch and French. Americans rank fourth.

But the sprawling site is generally quiet. There were only two other tourists at the Son My Memorial when I arrived. The first stop is the tacky, shambolic visitors' centre, with its bust of Ho Chi Minh and inexplicable collection of seashells. A documentary made by Al Jazeera plays continually on a modest television set. It tells the story of the return to My Lai of one of the veterans of C Company, 1st Battalion, 20th Infantry Regiment, 11th Brigade of the 23rd (American) Infantry Division, the unit that perpetrated the massacre. Kenneth Schiel, a veteran from Michigan, had been accused of murdering nine villagers, although the charges against him were dropped. The film shows him meeting with the director of the site museum, Pham Thanh Cong, whose mother, sisters and six-year-old brother were murdered, and who was himself badly wounded. Schiel says only that he is sorry, and that what was done at My Lai was wrong. It is the smallest of confessions and Cong is uncomprehending and unforgiving, but it is obviously a huge step for the tormented Schiel, who was never convicted of any wrongdoing. In the absence of justice, it seems, the guilty punish themselves.

The museum displays photographs that are virtually impossible to view, pictures of entrails spilling from corpses, and an image of a dead little boy who has thrown himself on the body of his younger brother to protect him from gunfire. But worse are the pathetic, primitive children's toys that survived the destruction of the hamlets – stone marbles, a plastic crab – the property of people who had almost nothing. Outside the museum, the foundations of homes are all that remains, as the Americans bombed everything that they had not burned, to erase the evidence. One thatched clay house has been recreated, to show the daily lives of people who once cooked, slept and played music here, but everything else is gone.

The only exhibit relating to Australia illustrates Australian support for the anti-war movement. The same is true of the museum at Hoa Lo Prison (the 'Hanoi Hilton') in Hanoi. The Vietnamese government barely acknowledges that any Vietnamese fought on the American side, let alone that the US had international allies.

So, why do men feel blamed when they are not? Perhaps simply because they once were, by Colonel Trung and atrocity-hunting journalists or – arguably – by Nadine Jensen and some placard-wielding demonstrators. But why do men like Michael – if he really was a veteran – or Claire Hall's New Zealanders, 'admit' to crimes of which they have never been accused?

Perhaps the answer can be found in the words of former engineer Tony 'Bomber' Bower-Miles, who talks about attaching Claymore mines to Vietnamese corpses and destroying the bodies so as to 'piss off the ones that are still alive': 'This was the reality of what went on over there,' wrote Bower-Miles, 'and why we're all suffering now.'[48]

In other words, the act of committing an atrocity damages the perpetrator as well as the victim – and, in fact, as time passes, turns the perpetrator *into* the victim. This is an idea that works for left and right alike. For the left, since war forces men to commit acts that will ultimately destroy them, it must be right to protest against war. For the right, since men were forced by war to do what they did, they cannot be held accountable. For the left, this pushes the responsibility onto the government, which is always the target of choice. For the right, which has historically resisted the idea of the VC as a genuine guerrilla force raised in the South, it can sometimes shift the blame onto the Vietcong, for fighting a war in which fighters were indistinguishable from local civilians and thereby exciting mistaken retaliation against the innocent.

6
Seething from a jet plane
The myth of airport demonstrations

The trauma of homecoming for some Australian soldiers was ample testimony to a new ambivalence in Australian society. Nowhere was this ambivalence sharper than at the airports when soldiers arrived from Vietnam to face demonstrations.
– Peter Cochrane, 1990[1]

Two giant U.S. Starlifter transport aircraft landed at Kingsford Smith Airport yesterday, bringing 180 Australian troops home from Vietnam. Crowds of relatives and friends gave the returning troops a hearty welcome … 'This is the best Christmas present I've ever had,' Mrs E. Harvey, of Sylvania, said as she waited for her 20-year-old son. 'It's been a year since I've seen him.' … The soldiers looked tired after their long flight, but all were glad to be home.
– Sydney Morning Herald, *12 December 1966*

In *Dust, Donkeys and Delusions*, the author Graham Wilson undertakes a fascinatingly thorough – not to say obsessive – quest to fact-check the much-loved story of Private John Simpson Kirkpatrick, who is supposed to have saved 300 lives at Gallipoli in 1915 by picking up wounded men – often while under fire – and transporting them to medical facilities on the back of his donkey. Wilson demonstrates that the soldier who became known simply as 'Simpson' could not possibly have saved 300 casualties in the 23 working days between his landing at Gallipoli on 26 April and his death on the morning of 19 May. He cites the actual distance (expressed in miles, yards and kilometres) that Simpson would have had to travel with his donkey to make a round trip with a wounded man; the average walking speed of a human being; the average walking speed of a donkey, both laden and unladen; the temperament of donkeys; and the time it would have taken to load and unload a wounded man. He quotes hauling and tillage studies that have recommended individual donkeys should carry no more than one-third of their body weight ('that is, 40 to 60 kilograms depending on the size of the donkey') and warning that donkeys are too small to carry large human beings. Later, Wilson introduces further factors and variables such as the phases of the moon, the difficulty of the terrain and the accumulated fatigue of man and donkey, as well as the recorded flow of wounded men. He ploughs on unrelentingly before arriving at his next question: what kind of casualties could have been transported by donkey? His answer is, in brief, none with life-threatening wounds and probably none who could not have walked. Simpson, according to Wilson, saved nobody.[2]

It was with Wilson's example in mind that I approached the subject of the demonstrations that are supposed to have greeted returned servicemen at Sydney Airport. The idea that this happened cannot be examined without taking into account the logistics of organising a demonstration at an airport at night; the actual circumstances of the returning flights; the dates on which the demonstrations are supposed to have occurred – and what else was taking place at the airport at those times; and a host of other quantifiable factors.

The idea that returning Australian soldiers faced demonstrations at Australian airports emerged in the early 1980s, between the formation of the Vietnam Veterans' Association of Australia (as the Vietnam Veterans' Action Association) in 1979 and the staging of the welcome home march in 1987. The Qantas charter flights that carried most troops home from South Vietnam flew into Sydney either first thing in the morning or last thing at night. Among veterans, there is a common belief that these schedules were maintained to avoid protesters. Initially, I had thought that perhaps the scheduling of the flights had produced the idea that there were protests to be avoided, and therefore the conviction that protests must have happened. However, I now believe it was a simple and direct appropriation of the US experience – which, in its turn, grew out of fictitious representations of the aftermath of the war in the movies *First Blood* (1982) and *Coming Home* (1978). The existence of the same impossible stories in the US, Australia and New Zealand make it difficult to allow any other conclusion.

In *Vietnam: The Australian war*, Paul Ham wrote that most troops sailed home aboard HMAS *Sydney*.[3] In fact, the majority of veterans came back on flights that were mainly chartered from Qantas. Up until 1967, these seem to have been overnight flights. By 1968 and up until at least 1971, the flights left Saigon during the day and arrived in Sydney that same evening. The idea that veterans were brought back late at night to avoid protesters seems to have first been published in Rintoul's *Ashes of Vietnam* in 1987. A caption in the picture section of the book, beneath a photograph showing soldiers in darkness, disembarking a Qantas jet, with their sleeves rolled up to their biceps – the lead man carrying a weapon – reads 'Returning Australian troops often flew back into Sydney's Mascot airport after dark to avoid demonstrators', although the picture looks like troops arriving in Vietnam, rather than Sydney. While the idea that flights were scheduled to avoid protests might well have existed among the men during the Vietnam War, it was never canvassed in the media, since any journalist's phone call could have uncovered the truth. As former Qantas cabin crew Alan Kitchen wrote in *Vietnam Logistics and Support 1962–1975*, 'There is no truth in the story that the flights took off late at night to sneak them out of Sydney. Leaving at that time was purely the best way to operate as Qantas lost only one day of commercial use. The aircraft would leave at night, usually 11 pm, having possibly operated to New Zealand and back during the day in time to have the 20 first class seats replaced by 45 economy seats ... After the aircraft and its crew had been on the ground for several hours in Saigon 165 very happy Aussies boarded for the flight to Sydney. The flight was usually the first in at 6 am giving Qantas time to reconfigure the aircraft for a commercial flight as soon as possible.'[4]

One of many logical inconsistencies of the folkloric flight-scheduling story is that if the arrivals moved to night time to avoid demonstrators, there must have been demonstrations in the mornings – but none have ever been reported nor, to my knowledge, even alleged. Alan Kitchen is an official of the flight crews veterans' organisation the Skippy Squadron, and has occasionally attempted to set the record straight in the media. As early as April 2003, Kitchen had told the *Sydney Morning Herald* 'that planes arrived and departed at night so they could be reconfigured for commercial daytime flights'.[5] And yet many years later, many journalists – including me – remained happy to regurgitate the old canard.

Archives of the Flight Stewards' Association of Australia are held at the ANU Library in Canberra. They contain scores of documents relating to the Vietnam charters, including the receipts for members' insurance for every flight, from which it is possible to reconstruct the changing flight schedules. Conference notes show Qantas explaining that it had to 'fit use of planes on military charter into its total plane utilization' and 'planes would not stay overnight at Saigon but turn around there quite smartly'.[6] All of the relevant documentation points to the fact that all of the worries of the airlines and crew were related to what might happen at the airport in Saigon – from dangers posed by 'habitation nearby that could be hostile' to 'uncontrolled military aircraft' – not at the airport in Sydney.

The union files include a report by a cabin crew member of a May 1969 flight to Saigon. On the evening before he left, in the midst of a general guerrilla offensive, Tan Son Nhut had been the target for a rocket attack. He rang from Singapore to ask the union to issue a directive to crew that they would not operate in Vietnam until their safety could be reasonably guaranteed. He wrote, 'As the troops boarded the aircraft, I was approached by the officer commanding the troops – he asked if we were continuing the flight into Saigon. His information was of the possibility of our going elsewhere in view of the situation existing in Saigon. I offer this as evidence that circumstances involving our flight safety were also the subject of concern to the authorities ... Upon arrival in Saigon, ground personnel informed me that in the previous 24 hours six 122 m.m rockets had hit the airport area and they had received two mortar attacks.'[7]

These were the actual conditions that concerned those who flew and crewed the planes. The absurdity of the idea that schedules were set to avoid demonstrators is clear when considering that it would have meant landing reinforcements in a possible war zone at Tan Son Nhut at some arbitrary time dictated by the chance of a demonstration meeting the return flight at Mascot.

Some of the same people who believe the flight schedule was devised to avoid protesters also hold that demonstrations took place notwithstanding these precautions. For example, 6RAR veteran Gary McMahon has said, 'We flew into Sydney at about one in the morning to avoid demonstrators. Even at 1 am, though, the demonstrators were there.'[8] There are published accounts of fewer than a dozen airport demonstrations, and the same couple of stories are retold over and again. Logically, the first step towards authenticating reports of the protests would be to establish when and where the witnesses returned to Australia. The DVA's Nominal Roll of Vietnam Veterans is not perfect, but it is usually possible to use the roll to establish the dates on which individuals flew home from Vietnam. On those occasions where veterans have used their real names in published accounts, it should be simple enough to compare their remembered hostile homecoming stories with contemporary accounts.

However, there are no contemporary accounts of hostile homecomings. None at all.

The first published description of a demonstration against returned troops at an Australian airport appeared in the first Australian anthology of veterans' writings, *Desperate Praise*, published in 1982 by Artlook Books, WA, and edited by John J Coe, a historian and Vietnam veteran. It surfaced in a piece entitled 'Vietnam – So what?' by Terry Spriggs, a regular soldier who served as a lance corporal in 6RAR. Spriggs wrote about arriving at Sydney Airport in June 1970: 'Into the terminal came .. shitwitted protestors. Hundreds of people in that terminal that night, were cheering and clapping their families home and then these motherfuckers come bursting in carrying placards. One I'll never forget as long as I live, this poxy ridden excuse for a female, screeching and carrying a placard saying "CHILD KILLERS". If I had been able to get through the crowd and if the police wouldn't stop me, I would have pulled her head right off her shoulders and played soccer with it.'[9]

According to the DVA's Nominal Roll, Spriggs returned from Vietnam on 17 May 1970. No Sydney newspaper reported a demonstration at Sydney Airport on that date. However, the *Sydney Morning Herald* reported a large crowd of journalists and onlookers at Sydney Airport that night, as Canadian Prime Minister Pierre Trudeau arrived in the new international airport terminal. Trudeau was met by Prime Minister Gorton and 'a group of about 18 loyal Canadians, waving the Maple Leaf flag'.[10] It's possible that – if he were one of the first men off the plane and the Canadian welcoming party lingered in the airport – Spriggs, from a distance, mistook patriotic Canadians for placard-wielding anti-war demonstrators.

Deeper in the *Sydney Morning Herald* was a report of a Sydney City Council move to place restrictions on processions and marches through the city 'because of the number being held and the increasing disruption they cause to traffic'. If the editors of the paper, which had journalists at the airport, had not felt a demonstration against Australian soldiers was worthy of a news item of its own, it could have been tagged on to this story – but it was not. If Sydney City Council had felt it was worth restricting demonstrations because of the disruption they caused to traffic, local councillors would, presumably, have been even more concerned with the disruption they might bring to the operations of the new international airport. However, the paper does not record the time of Trudeau's landing and, of course, everyone

– press, politicians, police and Canadians – might have left the airport by the time the troops arrived.

Artlook Books also published the sometime author and journalist Hal Colebatch, who is thanked in the acknowledgments of *Desperate Praise* for his 'constant advice and criticism'.[11] Surprisingly, when *Desperate Praise* was reviewed in the *Bulletin*, the review was written by the selfsame Hal Colebatch, who suggested the collection might 'give some perspective to the mythology' about the Vietnam War.[12] In fact, it helped create that mythology – as did Colebatch's review, which quoted three paragraphs of Spriggs' story about the airport demonstration. The demonstration story was also quoted in reviews in *Army*[13] and the *Daily News* (WA)[14] and immediately gained an audience far larger than might have been expected to read the book itself. Neil Jillett, former Southeast Asia correspondent for *The Age*, denounced the book as a failure – 'most of the writing is turgid and passionless,' he wrote, 'like the evidence given by a stolid policeman in a dull court case'[15] – but even Jillett singled out Spriggs' work as 'the best piece'. Faintly comically, and slightly bafflingly, Spriggs' story was later quoted in Robin Gerster's essay, 'Occidental tourists', wrongly credited to 'the repatriated Gary McKay',[16] whose genuine story is reprised earlier in that same essay.

For all its flaws, *Desperate Praise* was a groundbreaking book that put the veterans' own experience at the heart of the Vietnam story. It sat lonely on the shelves until 1987, the year of the Sydney welcome home parade, which saw a wave of books about the Vietnam War storm out of the shell scrapes, yelling and screaming and shooting in every direction. The most popular title was Stuart Rintoul's *Ashes of Vietnam*. As we have seen, there are certain difficulties with this book too, chief among them that Rintoul allows his most controversial contributors to remain anonymous, so their stories cannot be verified. Rintoul's narrative has naïve conscripts fighting a dirty war, committing and witnessing atrocities, coming home to face protests, and drifting towards alcoholism, mental illness and suicide. This was probably the dominant image of the life of a Vietnam veteran in 1987 – and, to some extent, may remain so today. Rintoul quotes an engineer named Bob Pride, whom the Nominal Roll records as Robert George Pride, who served with 17th Construction Squadron until 11 February 1969: 'I think we landed at Sydney airport at about ten or eleven o'clock at night, went through customs and got our pay. When the doors opened up there were these people waving placards and someone was holding up a page out of a newspaper about women and children being killed.'[17]

Once more, there are no reports of airport demonstrations in the Sydney press on 12 June 1969. Pride's story appeared again, sourced to Rintoul, in Peter Cochrane's essay 'At war at home' in *Vietnam Remembered*, to illustrate the contention made by Cochrane at the head of this chapter. Pride was also quoted uncritically in 'Australia and the Vietnam War',[18] a 2007 DVA publication meant as classroom teaching materials.

Probably the most famous of all the airport demonstration stories is also the most unlikely – the riot described by 'Mike' from Perth that led to my initial interest in the idea of the protests. Mike's story appeared in the pamphlet *Homecomings*, which was first published as part of the Vietnam Veterans Counselling Service (VVCS, now Open Arms – Veterans and Families Counselling) contribution to the 1987 welcome home parade. The editor, Noel Giblett, was a counsellor at the VVCS, and the book comprises pseudonymous, uncorroborated, apparently oral testimonies from veterans and their wives, selected because they were known to the staff at Perth VVCS – that is, they were probably disturbed and sought counselling. Ten thousand copies were sold within months of the parade – the majority of them, it's reasonable to assume, to veterans and their families.

Mike wrote, 'We were pelted with tomatoes and spat on. But we got our satisfaction afterwards – 150 toey, angry lads from Vietnam versus 400 demonstrators – they didn't stand a chance. The cops were very good about it. They seemed to be otherwise occupied for a while. It's impossible to describe what it feels like to have been away at war for your country and come home to that kind of treatment. It's something you never forget.'[19]

This is the only airport demonstration story in *Homecomings* and it's notable that, as in Rintoul's book, the most sensational account in the book originates from a pseudonymous, unverifiable source. An airport riot involving 550 people would have been the worst incidence of political violence in Australia since 1968, and the only time a large number of returned soldiers battled with demonstrators. It would have been the biggest clash ever around the Vietnam War to that date.

The Qantas charter was a weekly service, and the Flight Stewards' Association of Australia's archives show flights returning on a Wednesday, which would have them arrive in Sydney at 10.30 pm on 7, 14, 21 and 28 January. However, there are no airport demonstrations reported in the Sydney press on a Thursday – or, indeed, any day in January 1970. In addition, students are on vacation throughout the month of January and, as Paul Ferry wrote in *The Rise and Fall of Practically Everybody*, 'student activity is naturally non-existent during the long summer vacation'.[20]

In his 2007 bestselling history, *Vietnam: The Australian war*, Paul Ham assembled a selection of the best-known airport demonstration stories, and presented them as fact, in a chapter headed '"Baby-killers"'. He began with the Spriggs piece, then pronounced, 'Spriggs escaped lightly. On another flight a soldier wept as a plane banked above the lights of Sydney; moments later, outside Mascot airport, hundreds of demonstrators pelted him and his fellow troops with rotten fruit.'[21] Ham's reference for this incident is Mike's story in *Homecomings*, the riot that apparently went unreported and unremarked upon for 20 years. Next in Ham's assemblage was Gary Blinco's story from *Down a Country Lane to War,* first published in 1997. Blinco was a conscript with 6RAR who, by his own account, extended his national service then signed on with the Regular Army. The Nominal Roll shows he returned from his first tour of Vietnam on 29 April 1970, and from a second tour on 25 November 1971. His arrival at Mascot is described in the final paragraph of the book as if it had occurred after his final service, but his description of the weather in Sydney and the date ('May') locate it in the earlier period: 'There were some anti war protestors waiting near the baggage area, a motley crew of hippies waving placards ... A protester, with a pimply face, and long greasy hair, pressed close to me. "How many women did you rape? How many children did you murder?" he spat. I shoved him roughly as I pushed past. "Get fucked dickhead, or I'll break your neck" I hissed quietly in his face.'[22]

It is notable that, although the protester doesn't physically spit at Blinco, his words are 'spat'. However, there is no mention of a demonstration at Sydney Airport in the Sydney press on 30 April 1970, but a large piece towards the back of the paper – entitled 'A debate about the Moratorium' – included photographs of Prince Philip in conversation with a 'pretty sixteen-year-old schoolgirl' with a Moratorium badge, and Princess Anne with a 'bearded' student wearing the same badge.[23] An anti-war protest at the airport would surely have been mentioned here.

Both Gary Blinco and Terry Spriggs were soldiers with 6RAR on the battalion's second tour of Vietnam. As we have seen, theirs was the only battalion to return home entirely by air; it did so at around the time of the first big Moratorium demonstrations; and it did not receive a welcoming parade through its home city. Of all the infantrymen who believe they were ignored or rejected upon their return, the veterans of 6RAR's second tour have the strongest case. However, the fact there were demonstrations in the streets against the war does not mean there were protests at the airport against the soldiers.

In 2005, in a generally overlooked claim in Charles Mollison's *Long Tan and Beyond*, Gary McMahon, a regular soldier, says he came home at the end of his second tour of South Vietnam to meet demonstrators at the airport.[24]

McMahon returned to Sydney on 30 June 1971, making this the latest reported incident of an airport demonstration. June 30 was the date of the last round of Moratorium demonstrations in Australia, which could well be the source of McMahon's story. There was certainly a large anti–Vietnam War demonstration held in Sydney that day – and even if it was not directed at specific returned servicemen, McMahon might naturally have taken it that way. While there was trouble in other capital cities, most notably Adelaide, the march in Sydney was comparatively low-key. According to the *Sydney Morning Herald*, 'The crowd's only distraction was a city council street cleaner who slowly swept the gutter from Bathurst Street to Park Street, clambering over seated protesters.' It was a sign of things soon to come that although 'the speeches had an anti-Vietnam war theme ... some urged support for protests against touring South African sporting teams and others sought free abortions'. The heat had gone out of the Vietnam debate. 'When it became apparent the demonstrators were peaceful,' wrote the *Sydney Morning Herald*, 'and that there were fewer of them than expected, a number of police were withdrawn and held in reserve.'[25] In Canberra, extra police were posted at Parliament House after an anonymous caller threatened that Prime Minister McMahon would be killed at 10 am. They were withdrawn at 10.20 am when nothing had happened, and William McMahon worked in his office through the 20-minute emergency. In such a climate of indifference and ennui, it seems unlikely that peaceful demonstrators, at the end of a day spent marching around and sitting down, would reassemble at the airport to spit on returning veterans – and incredible that such an event could remain unreported.

To the standard narratives of Spriggs, 'Mike' and Blinco, Paul Ham added new anecdotes derived from his own research. 'Among the more disturbing stories,' wrote Ham, 'was that of David Morgan, a diligent young signaller, who landed in Sydney at 1 a.m. amid the usual emotional scenes. His connecting flight [to Brisbane] left the next day, so he and a mate, Scotty, spent a night in Kings Cross. Next morning, they returned to the airport, in their uniforms, where a large group of demonstrators waited: [Ham then quotes Morgan] "... They yell at us with obscene language, calling us killers of little Vietnamese children, murderers, and that we should be in jail. They jostle and heckle, as we try to make our way to the entrance. As I am about to enter ... I notice a woman lunging towards me, with her head in a forward motion. The next thing I know a large gob of spit hits my left cheek."'[26]

Morgan's story, taken from an unpublished manuscript sighted by Ham, is one of the oddest of all, with the motivations of the protesters particularly impenetrable. The week's flight back from Vietnam had arrived the night before, so if there was a 'large group of demonstrators outside the airport', they were either a day late for the previous demonstration or a week early for the next one. The only possibility is that the 'large group of demonstrators' knew the Saigon flight had returned and were staking out the airport the next day in the specific hope of finding interstate soldiers going home in uniform, so as to spit on them. According to the Nominal Roll, Corporal David Morgan, a regular soldier with 104 Signals Squadron, left Vietnam on 7 January 1970, during the university summer vacation. His connecting flight would have been on 8 January 1970, and any protests would have been reported on 9 January. Once again, there were no such reports in the Sydney press, although the *Sydney Morning Herald* ran stories about the trial in Vung Tau of Peter Denzil Allen, a 9RAR soldier who 'fragged' an officer; a quashed rumour started by Jim Cairns that the troops had been told they would be home by June; and the announcement of the eleventh registration for national service.[27]

When national serviceman Greg Smith, author of the 2007 memoir *A Pogo's Perspective*, returned home from Vietnam, the protesters were casually ubiquitous, mingling with the welcoming crowd, who apparently accepted them as inevitable, an unavoidable presence day or night: 'After we had cleared customs and moved through the relatives and a number of protesters, my group was ushered into the back of an army truck,' he wrote. But if the cold weather of an April night in Sydney was a surprise to the diggers, wrote Smith, 'So to [sic] was the abuse and screamed comments from people on the footpaths or from other vehicles on the road ... I remember thinking that these people (away from the airport) couldn't know that we had just returned from Viet Nam.

And therefore assumed that the groundswell of opposition must be so strong as to be directed at anyone in uniform. There was no doubting the dedication of those protesters at the airport, out at that hour in the freezing cold to hurl abuse at those returning.'[28]

Smith came back on 7 April 1971. No demonstrations at the airport were reported in subsequent editions of the *Sydney Morning Herald* but, in contrast to Smith's idea that no man in uniform could venture out without courting insult, a front-page story in the paper's 8 April edition chronicled the granting of freedom of the city of Sydney to RAAF Richmond Air Base: 'An RAAF colour party and 170 men assembled in Hyde Park and marched through the city centre. At the intersection of George and Druitt streets the marchers were halted ... by Police Superintendent E. Baldwin. The parade commander, Air Commodore H. D. Marsh, showed Superintendent Baldwin the scroll from the City Council giving the base freedom of entry to the city "in full panoply, with bayonets fixed, drums beating, bands playing and colours flying." There was a fly-past of Hercules planes.'[29]

This event occurred on the same day as Smith's arrival at Sydney Airport. On 8 April, the last date on which a protest which spilled into midnight on 7 April might be recorded in a morning paper, the *Sydney Morning Herald* published a front-page story about the kind of treatment meted out to anti-war protesters who turned up where they were not wanted. Under the headline '5 mothers are jailed', the paper reported that five supporters of Save Our Sons had been imprisoned for 14 days for wilful trespass at the offices of the DLNS on 8 February.[30]

In 2012, RAAF veteran Greg Mead said his 'weekly QANTAS military charter flight' back from Vietnam was met by 'an un-Australian and uncharacteristically hostile welcoming party offering jeers, insults and derision'.[31] Mead came home on 14 May 1969. There are no demonstrations reported in any of the Sydney press on 15 May, but the *Sydney Morning Herald* included a piece about the government's reaction to the problem of 'student violence', which chronicled the rejection by the government of a demand from backbenchers for a 'comprehensive statement on student violence in Australia',[32] and also noted a backbench push to raise the RSL national executive's demand for a white paper on communist dominated or influenced political organisations in Australia. If there had been any student protest against troops on the previous day, it would surely have been reported here.

A fuller account of David Morgan's airport ordeal of 1970 was published in 2014, in Morgan's memoir, *My Vietnam War: Scarred forever*. The protesters had acquired placards and, rather than jostling Morgan and his mate, they actually rushed towards them 'yelling foul language'. Morgan wrote, 'They called us baby killers, and shouted that we should both be in jail ... When we reached the main doors, a woman lunged towards me. A blob of spit hit my left cheek as we push through the terminal doors and left the demonstrators singing, "We shall overcome".'[33]

It's impossible to know how much of this detail was in the manuscript shown to Ham, but the phrase 'killers of little Vietnamese children' has been modified to 'baby killers' in harmony with the title of the chapter in Ham's book which quotes Morgan's story.

There is nothing strange about a story changing with time. As the historian Alistair Thomson wrote in his study of war memory and mythology, *Anzac Memories*, 'The creation and repetition of the story about an event converts that event into a meaningful experience and consolidates it in memory. The story is never fixed – every time we return and remember the event for a different audience it might change in subtle or even significant ways and take on new meanings – but much of the fundamental detail will be retained.'[34]

However, the narrative in Morgan's published memoir has him encounter another demonstration when he lands in Brisbane.[35] This would seem to be the only suggestion ever made that there were anti–Vietnam War demonstrations held at Brisbane Airport and, once again, it is impossible to discern the purpose of the protest or its intended target – and, of course, there is no mention of the demonstration in the Brisbane *Courier-Mail*.

As far as I can ascertain, these are the only published veterans' stories of airport demonstrations meeting the Qantas flights – although I could, of course, have missed one or two. The highly respected SAS soldier Harry Whiteside is quoted in *Vietnam: The Australian war* as facing a protest when he stepped off a Pan Am R&R charter, but I have no information about these flights and the dates of Whiteside's service do not appear in the Nominal Roll.

To my knowledge, only one civilian has ever reported witnessing an airport demonstration against returned men – *Desperate Praise* reviewer/supporter Hal Colebatch. In a crafted, angry and convincing polemic-cum-memoir wrapped in an elegant cape of literary criticism and published in 1987, Colebatch wrote of the early years of Australian involvement in the Vietnam War, and the rise of the protest movement in Western Australia. 'Clergymen helped throw blood and garbage at Australian servicemen disembarking from aircraft at the end of their tours of duty,' he claimed.[36] Colebatch was a journalist at the time, but he is also a poet, and this essay appears to contain elements of poetry. Even under direction from the helpful and courteous Colebatch, I could find no other written reference to an incident in which clergymen helped throw blood and garbage at soldiers in WA – nor, for that matter, a verifiable account of anyone throwing blood or garbage at soldiers anywhere in Australia, nor any other protest aimed at returning soldiers at Perth Airport. It appears there was no press coverage of even this spectacular and disgusting protest. There are no records of any action taken against soldiers in WA in any of the religious publications that took a stance against the Vietnam War, from *Catholic Worker* to *Beacon*, the magazine of the Unitarian Peace Memorial Church. One likely source of the story seems to be an assault on Brisbane Stock Exchange on 15 May 1972, in which students were led through the building by an Anglican deacon, throwing animal blood around the trading room. They were charged with wilfully damaging two quotation boards, private papers, a table and floor belonging to the Exchange. As far as I can ascertain, this was the only action in Australia throughout the Vietnam War involving both clergy and animal blood. Not only was it heavily reported, but the protesters were arrested and (briefly) imprisoned, and leaflets campaigning for their release, such as 'Blood on the Stock Exchange was to STOP THIS!', have survived in archives such as the Riley Collection at the National Library of Australia.[37]

The Stock Exchange incident actually happened, but it does not fit into the narrative that has grown up around the veterans' return, in which they were personally blamed and attacked by the anti-war movement. It wasn't even directed against the Australian war effort, which was largely over. According to a report in the *Courier-Mail*, it was a protest against the US announcement on 9 May of a blockade of North Vietnam. The protesters feared this 'had brought the world to the brink of a nuclear holocaust' and felt the Stock Exchange 'was party to the war as it was the link between the companies supplying war materials'.[38]

Colebatch's possible confusion aside, the apparent unreliability of many veterans' memoirs when it comes to the airport demonstrations does not necessarily reflect on the veracity of the balance of their testimony. I do not suggest there have been deliberate distortions: the authors are sincere men, recounting their life experiences as they remember them now. It's clear how, with the erasure from history of any pro-war sentiment or organisation (as we have seen in the distorted recollections of the welcome home marches), the boisterous crowds of well-wishers (sometimes waving signs) could become angry mobs of demonstrators brandishing placards. Most of the men who wrote longer memoirs have relied upon their diaries as the base for their books. As Stephen Garton noted in relation to the personal testimonies of Australian veterans of all wars, 'What is remarkable about so many of the diaries, autobiographies, and memoirs of returning servicemen and women is how many of them finish with the cessation of hostilities. Even a description of the actual return journey is rare.'[39] Morgan, for example, reproduces his diary entries at the end of his book. They finish as he leaves for Australia, and therefore offer no record of his remembered airport encounters.

These contemporary personal records of airport demonstrations would be unlikely to exist even if the demonstrations had occurred. While life in army training establishments or overseas in South Vietnam might be recorded in letters home, it seems improbable that many soldiers would have written home to describe their homecomings. There is no conspiracy here, and no deliberate attempt to mislead, but perhaps there is the adoption of a collective memory on behalf of the veterans and a surprising degree of credulity exhibited by some researchers. However, if the events never happened at the time, the injustice they apparently signify – a rejection by the civilian population of the troops who had fought the war – was certainly remembered by the veterans in later years. The significance of the airport demonstration stories may lie less in the fact that the accounts are false than the feeling that their meaning is true for those who remember them and believe they were the victims of an organised campaign of public harassment and shaming.

One way to gauge what evidence might be left of a large demonstration at Sydney Airport is to look at a protest that really happened: on 23 March 1971 there was a confrontation between uniformed men and left-wing demonstrators which became known – to those who participated in it, if nobody else – as the Battle of Mascot Airport. A South African surf-lifesaving team flew into Sydney, to compete in Australia in contravention of a sporting and cultural boycott called by the African National Congress. They were met by about 100 anti-apartheid demonstrators, who were, in turn, confronted by four uniformed members of the Australian National Socialist Party – Ross 'The Skull' May, Alan Parziani, Ken Gibbett and Peter Wells.

This is significant for several reasons. It was an airport demonstration that genuinely occurred, and as such was heavily reported – even though no arrests were made. There was a TV cameraman present from Channel 9 – who was punched by May, and who punched May in return – and the story made the front pages of *The Australian* and the Sydney *Daily Telegraph*, and page two of the *Sydney Morning Herald*, because a demonstration at Australia's gateway airport was of national significance – particularly since it turned violent. The left was only able to muster 100 people to come to the airport, and they were such a soft target that four Nazis felt confident to disrupt their protest. Photographs exist of several clashes between individual Nazis and individual leftists, including a tussle between Ross May and the prominent activist Denis Freney. The protest was written up in the left press – an account appeared in the Communist Party's *Tribune* newspaper – and is acknowledged (and even celebrated) by the Nazis and the left, both of whom claim it as a victory. Photographs and an exhaustive account of the 'battle' appear in the book *Everyone Wants to be Fuehrer*[40] by David Harcourt, and the events from Freney's point of view are presented in his memoir, *A Map of Days*.[41]

Many of the anti-apartheid demonstrators would also have been anti–Vietnam War demonstrators, and the small group of Nazis who attacked them also – by their own account and those of others – regularly assaulted anti–Vietnam War demonstrators. There is a possibility that this single and singular clash – unrelated to the Vietnam War except for the identities of the parties involved – helped give rise to the broader myth of airport demonstrations. If airport demonstrations against troops returning from Vietnam had really happened, they would have been nationally reported and remembered by the left and the right. These clashes would have become war stories for the left, just like the 'Battle of Mascot Airport'. Indeed, they would have had a similar cast of characters.

Intriguingly, there are press photographs of a three-person protest at Brisbane Airport in 1971, against the arrival of child psychologist Benjamin Spock, an opponent of the Vietnam War. The demonstrators, Australian Nazis led by a mysterious character named Gary Mangan and including a woman, carry banners, one stating: 'Back to babies Benny you bum'.[42] It's possible that some people, having seen this photograph, might have reimagined the scene as a small group of anti-war protesters gathered at Sydney Airport waving signs at soldiers reading, 'Baby killer bums'. Whether or not this is true, the existence of the picture and news story of Mangan and his tiny crew of cohorts suggests even the smallest of demonstrations at an airport would have received press coverage.

As I mentioned at the beginning of this book, I initially believed that the sometimes opaque workings of the national service scheme – and, perhaps, the lack of military experience of the conscripts – might lie at the root of various mistaken beliefs about Australia and the Vietnam War. As a control to gauge how homecomings from the war might have been remembered in the absence of national servicemen, Australia, fortuitously, has the example of New Zealand. However, when close comparisons are made, there appear to be few distinctions between the mythologies which have developed among veterans in Australia and New Zealand, even though there were substantial differences in the logistics of New Zealand soldiers' return from Vietnam. While many troops came home in small groups at the end of their tours, the NZ companies of the ANZAC infantry battalions flew back from Vietnam to other parts of Southeast Asia, where they were reabsorbed into 1RNZIR.

The New Zealand infantry served as V ('Victor') and W ('Whiskey') companies in Australian battalions. Ian McGibbon, the de facto official historian of New Zealand's Vietnam War, wrote, 'The initial V Company comprised many men near the end of their engagements, and they returned to New Zealand soon after leaving Vietnam. The military chiefs considered the possibility of the company parading on their return … but, with 30 per cent of the company remaining in Malaysia, practical difficulties ruled out any action.'

In New Zealand, as Australia, 'The circumstances of the Vietnam troops' return would also become a persisting source of anger for many of them,' wrote McGibbon. While New Zealand troops returned to Royal New Zealand Air Force (RNZAF) Base

Whenuapai rather than a civil airport, 'Flight schedules dictated that aircraft landed at Whenuapai during the night. Most men, after arrival formalities had been completed, immediately went on leave with orders to report back in some weeks. Advice to wear civilian clothes rather than uniforms came, in retrospect, to be seen as part of a sinister pattern in which the government sneaked them back into the country in the dead of night to avoid anti-war protesters [but] many of the returnees from Malaysia/Singapore were not Vietnam veterans. Since most flights into Whenuapai were routine operations, and RNZAF aircraft brought back formed units from Vietnam only in 1965, 1971 and 1972, there was nothing specific to connect such flights with Vietnam, and little likelihood of protesters appearing, let alone causing problems at an air force base where they could easily be excluded.'[43]

In the book *Grey Ghosts: New Zealand Vietnam vets talk about their war*, author Deborah Challinor writes, in her rather unusual style, 'Although many New Zealand soldiers were not met at the airport by protesters (the flight arrival times suggesting that this was deliberately orchestrated), others were and found the experience to be confusing, disappointing and, in some cases, very annoying.' She goes on to quote the story of an inevitably anonymous 'Matt G' who landed with his company, Whiskey 1, at Whenuapai. Challinor says, 'They were completely perplexed when a policeman immediately boarded the plane and advised them to stay in their seats because [she quotes Matt G] 'You'll see people out there, they've got placards saying "Babykillers" and Christ knows whatever else, he says ignore them, don't even look at them, just get out of the plane and take off into the bus ... Plus you no sooner stepped out of the plane and these people are YAH! Shoving these placards in your face. Soldiers just straight over the ropes having a hua of a great scrap about two o'clock in the morning ... A few of the bloody placards got broken over the soldiers' heads and the soldiers grabbed the broken sticks and whacked a few people around the bloody heads, including a policeman, and bloody police dogs got in the road and everything else.'[44]

It becomes faintly dispiriting to wade through these anonymous narratives, which imagine in such fine detail events which are fantastically unlikely to have happened on a military base after dark, and impossible to conceive of occurring without mention in the press. It begins to seem that, no matter what the objective circumstances, the same stories will arise and be recorded with similar credulity by researchers whose reluctance to question a veteran's testimony – even when that testimony directly contradicts other veterans' accounts – leads them to become, at best, folklorists rather than historians.

In Australia, there appears to have been little attempt made to apprehend the administrative processes involved in repatriation from Vietnam. Army records show the returned men did not simply spill out of the plane and into the terminal, haul their luggage off the baggage carousel and walk out the door. At the airport, every man was met by a team of soldiers, largely from Eastern Command Personnel Depot, who compiled his leave entitlement, made up his pay book, issued him with cash and, if necessary, his rail warrants, and gave him an informal customs briefing. It could take between three and four hours to process a planeload of men.

For example, in October 1967, it was reported that the charter landed at 6.20 am, the last man passed through customs at 7.20 am, the last leave pass was raised at 9.30 am and the last pay at 9.35 am.[45] During this time, the returned men were under the care and protection of the Army – but there would have been civilians in the airport.

The same logistical considerations applied in 1968 and beyond, when the planes left Saigon in the morning and arrived in Sydney at 10.30 pm. Army records show military staff at Mascot in 1968 included one liaison warrant officer; three pay clerks; two leave clerks; a co-ordinator; two paymasters (civilian); a captain in charge of movements; two Military Police officers acting as pay escorts; and three drivers. It took 19 personnel with three vehicles up to four hours to process 160 men. The last soldier off the plane would not have been paid out until 2.30 am. This explains why some men say they arrived in the early hours of the morning, but it effectively precludes most men from any casual contact with civilians. In July 1968, the Army experimentally altered the system so that more pre-leave paperwork was completed in Vietnam, which reduced the number of staff required in the airport to between nine and 12 (with only two vehicles) and cut the processing time by more than a third.[46] It is not clear from the documentation if this modification continued until the end of the war, but it would still have been later than 1 am before the last soldier from a full flight left the airport, at which time the roads, streets and terminals would have been deserted.

One of the more puzzling aspects of Australia's airport demonstration stories is the idea of the media propagated by the popularisers of the mythology. In their judgment, it seems, great waves of wildly newsworthy delinquent behaviour went ignored and unreported by a fathomlessly incompetent press. This idea of a media that is either deliberately blind or, at best, lacking in the physical, intellectual or logistical resources to cover what would surely have been one of the biggest news stories of the 1960s, seems as folkloric as the concept of directionless and bafflingly motivated, historically invisible hippie protesters. This is particularly odd since some of the propagators of the myth are journalists or former journalists.

Another unusual aspect of the world view that apparently informs the airport demonstration stories is an apparent disregard for the well-documented role of the security services in the surveillance and penetration of left-wing organisations. The media was not the only agency keeping a close watch on the anti-war movement. The Australian Security Intelligence Organisation (ASIO) took a forensic interest in the activists and their activities. According to ASIO's official historian, John Blaxland, the agency began to deploy 'considerable resources' to monitor the anti-war movement in 1965. Organisations from the Youth Campaign Against Conscription (YCAC) to the Women's International League for Peace and Freedom (WILPF) to Save Our Sons (SOS) were penetrated by ASIO agents to 'provide prior warning of their intentions'. This effort diverted a significant amount of ASIO's energies from more traditional tasks such as counterespionage and protective security.

Blaxland cites John McFarlane, an ASIO operative charged with monitoring the dissenters, as claiming 'there had never been so much pressure from government for reporting as on the protest movement'. Blaxland writes that ASIO agents in every state were 'tasked to obtain the confidence of the targets and be directly and enthusiastically involved with anti-Vietnam War protests'. ASIO's monitoring of early protesters was sufficiently intense that it could report to Prime Minister Harold Holt that, of those people involved in demonstrations in Sydney from February to July 1966, at least 100 had attended two or more protests. When Monash University students formed their committee to raise funds for the NLF in June 1967, ASIO conducted a photographic 'sweep' of the students' homes. The central concern of ASIO had been the role of the Communist Party and its front organisations in the anti-war movement, but as the political importance of the CPA declined and the so-called 'New Left' came to the fore, ASIO continued to enthusiastically infiltrate the protesters. Agency Director-General Charles Spry was in Europe in July 1968, when he wrote to his deputy that 'gathering intelligence as to the intentions of the protestors remained vital so that police could be alerted speedily and accurately'. ASIO therefore should 'continue to effect penetration on as wide a scale as possible'. It eventually became apparent that the CPA was actually 'opposed to militant action and was seeking to prevent or control extremists' actions'. If there was trouble on the streets, it would come from the Maoists, Trotskyists, anarchists and radical students. Blaxland writes, 'ASIO field officers such as Lawrie Pollard, who was often present among demonstrators, recalled there was enormous pressure from headquarters to know who was at the demonstrations "immediately". Demonstrators would gather from about three o'clock for a demonstration that started at about 4 p.m.' Blaxland quotes Pollard: 'We were tasked to report back answering a range of questions. Who was there? What placards were they carrying? Was it violent? Who were the guest speakers? ... I went to Robert Stephen Gould's bookshop in Goulburn Street, and I'd mix with these people. I'd go down on a Wednesday night and we'd sit around with them and get pissed and they'd do the usual thing offering you a joint to see if you were an ASIO or police special branch agent and they'd have their planning sessions for the Thursday and the Friday.'

'Regional offices,' writes Blaxland, 'were exhorted to continue to "make every effort" to identify student protesters and forward the relevant details to headquarters.'[47]

In 1969, ASIO began an intelligence-gathering effort that came to be known as Operation Whip, collating 'detailed information, photographs and comments' on leading New Left radicals in each state. Protester events were given Whip numbers. In January 1970, ASIO ran operations numbered Whip 8 and Whip 9. Whip 8 involved surveillance of the protests greeting US Vice-President Spiro Agnew when he arrived in Australia for a two-day visit. Whip 9 recorded an anti-war conference in Sydney. January 1970 is also the month in which 'Mike' from Perth was apparently involved in a huge confrontation at Sydney Airport. Whip 13 was the visit to Australia of Canadian Prime Minister Pierre Trudeau in May 1970. As we have seen, Trudeau arrived at Sydney Airport on the same evening as Terry Spriggs claims to have been met by screaming protesters waving a 'CHILD KILLERS' banner. On that specific night, ASIO were monitoring the New Left, the Old Left and the Trudeau visit, and would certainly have had agents at the airport.

Operation Whip was a major effort on the part of ASIO to gather information about protesters and produce intelligence that could be employed against them. Yet there is no mention in Blaxland's history of ASIO, or any other study of ASIO, of demonstrations against returning troops at Sydney Airport, and Blaxland found no files that related to these supposed protests.[48] A rash of books in which former political activists publish and comment upon extracts from their own recently released and heavily redacted ASIO files contain no reference to airport demonstrations. Apparently, ASIO successfully penetrated and monitored most of more than 100 left-wing groups it identified, with the exception of some draft-resistance organisations – which were perhaps the least likely groups to protest at the safe return of drafted men from Vietnam – but the agency never learned of three years of violent and vulgar confrontations at the largest international airport in the country. None of its agents was able to give warning that a group was planning an airport protest on the very night of the visit of the Canadian prime minister – with whose protection ASIO had been specifically charged – and none of its informants noticed when it occurred.

While the idea of the airport protests displays a limited understanding of the role of the media and the security services, it also shows a certain incomprehension of the logistics of demonstrations and the goals of the anti-war movement. The stories seem the provenance of people with little experience of political organisation, who assume that demonstrations might form either spontaneously or out of drugged-up conversation between bored hippies in a share house around midnight. During the war years, the point was repeatedly made by pro-war (or, at least, anti-anti-war) elements that this was not the case. The chief charge was that the protests were orchestrated and planned in advance. This was undoubtedly the case for the majority of demonstrations of any sort in the days before social media. It could take weeks to build even a small demonstration. Many potential protesters would be reluctant, apathetic or frightened – and the airport demonstrations would have been particularly intimidating for the demonstrators, who would be walking directly up to men they regarded as trained killers with the explicit intention of accusing them of murder. Even the most cursory examination of the methods and memorabilia of the left reveals that the period before a demonstration generally involves leafleting, posters and meetings, in which potential slogans to be aired are debated or mandated, depending on the level of internal democracy in each particular organisation. For example, before the very real demonstration at 9RAR's welcome home parade in Adelaide in 1969, according to draft resister Bob Hall's account in the Adelaide *Advertiser*, the demonstrators met to choose 'the least emotional banners we could find'.[49] It was not simply a case of scrawling 'Baby Killers!' on a piece of cardboard and nailing it to the top of a stick.

To consider more concrete examples, the files of the YCAC are held at the State Library of Victoria. They comprise an extensive collection of flyers, leaflets, newsletters and notes that give a comprehensive picture of the workings of the organisation. In 1966, the YCAC organised a demonstration at Central Railway Station, Sydney, as the second group of conscripts left for training. There are a number of newspaper reports of the demonstration taking place but, if its provenance were to be called into question, the State Library holds a YCAC flyer which states, 'The Youth Campaign Against Conscription is organizing a demonstration on Central Railway Station, as the second group of conscripts leave for the training camp in Victoria.'

The fact that the demonstration took place would have been of little surprise to anyone monitoring the movement as the details of the action were clearly set out in the flyer:

PLACE: CENTRAL RAILWAY STATION,
COUNTRY PLATFORM
DATE: WEDNESDAY, 29th SEPTEMBER
TIME: EVENING 7.00pm[50]

In the absence of this type of material, in the days before many student houses even had telephones, it would have been extremely difficult to organise a demonstration, since nobody would have known when or where to demonstrate. At the bottom of the flyer is a coupon for would-be demonstrators to fill in and return with their names and addresses, presumably to give the organisers some idea of how many might be expected to attend and a means by which to contact potential demonstrators with details of future demonstrations. The same Victorian archive holds *Viet Protest News, the Bulletin of the Vietnam Day Committee*, one single edition of which included a 'Coming Events' calendar listing forthcoming demonstrations beginning with a 24-hour vigil at the US Consulate on 3 July and ending with a Hiroshima Day Parade on 7 August, and with ten more meetings, vigils, forums and debates in the days between.[51] If there had been regular airport demonstrations – rather than, for example, one single spectacular act – they would have been publicised in this way.

It is also worth considering who the airport demonstrators could possibly have been. The pool they had to draw from was far smaller than might be imagined. The anti-war movement is now regarded as having been huge, even hegemonic, primarily because the first Moratorium demonstrations were very large but, as Grey noted, 'The link between involvement in a street demonstration and a commitment to political activism is impossible to establish through quantification'.[52]

The Maoists of the CPA (Marxist-Leninist), dominant in Melbourne, would appear to have been the most violent and volatile group on the far left in the 1960s, but they were not a significant presence in Sydney, where the Sino-Soviet split had left the Stalinists in control of the Old Left and the New Left was strongly influenced by Trotskyists.[53] Even Melbourne's Maoists had no apparent record of confronting Australian veterans: the targets of their demonstrations tended increasingly to be symbols of US 'imperialism' in Australia, such as the US Consulate.

However, the actions of Monash University Maoists in raising funds for aid to the NLF spawned the Maoists' own Vietnam

War myth: Rhys Pollard's novel *The Cream Machine* includes a fictitious episode in which 'bandages with the "Monash University" stencilling are found on the corpse of a VC guerrilla'.[54] Although no such discovery was ever reported during the war itself – and it would be making an enormous understatement to say this would have been a huge news story – the idea that it actually occurred later featured both in academic work and various veterans' memoirs. In 1982, Terry Spriggs wrote of searching a VC and 'finding cigarettes from Australia in his pockets, compliments of the students of a certain Australian university',[55] although there had never been a suggestion that students were sending cigarettes – rather than money – to the NLF. In 1999, David Savage, a captain with the AATTV who was training Montagnard mercenaries in Pleiku in the Central Highlands from late 1968, remembered finding medical supplies that 'came originally from Australia, via Cambodia'[56] – which was the route taken by the Maoist Michael Hyde to channel the aid from Monash University.

In 2004, Janine Hiddlestone wrote, 'The fact that the Monash group's assistance to the NLF was small was no consolation to a soldier in a war zone, who when seizing enemy supplies, found boxes marked Monash Medical School'.[57] This sentence is footnoted, as if to offer substance to the claim, but 'Monash Medical School' appears to have been a specific addition to the tradition. The footnote reads simply, 'For details of assistance given to the NLF by some of the radical anti-war organisations see: Langley, *A Decade of Dissent*.' While Greg Langley's 1992 oral history of the anti-war movement includes the story of Hyde taking Monash money to Cambodia, it says nothing about medical kits, Monash Medical School or anything similar. In 2011, former regular soldier Tony Bower-Miles recalled finding 'medical supplies from Monash University'[58] in the Long Hais in 1969, even though no money had been raised at Monash for medical aid to the NLF since 1967. By 2012, the medical kits had, alarmingly, transformed into tinned fish. Richard Barry, a former national serviceman with 6RAR, wrote in his extensive national service memoir, *The 10th: Reflections of national service and life in the Australian Army, 1967–69*: 'I was informed by a reliable source of something that made my blood boil. The morning after a particular successful ambush the engineers were sent in to destroy a bunker system. As they were laying charges they dug up numerous cans of sardines and herrings laced with tomato sauce plus tins of Quick [sic] powder. Enquiries were initiated and with some detective work they found that this food was sent indirectly to the enemy by university sympathisers in Melbourne.'[59]

The myth of Monash-donated equipment on the bodies of the dead is perhaps the easiest of the Vietnam War myths to trace, and also the easiest to understand. While the students at Monash did not send any equipment to the NLF, the money they raised was certainly supposed to buy supplies for the guerrillas. Although nothing was ever found stamped 'Monash University', some VC medical kits might conceivably have been purchased using money from Monash students – in truth, it was impossible to say, but they could have been; almost should have been. The claim that they *were* allows veterans to tell a dramatic story that may be false in its detail but true at its core, one that describes many troops' conviction that Monash students were effectively proxies for the NLF and gives flesh to that feeling by turning the students into personal enemies of individual Australian troops. Without the medical kit stories, the Monash story might not be retold, and the alienation and disillusionment of some veterans would be less easily understood. It is less clear what function might be served by the medical kits becoming tinned fish, but the 'Chinese-whispers' style process by which this came about can be readily apprehended.

While the Maoists were, by some distance, the most likely of all Australia's revolutionaries to have contemplated a demonstration against returning men at an airport, their strongholds were in Melbourne and Adelaide rather than Sydney, and their talent for attracting publicity was such that it is inconceivable to think a Maoist-directed demonstration at an airport would have been overlooked by the media.

Another significant revolutionary organisation was Students for Democratic Action (SDA), which had formed in 1966 in Brisbane, where its anarchistic ideals were, for a period, dominant among local anti-war campaigners. Barry Heard's memoir, *Well Done, Those Men*, cites a genuine example of apparently homicidal hostility towards Australian troops from the anti-war movement[60] – a pamphlet featuring instructions on how to disable a Huey helicopter, the same 'dust-off' chopper that saved the lives of so many wounded in Vietnam. The pamphlet was, in fact, a 1969 edition of *Student Guerrilla*,[61] the short-lived magazine of the SDA, and Heard's description is accurate. Copies of *Student Guerrilla* still exist, as items that are genuinely published and distributed do not, generally speaking, disappear.

The roughly equivalent organisation in Sydney was Students for a Democratic Society (SDS), which, as its name suggests, was largely made up of students. Since at least two of the reported airport demonstrations – including the largest of them all – took place during the university vacation, SDS was unlikely to have had the capacity to organise them. In addition, SDS leaders such as Mike Jones were well known to the police, politicians and the press. A demonstration would not have taken place without them, and a demonstration that involved them could not have evaded scrutiny.

At the Adelaide welcome home parade clash of 1969, the silent demonstrators were described (apparently via draft resister Bob Hall) as 'the Women's International League for Peace and Freedom, Provo, and "an anarchist group"'.[62] Provo was a Netherlands-based, vaguely Situationist sect noted for its humanist opposition to the Vietnam War.[63] In South Australia, Provo seems to be the name adopted by the founders of the local SDA.[64] In effect, this leaves the only suspect for Sydney's mythological airport demonstrations as the WILPF.

And the WILPF had form – it had genuinely been sighted demonstrating at Sydney Airport, in 1965, when six members picketed the departure for South Vietnam of Sydney's Anglican Archbishop, Hugh Gough. Their tiny, silent protest made the front page of the next day's *Sydney Morning Herald*. The paper reported the women stationed themselves in the departure lobby with a banner containing a text from St Matthew in foot-high letters. It read: 'Inasmuch as ye have done it unto one of my brothers, ye have done it unto me. Matt. 25.40.'

It wasn't quite 'Baby Killers!' – but nonetheless there was violence simmering under the calm at the airport as 'the women pushed people aside to unfurl the banner'. The mastermind of the protest was revealed as the sinister 'Mrs M. Holmes, who attends St. Luke's Church of England, Mosman'. 'Did the Minister of St. Luke's, the Rev. Noel Delbridge, know she was organising the demonstration?' asked the journalist. 'He certainly does not,' replied Mrs M Holmes, 'But he knows my opinion.' The paper could not resist the final line: 'Dr Gough, who had been to a private farewell in an airport lounge, appeared shortly before his flight was due to leave and walked past Mrs Holmes before she saw him.'[65]

Once again, the reporting of the WILPF action shows that any airport demonstration, no matter how small, was noticed and noted, and was potentially front-page news. It was photographed and the leader was identified, which is what might be expected in any similar circumstance. The WILPF had also directly protested against at least one troop movement, when another of its banners oversaw the departure of 1RAR in 1965. This was, once again, the work of Mrs Holmes, a doctor's wife and mother of six. As a Radio National profile of Margaret Holmes in 2006 noted: 'She attended prayer vigils and a candlelight vigil the night before HMAS *Sydney* departed. As the ship sailed out of Sydney Harbour she was amongst WILPF members who went to North Head to unfurl a large banner over the cliff proclaiming "YOU GO TO AN UNJUST WAR". The following day, Margaret retrieved it, changed the wording to read THEY WENT TO AN UNJUST WAR, positioning it at The Spit.'[66]

Only the WILPF had the personnel and the history that might suggest it would turn up at an airport to shame the soldiers, but the WILPF was always a small organisation in Sydney, and it seems likely that The Spit was the closest Mrs Holmes ever came to spitting. And, far from shouting slogans, the women of the WILPF seem only to have been reported in silent demonstrations.

In addition, there is no memory of airport demonstrations – staged by the WILPF or anyone else – on the left. The three largest archives of materials relating to the anti-war movement in Australia – that held at the Australian War Memorial; the large Saunders Collection at the University of New England; and the huge Noel Butlin Archives at the Australian National University – contain neither documents nor memorabilia relating to airport protests. There are no flyers or posters exhorting would-be pro-testers to converge at Sydney Airport. There are no cuttings from the left press advertising these demonstrations, or even criticis-ing them as a tactic. In such a furiously sectarian and divided milieu, it seems barely possible that such a confrontational and controversial action could have passed undebated over a period of several years. Nor do the small number of memoirs of Australian anti-war protesters make any mention of airport demonstrations. The National Civic Council's *News Weekly*, the scourge of the student left and tireless chronicler of radical outrage, recorded no airport demonstrations either.

For an indication of the kind of debate to which the airport demonstrations might have given rise, had they in fact occurred, one need only look to the positioning statements in the first issue of the Trotskyite Socialist Youth Alliance's news-paper, *Direct Action* which, as is the custom among followers of Trotsky, dissected and condemned the actions and ideologies of every competing left group. The 'remnants' of Students for a Democratic Society are singled out in particular for their alleged propensity to 'glorify karate and urge people to attend demon-strations wearing crash helmets'. *Direct Action* pronounced this as 'lunacy' which 'must be avoided and refuted', pointing out that 'the only way we can be effective here is mass action, not guerrilla heroics, and shock tactics'.

Direct Action also denounced the 'Melbourne Maoists' for their policy of seeking confrontation with state authority, and instead advocated actions which 'do not have as their aim a punch-up with the police'. Nor was the paper 'impressed by an emphasis on candle carrying and the names of our dead, etc [which] obscures the real victims of the war and the political nature of it'. It did not like the ultraleft or 'new left' currents either, and had no time for the CPA's position, which it described as 'little different from that of the liberals'. Many of the airport demonstrations are supposed to have occurred in the Socialist Youth Alliance's stronghold of Sydney in the year the paper was launched, but *Direct Action* neither blamed the soldiers for the war, nor saw them as the enemy. It looked instead for a means to recruit them. 'We must seek to develop an approach that allows us to effectively contact all conscripts before and after they join the army,' said *Direct Action*. 'We must recognise that the majority of young men will in fact go in and therefore not direct the weight of our propaganda towards the immorality of this act. This cuts us off from the forces we should be trying to organise. Obviously the key to the problem lies through mobilizing these forces against the war itself.'[67]

As for the young Trotskyists and their fellow travellers in Bob Gould's bookshop, their ASIO-infiltrated Wednesday night meetings led to the production of a VAC 'Calendar of Anti-Vietnam War Activities', copies of which have survived in archives.[68] They signal marches, meetings and mobilisations – any actions that might attract people to the cause – but no trips to Sydney Airport to protest the return of men whose return they had been demanding since the Australian commitment began.

The airport demonstration stories have a particular meaning – that is, to show anti-war protesters to be specifically opposed to the troops. There is no motivation for their actions beyond a desire to antagonise returning soldiers, confront them physically, and make them aware of their guilt. There is no doubt that this is how the veterans characterised Nadine Jensen's lone protest at the homecoming parade of 1RAR in 1966. Jensen smeared their leader with 'blood', and they have been smeared and blood-libelled ever since. The chief problem with the stories is not that the sentiments attributed to the protesters did not exist – at some level, in the minds of some, they undoubtedly did, although this would seem to be more prevalent in the 1980s than the war years – but that airport demonstrations would have been a tremendously inefficient way to make that point. Although they would have been seen by small numbers of soldiers, they were never once reported in the press. Had they occurred, they would have been the least successful of any publicity strategy ever adopted by the anti-war movement, which generally had no problem attracting hostile, mocking, or even, by 1970, moderately sympathetic press coverage. The mainstream media generally reviled the militant left but it won attention far beyond its numbers, reach and influence, probably because, as Chelsea Mannix has argued, 'the protest movement was a local story that could be covered easily and cheaply by the news media'.[69]

The anti-war movement was consistently lambasted and lampooned by politicians and editorial writers, social commentators and broadcasters, in the press and on TV, except when – we are supposed to believe – it indulged in its most controversial, bitterly remembered, wildly divisive, potentially explosive and yet persistently practised tactic of confronting soldiers at airports in the dark, in the presence of their family and friends (and armed military police). Even after several years of these purported demonstrations, no measures were put in place to stop these protests and nobody was ever arrested for taking part in them. And when the protesters in their turn were attacked by soldiers, none of them ever complained.

I have offered various explanations for the origin of the Australian myth, but the cradle of the post-war idea of airport demonstrations seems to be the United States. In his 1998 book *The Spitting Image*, Jerry Lembcke, a sociology professor who served as a non-combatant in Vietnam, pinpoints the first American airport demonstration as a scene in the 1979 movie *Coming Home*. The film shows the returning Marine, Bob Hyde, at the Marine Air Base, asking his wife, Sally, 'Where's all the demonstrators? The asshole on the plane told us there would be a bunch of flowerheads out there.' Sally replies, 'Well, there are some kids out there ... But they can't come in the gate.' In the following scene, a small group of anti-war demonstrators is shown circling the gate, chanting, 'One, two, three, four, we don't want your rotten war!' Lembcke claims this scene 'inverts the historical reality'. In truth: 'Anti-war activists protested the dispatching of GIs to Vietnam, not the return of veterans from Vietnam. At the entrance to the Oakland, California, army terminal, for example, protesters would sit down in front of the buses carrying soldiers into the base from which they were to be transferred to Vietnam. Their protests were couched in rhetoric that conveyed sympathy for the men being sent overseas. By moving the staging for the encounter from the entrance to the base (and metaphorically from the entrance to the war) to the exit from the base and the war, the film reframes the story as a movement against Vietnam veterans ... In the context of the scene, the "your" in the chant "We don't want your rotten war" can only refer to veterans.'[70]

7
'Rapists' and 'Baby killers!' Myths of blood, spit and jeers

*Among some veterans there is still an 'us and them' attitude …
because of the reception we got when we got home. Someone
from Women Against Rape in War threw red paint all over our
commanding officer.*
– Lt Norman Brown, 1RAR (Bien Hoa, Vietnam, 1965–1966)[1]

*The Union of Australian Women May Day float in 1965
carried anti-Vietnam slogans and a plea 'Must Children
Suffer?' The plight of women in war was mostly depicted as
being that of desperate mothers rather than as victims of
sexual assault.*
– Meredith Burgmann[2]

Although the chapter in Paul Ham's *Vietnam: The Australian
war* in which he collects and restates stories about veterans'
encounters with the anti-war movement is entitled 'Baby-killers'
in quotation marks, Ham appears to be quoting veterans who
claim to have been called baby killers, rather than protesters who
called veterans baby killers. There are thousands of photographs
of anti–Vietnam War demonstrations in archives throughout

Australia and I have been unable to find a picture of a banner reading 'baby killers'. If there had been such a placard, it would have been aimed squarely at returning soldiers, but the alleged epithet is perhaps a misconstruction of slogans such as 'Hey, hey, LBJ! How many kids did you kill today?' – which was directed at the president of the United States, rather than any returned man.

There are a handful of similar examples. In the Fairfax Syndication Archives, there is a photograph of a woman identified as Jean Curthoys protesting against conscription outside a Sydney court. Curthoys carries a handwritten banner reading, 'IS IT BETTER TO BURN A DRAFT CARD OR A CHILD?'[3] The Riley Collection in the National Library of Australia contains a large, coloured flyer, which could conceivably be used on a banner, reproducing photographs of napalmed children from *Ramparts* magazine's well-known story 'Children of Vietnam', under the slogan 'We cannot support a war against children!', and published by the Seamen's Union of Australia.[4] Elsewhere, there is a poster, published by the Committee in Defiance of the National Service Act and reproduced in Edwards' *A Nation at War*, which shows a wounded Vietnamese child in the arms of a villager at My Lai. Copies of the poster have been kept by the National Library of Australia and the Australian War Memorial. It bears the unpunctuated slogan 'before you register for national service Think'.[5]

This would appear to be the closest thing to a 'baby killers' banner produced by the anti-war movement in Australia. In the US, however, there was a famous poster by the Art Workers Coalition, a group of radical New York City artists. The poster is known as 'And babies'. It features the words 'Q: And babies?' at the top and 'A: And babies.' at the bottom, imposed on an image of corpses at My Lai. The words are taken from a transcript of an interview with Paul Meadlo, one of the My Lai murderers, who admitted killing 'men, women, and children' then, when pressed, 'and babies'. Fifty thousand copies of the poster were printed, and they were circulated all over the world.[6] Although the poster was displayed in an exhibition of international political posters in Ballarat in 2013,[7] there do not seem to be any reports of it being carried as a banner in Australia, but it may have been brandished by somebody at some time somewhere.

However, it does not appear that Vietnam veterans were widely labelled 'baby killers' during the war itself. I can find no mention of the words 'baby killers' in any of the newspaper clippings files consulted for this study. The *Canberra Times*, which is digitised on the National Library of Australia's Trove archive, features scant mention of the words 'baby killers' in the 1960s and 1970s and, when the phrase did appear, it was in relation to either a virus that killed babies, or the problem of babies suffocating at home. The only occasion on which the words 'baby killers' appear in close proximity to the Australian military in the years 1962–72 was on 23 October 1969, where a brief story headlined 'Baby killers' abuts an advertisement for '100s of attractive highly interesting careers' in the 'navy, army and air force'. The story itself is about women in a Jakarta jail who had been imprisoned for killing their 'illegitimate' babies.

There was no mention of 'baby killer' as an epithet directed at Australian soldiers in the *Sydney Morning Herald* during the war years: the first instance in the *Herald* of its use in relation to Vietnam seems to have occurred in a story in 1981 about the left-wing journalist John Pilger's TV special, *Heroes*. The show was about the problems of American Vietnam veterans. According to Pilger, right-wingers in the US blamed the veterans for not winning the war and left-wingers still saw them as 'baby-killers and dupes'. The article also repeated a series of bizarre misrepresentations of the American Vietnam veterans' experience, including that 'a staggering 55 000 of them have apparently committed suicide, about the same number who died in the war'.[8] If this were true, it has been pointed out, the American national suicide rate would have been drastically affected, which it was not, since 'the *total* number of suicides for *all men* aged twenty to thirty-four for the decade from 1968–1978 does not equal the number of men who died in Vietnam'.[9]

The first instance of the use of 'baby killer' applied to Australian Vietnam veterans in the Fairfax/News digital archives searchable by Fairfax Media appeared in Rupert Murdoch's Adelaide *Advertiser* in May 1997, as part of Geoff Williams' account that included his being hit with a pole by the father of a deceased soldier.[10] The next mention came in March 2004, when a journalist on the Sunday *Herald Sun* wrote 'anti-war people spat on them and called them "baby killers"'.[11] In Gina Lennox's *Forged by War*, first published in 2005, the baby killers story took a particularly bizarre and interesting mutation. In Lennox's introduction, she wrote that men coming home from Vietnam were greeted by 'many' members of society as 'villains and murderers' and 'throughout this controversial war returning veterans were spat upon, ridiculed and condemned'.[12] This is perhaps the furthest any author has ever reached in their assessment of veterans' mistreatment, and none of the outrages mentioned are referenced.

Forged by War is a collection of oral histories of Australian veterans and their families, including several from the Vietnam War. One chapter focuses on the experiences of the Schulz family. Leonard Schulz served as a regular soldier in 7RAR in 1970–71. His children, Kathleen and Len Jnr, offer their accounts of their father's army life, dating from his enlistment in 1968. Len Jnr tells a story about an incident he believes happened after Len Snr returned from Vietnam in 1971 and left his father with nightmares that troubled him still: 'He had been out at Holsworthy on duty at the front gate. There were twelve of them facing a mob of 300 people who were protesting that Simon Townsend, a conscientious objector, had been locked in the guardhouse. When the protestors started charging the gate, the officer on duty ordered, "Present arms."[13] They stood there with their rifles forward, bayonets mounted. The protestors kept coming and one woman put her baby's neck on the bayonet of Dad's rifle.'[14]

The picture painted is a landscape of social collapse, with Australian soldiers training their guns on female civilians, a baby's neck on a blade. There are problems with this story, beyond the familiar issue that if it had occurred, it would have been reported in the press. The main issue is that Townsend was not at Holsworthy in 1971: he was locked up for 28 days in May 1968 and, since Townsend was the last conscientious objector to be held in an army jail, there was no protest of any kind at any military jail after Schulz had returned from Vietnam. A protest against Townsend's detention was recorded by the *Sydney Morning Herald* as having taken place at 'Ingleburn Army Camp'. It was the subject of quite a long news report, the central drama of which was captured in the headline 'Simon Townsend waves to his supporters'. The protesters held a roadside meeting outside the barracks, and a hand waved at them from a small window. The hand was identified by the crowd as belonging to Townsend, and the waving continued until someone shut the window. There were no rifles, no bayonets, no soldiers and no babies,[15] but, in the Schulz family narrative, the protesters themselves are forcing the troops to pose as baby-killers. At the conclusion of Len Snr's testimony in *Forged by War*, Schulz said he used to exaggerate the details of his Army service and admitted that, 'Looking back I've made up fairy tales about my whole life.'[16]

One question that might be asked of a particular type of veterans' story is why they often include women and spit. It would be apparent to even a casual reader of Australian Vietnam veterans' reminiscences in the media that the spitting incidents they recall are by no means confined to airports. In fact – or in fictions – veterans report being spat on anywhere and everywhere. However, there are no reports of Australian veterans being spat on during the war years, or the years immediately after the war, when the prime concerns of the veterans' movement were its conflicts with the DVA and later the RSL over Agent Orange.

The first veterans to report being spat on were Americans, and a number of American works have looked at the spitting mythology in detail. In *The Spitting Image*, Jerry Lembcke identified the fictional John Rambo in the 1982 movie *First Blood* as the first spat-on former soldier, although researchers – and the subject has attracted many, both amateur and professional – have since found two examples of veterans who had claimed in 1971 to have been spat on, although neither of them offered any corroboration.[17] In a syndicated newspaper column in the mid-1980s, journalist Bob Greene asked real-life US Vietnam veterans, 'Did anyone spit on you when you returned from Vietnam?' More than 1000 replied, and Greene published a selection of their responses in a book comprising 63 accounts of personal experience with spitting and 69 accounts of spit-free welcomes. Initially, Greene had doubted the spitting stories because of their clear similarities – they tended to feature an unkempt female hippie spitting on a clean-cut GI at San Francisco airport – but he became converted by the sheer weight of testimony. However, veteran Gary Kulik wrote, 'There are no named witnesses, none. You would think that at least one of these stories would involve two or more veterans who were friends and who could be remembered and named [and] there is not a single letter that claims to have witnessed a spitting ... Processing out of Vietnam was a form of mass production, not a one at a time activity. No soldier or Marine would have walked alone through the airports of Los Angeles, San Francisco, or Seattle–Tacoma at the mercy of vicious "flower children".'[18]

The first Australian spitting story would seem to have been published after the 1987 welcome home parade in Rintoul's oral history, *Ashes of Vietnam*. Rintoul quotes veteran Bob Gibson as saying, 'A woman who taught me at school spat at me. She was in Save Our Sons. Yeah, spat at me and I adored that woman.'[19] Gibson is perhaps unique in the annals of spat-on veterans in that he could name the woman who spat on him (although he did not). His story suffers slightly from the detail that of every organisation opposed to conscription or the Vietnam War, SOS – which saw the troops as victim-children – was perhaps the least likely to assault or abuse a returned man.

Strangely, the stories of spitting, which multiply and finally become ubiquitous after 1987, reach their peak not in the memoirs of national servicemen or regular soldiers – and certainly not in any of the history books – but in Narelle Biedermann's *Tears On My Pillow: Australian nurses in Vietnam*, published in 2004. Biedermann's book quotes one former nurse as saying that after serving in Vietnam until January 1970, then taking leave, she was posted to Watsonia in Melbourne, where 'I got spat on just about every time I came in and out of the front gates of the barracks when I was in uniform'.[20] Watsonia is home to Simpson Army Barracks and not a great deal else. It is 16 kilometres north-east of Melbourne's CBD. While there may have been iso-lated protests at Simpson Barracks during the Vietnam years, I have been unable to find mention of one (although there were anti-nuclear protests there in the 1980s). There had never been any previous suggestion that there had been any kind of picket outside the barracks, not least a daily protest aimed at the troops themselves. It might be thought that even in the most disciplined army in the world, if a *nurse* was being regularly spat on, someone in the military would do something about it, or at least think to call the police. Also in Biedermann's book, nurse Pamela Kelly, who served in Vietnam until May 1970, says that upon her return, 'All of a sudden we were all told not to wear our uniforms in public. We were not allowed to wear our uniforms in public because soldiers were being bashed and spat on and pushed off trains. Some of these soldiers had not even been to Vietnam, but because they were in uniform, people thought they had been to Vietnam.'[21]

There is a widespread belief that base troops in Melbourne and Canberra were ordered not to wear their uniforms on the street to save them from being identified and attacked. An early reference to this idea appears in Gary McKay's 1992 *Vietnam Fragments*, in which he writes, 'The wearing of military uniform in Canberra was actually stopped for a long period of time when it was felt that the presence of uniforms in public would incite violence or embarrassing demonstrations against service personnel.'[22] Many later memoirs include similar assertions but, as Jeffrey Grey wrote in *A Soldier's Soldier*, his biography of Sir Thomas Daly, this is a 'military "urban myth"': 'In fact, the move to have officers in Army Headquarters in Canberra (and in St Kilda Barracks in Melbourne) wear suits to work rather than uniform seems to have been a pragmatic one since officers were not to wear uniform in social or commercial settings, and this was clearly an inconvenience in a place like Canberra out of hours (on the way home from the working day, for example). The RAN already encouraged the wearing of civilian clothes.'[23]

What Grey failed to mention is that he himself was one of the propagators of the myth, as in 1991 he too wrote, 'Towards the end of the Australian involvement, service personnel were instructed not to wear uniform on public transport and in other public places because of the hostile reaction which it attracted from a minority of the general public.'[24] The assertion is footnoted, but the footnote leads not to a contemporary source (unlike the footnote in *A Soldier's Soldier*) but to the Commonwealth Parliamentary Debates for 28 October 1987, in which Senator Paul McLean of the Australian Democrats said, 'I recall having been a serviceman and having served under a standing order from my unit which told me not to wear my uniform to work ... That was from 1970 through to 1974, when they would have been harangued and ridiculed by virtue of the community attitude towards them in the post-Vietnam climate.'[25]

McLean was not a Vietnam veteran, nor is there any reason he would have been cognisant of the motive behind the order. However, the fact that Grey both disseminated and debunked the myth would seem to indicate that there is nothing deliberate or cynical about the spread of these stories, which cross any left–right divide: Rintoul was an opponent of the war, McKay a supporter, and both believed the Army hid the troops from protesters. Grey was, above all, a student of the war and, when his information changed, he changed his mind. There is a temptation to see conspiracy behind the relentless torrent of misinformation but I believe this is largely misguided: it is just a careless draft of history – and if the brilliant Grey could suffer a lapse, then anyone can.

To return to the nurses, the story of the nurse who said she was spat on whenever she wore her uniform outside the base, could not be true if Kelly's story (that she was ordered not to wear her uniform outside the base) was true, since they were both on the base during the same period. However, there seems to be an ingrained reluctance among oral historians to expect consistency from their informants. In addition, it should be said, there are no contemporary reports of soldiers – Vietnam veterans or other-wise – being pushed off trains.

As to spitting, it does not seem that spitting occurs regu-larly in Australian public life, or has ever been an acceptable or common means to register one's disapproval. However, this does not mean 'political spitting' never happened in Australia – or, for that matter, in South Vietnam. Probably the first mention of spitting in the context of Australia's Vietnam commitment appeared in *The Age* on 31 March 1966, in a short piece entitled 'Man of protest' about Trevor Ashton, the 22-year-old secretary of the Youth Campaign Against Conscription: 'It's not generally enjoyable to protest,' he said. 'In fact, it is unpleasant. You can be hissed, spat on, kicked or trodden on by a horse. Sometimes, on the other hand, you can be cheered and applauded and encouraged. Generally, people treat us with good-humored indifference.'[26]

The next time anyone was reported as spat upon in an Australian demonstration it was the prime minister. On 23 November 1966, Harold Holt addressed an afternoon meeting at Randwick and an evening meeting in Rockdale, both of which were disrupted by demonstrators protesting against the arrest of conscientious objector William White. EH Cox, for the

Melbourne *Herald*, reported: 'There is no precedent for the noisy, vicious attack organised against Mr Holt when he was buffeted, struck and spat at as he left the Rockdale meeting soon after 9 p.m ... A newspaper poster saved for the occasion – "mass killer in Sydney" – was waved above the mob ... Women spat viciously at him and shrieked insults ... The street afterwards was littered with women's shoes, a woman's hairbrush, spilled packets of cigarettes, handkerchiefs, pencils and general contents of women's handbags.'[27]

This account, written immediately afterwards, contains many details which also appear in subsequent, apparently mis-remembered narratives of protests which do not appear to have occurred, and gives credence to the ideas of women spitting and protesters holding up newspaper cuttings. Here, the demonstrators wave a newspaper poster, women spit and 'shriek' insults. When the violence is over, it is 'women's shoes' that are left behind, a 'woman's hairbrush' and 'general contents of women's handbags'. Also present at the Rockdale demonstration was Alan Ramsey, a left-wing journalist with *The Australian*. The third-deck headline to Ramsey's report of the protesters' attack on Holt is 'Girl spits as police lift him into car'. When all the Vietnam-era spitting stories are read together, it seems as if the same young woman toured the world spitting on veterans in the US, Australia and New Zealand. I had begun to believe she was apocryphal until I found Ramsey's report – because there she was in Rockdale, New South Wales, of all places, 'a girl of about 15' who saw Holt and 'spat in his face'.[28] Although it was not common, it could happen.

Another reported case of spitting at an Australian demonstration, with only the loosest connection to the Vietnam War, happened at May Day celebrations in Melbourne in 1972. Once again, it is connected with the tiny Australian Nazi movement. When eight members of the National Socialist Party of Australia distributed pamphlets in the City Square, Nazi Claud Woods was hit in the face and lost a tooth and 'as Nazis in uniform handed out leaflets, an elderly woman spat on them'.[29] Woods had been involved in various actions against the anti-war movement, and was photographed in December 1968 leading a demonstration targeting the Red and Black Bookshop in Brisbane, carrying a sign reading 'FREE GASOLINE AND MATCHES FOR THE N.L.F.'. A press report said the group (essentially a procession of ten people) was 'protesting against a militant student group which, they alleged, was supporting the Viet Cong ... A small crowd gathered to watch and their scattered reactions ranged from shouts of "Heil Hitler" to attempts to spit on the demonstrators.'[30] If the spit had hit Woods, it would have made him the only Vietnam veteran to have been seen and recorded as being spat on during the 1960s – although, at the time of the spitting, Woods was not yet a veteran. However, he eventually was conscripted and served in Vietnam from March 1970 to March 1971, not as a stormtrooper on the front line but as a member of the Australian Army Catering Corps at 1ALSG in Vung Tau.

The stories recounted above demonstrate that spitting was not unheard of at political protests in Australia, but also that it was possible to witness and report spitting, and that the act was sufficiently rare and transgressive to merit treatment as news. In the face of these reports, it is impossible to discount every story of a returned Vietnam veteran being spat on during a clash between soldiers and organised anti-war demonstrators, but it remains unclear whether more than a handful of such clashes occurred. In those few instances where protesters demonstrably came into contact with returned servicemen – most notably in Sydney in

1966 and Adelaide in 1969 and 1970 – there is no suggestion anyone from either side spat. The spitting nearly always occurs at demonstrations that did not happen. However, as early as 31 October 1966, the journalist John Sorell wrote in the Melbourne *Herald* of the village of Hoa Long, 'Men of the Australian Task Force today carried out an operation that underlies the difficulty of winning over the hearts and minds of people who still spit as the soldiers walk by.'[31] Nearly five years later, Pat Burgess in the *Sunday Australian* wrote, 'Vietnamese children in Hoa Long village sometimes spit at Australians. The adults are sullen, their anger contained. You feel the hatred rather than see it.'[32] It's possible Australian troops were actually spat on in Vietnam by the South Vietnamese, rather than in Australia by Australians.

But for the spitting to serve its purpose in popular historical memory, it cannot have occurred in South Vietnam, just as it cannot have been directed at politicians, nor, obviously, anti-war campaigners.

In May 1970, the month of the first huge Moratorium demonstrations, the city of Adelaide was shaken by the only large clash between demonstrators and servicemen recorded in Australia during all the years of the Vietnam War. Soldiers were not abused and spat on by women – they abused and beat up women. These events were not rumoured or recounted for the first time many years after the fact – they were photographed and reported in the press the next day.

On 8 May 1970, two days before Adelaide's 'official' Moratorium demonstration, a crowd of 1000–1500 students took part in a 'March Against Imperialism'. They were met by soldiers from Woodside-based 3RAR, dressed in civilian clothes.

The soldiers first jeered the marchers, then charged at them. According to the *Advertiser*, the soldiers 'kept up a running battle with 1000 peaceful Moratorium marchers', attacking them 'at least 20 times'. The soldiers grabbed NLF flags and tore them to pieces, or set them alight and threw them back into the crowd. Nineteen-year-old Margaret Barry of Murray Bridge was punched unconscious. She said her attacker had rushed into the marchers, striking wildly with his fists, and hit her on the side of the head. A spectator joined in the attack on the marchers, and hurled two large ice-creams into their ranks. Later, the soldiers linked arms and spread across the street, to block the passage of the march. When the marchers tried to return to Adelaide University, the soldiers ran ahead of them and slammed the gates closed. The gates were forced open by police and demonstrators.

Later that evening, there were further clashes outside Parliament House. Officers from Woodside came down and persuaded the men to leave, but they returned half an hour later, chanting 'We'll kill the Communists', and staged a sit-down protest.[33] The *Advertiser* headlined the story on the front page, and included photographs of soldiers with burning NLF flags and the young woman being carried unconscious from the crowd. According to reports collected in the radical *Revolution* newspaper, the soldiers, described as 'drunken Nashos', 'attempted to smash placards, break flag-bearing stakes and used these to bash demonstrators. At least two girls were attacked, one being knocked unconscious' and 'despite the intense and continuous provocation hardly a punch was thrown by demonstrators'.[34] The soldiers involved later told their story in a privately published unit history of 9 Platoon 3RAR: 'The diggers were into the crowd of demonstrators like bandicoots through a blackberry bush. North Vietnamese flags were soon burning up and down the footpaths. One digger even set one alight from the roof of a fruit cart. Speaking of fruit carts, those that were in the vicinity sold out of tomatoes like lightning – and a hail of vegies ended up in the crowd of protesters a split second later. It was huge fun.'[35]

The Adelaide incident – the only large confrontation between Australian demonstrators and soldiers ever recorded, rather than imagined – is not mentioned in Paul Ham's book, and the RAR's regimental history *Duty First* presents a sanitised version, claiming, 'Some 50 members of 3 RAR who were in town in civilian clothes decided to join other anti-moratorium demonstrators in an anti-protest march. There was a lot of shouting, pushing and shoving but no major incidents. Fortunately word had got back to Woodside and all available officers and senior NCOs, plus some staff from Keswick Barracks, hastened to the scene and persuaded the soldiers to disperse.'[36]

The press reports of the Adelaide demonstration give a clear picture of what might really happen anywhere in Australia if a large number of students – including a large number of women – were confronted by a far smaller number of trained and disciplined male soldiers: the soldiers would take them to pieces.

A footnote to the events of 8 May is offered in sportswriter Ric Teague's recent biography of Aboriginal national serviceman Allan Aldenhoven, a much-loved former member of 7RAR. Aldenhoven's national service takes up about half the book, and Teague looks to it for an explanation of Aldenhoven's postwar criminality. According to the dense back cover blurb, 'the abhorrent treatment dealt to Vietnam veterans made him angry'. Curiously, according to the book itself, when Aldenhoven returned from the war he slid effortlessly into the counterculture. He hitch-hiked from Adelaide to northern New South Wales, surfed up and down the coast, 'grew his hair long and allowed his moustache to droop', joined a milieu where there were 'plenty of parties and everyone was smoking marijuana', returned to South Australia to become 'immersed in the club and party scene' and 'joined the throng at the Myponga Rock Festival' where 'hippies and topless women were among the thousands dancing to loud music in the open air'. Aldenhoven became a popular boxer and man-about-town who 'cut a fine figure in early seventies attire of bell-bottom trousers and tight fitting shirts' and who had 'an amazing advantage in his endless pursuit of attractive women'.

There is nothing in Teague's book about Aldenhoven being taunted by anti-war protesters, just a repeat of the back cover generalisation that returning men were branded as 'baby killers' and a mention of a 40-year-old conversation with a boxing trainer, in which the trainer recalled Aldenhoven saying he was 'angry about the public rejection of his Anzac legacy'. In fact, the book mentions only one instance in which Aldenhoven encounters a former protester. Aldenhoven, by now a marijuana dealer, is working as a bouncer at a Deep Purple concert when he notices a familiar face in the crowd: 'She was short, pretty and curvaceous ... He ran forward, lifting the young woman off her feet with both hands and threw her into the air before safely catching her. She was surprised yet laughed when she realised who it was and wrapped her arms around him and kissed his cheek.'[37]

The woman is Margaret 'Silver' Smith (nee Margaret Barry) and – although Teague does not appear to be aware of this – she was the protester bashed unconscious in Adelaide in 1970. Apparently both the ex-girlfriend of Sam Ward of 7 RAR, and the ex-wife of anti-war radical philosophy lecturer Graham Smith of Flinders University, if any former protester had a good reason to carry a grievance against former soldiers, it was Margaret Barry. However, when she saw Aldenhoven, she did not spit on the veteran – she kissed him.

One of the most popular pieces of Australian literature to emerge from Vietnam was the ballad 'I Was Only 19 (or A Walk in the Light Green)' written by John Schumann of the radical folk-rock band Redgum and released by Redgum in March 1983. In spectacular contrast to the American – or even the British – popular cultural experience, Australia's first popular protest song to deal explicitly with the Vietnam War was not released until more than ten years after Australia's part in that war was over, and was exclusively and sympathetically devoted to the concerns of veterans. Redgum had been formed by students at Flinders University in 1975 as a musical project for a Politics and Art course taught by a Maoist, Professor Brian Medlin. Redgum's first recording was made at the ABC's Adelaide studios by the Maoist Darce Cassidy, and there were certainly communists in the band, but Schumann's song was based on interviews with his brother-in-law, 6RAR forward scout and national serviceman Mick Storen. Storen had been involved in an incident in South Vietnam on 21 July 1969, in which Platoon Leader Lieutenant Peter Hines was killed when he stepped on a mine, and others, including Private Frank 'Frankie' Hunt, were seriously wounded.[38] After Schumann had written his ballad, Redgum went on tour and Schumann met Hunt for the first time in Bega, New South Wales. Once the recording was made, wrote Schumann, 'Frank Hunt joined me in Sydney and he and I did endless media interviews together'.[39] The song speaks of a passing-out parade at Puckapunyal, training at Canungra and Shoalwater, 'contact' and 'dust-off' and the Grand Hotel in Vung Tau – all essential components of the infantryman's experience in Vietnam. It tells the story of the mine incident in verse, then names its consequences in chorus: the veteran remembering the story cannot sleep; the sound of a helicopter takes him back to Vietnam; he has a rash that, it is implied, might be the result of exposure to Agent Orange.

'I Was Only 19' does not claim to be a historical document. It has Hunt kicking the mine rather than Hines, apparently in deference to the feelings of Hines' widow. It helped popularise the misbelief that many national servicemen in Vietnam were 'only 19' whereas, in fact, none were. Mick Storen was 20 years old in July 1969, although Frankie Hunt, a regular soldier, actually was 19. 'I Was Only 19' became a political anthem – not of the anti-war movement, which had passed into history by 1983, but of the veterans' movement, which was gaining in energy. All profits from the song continue to be channelled to the VVAA.

'I Was Only 19' includes the first retelling of the story of Frankie Hunt. In the song, Hunt is remembered only as drinking cans of beer in the Grand Hotel on R and C (rest and convalescence leave) in Vung Tau, and then for lying screaming in the jungle until a medic silenced him with morphine. Schumann has noted, rather dryly, that 'Over the years, Frankie Hunt has assumed a prominence with regard to *I Was Only 19* that is understandable, if not entirely justified.'[40] As we will see, Hunt was to add substantially to the song's picture of his life in the years to come. The alterations and additions to Hunt's narrative, as published in 1987, 2005 and 2015, tell their own story of the changing memory of the Vietnam War.

In 1983, the veteran experience, as recounted by Storen to Schumann and described in interviews by Hunt, did not involve red paint, spit or confrontations with protesters, and still included the people of Townsville lining the footpaths to farewell the troops. Three years after Frank Hunt's 'endless media interviews', Hunt told his story once more to the TV cameras, when he was interviewed by Russell Braddon for the ABC show *Images of Australia* in 1986, the year following the report of the Evatt Royal Commission. The unedited footage of Hunt's 26-minute interview was later deposited in the Australian War Memorial, and is available for public viewing. Hunt is interviewed on a beach, and some of his words are difficult to hear, the sound perhaps drowned by the wind blowing in from the sea, but he recounts the story of his time in hospital, when he was recovering from his wounds in Australia. Every week, he says – if I hear the audio correctly – he was visited in his ward by sympathetic students from La Trobe University, who brought him gifts of food.[41] The show was broadcast in 1987–88, but an edited version is not publicly available.

Hunt was also interviewed for Rintoul's oral history *Ashes of Vietnam*, published in 1987. In 'Aftermath', the final section of Rintoul's book, Hunt talks of his post-war years. He says he was one of the lucky ones, as his wounds made it obvious to all that he had suffered in Vietnam, and people were sympathetic. When they saw Hunt limping along with his calipers, they thought he was a 'poor bastard'. Hunt contrasted the compassion he received with the incomprehension faced by veterans with invisible war wounds such as mental illness.[42] Frank Hunt appeared on stage at the 1987 welcome home parade, wheeled out in his wheelchair by former army nurse Colleen Thurgar. Hunt and Thurgar wept in each other's arms while Schumann played 'I Was Only 19'.[43]

In 2005, an interview with Hunt was published in Gina Lennox's *Forged by War*, and his reminiscences are entirely different from anything he had remembered before. In 1986, Hunt was saying university students had brought him food in hospital. By 2005, he was saying they had assaulted him with food in his wheelchair. The returned man attacked by students is a familiar story among veterans. For the narrative to function properly, the returned man has to be instantly recognisable as a veteran, but also in a weaker position than his long-haired assailants, or otherwise prevented from retaliating physically, perhaps because his attacker is female. After Hunt was wounded in Vietnam, he returned home on 29 July 1969. He says he spent nineteen-and-a-half months in hospital. At some time during this period, his nurses decided to take Hunt and two companions to a cinema on Bourke Street. Hunt claimed, 'We were all in wheelchairs, wrapped in dressing gowns with drips hanging off us. I was still in a plaster cast; one fellow had one leg, the other had no legs. We came out of the movies and suddenly there's a shout: "Child killers!" About twenty long-haired people joined in chanting "Murderers, rapists, child killers." I copped eggs, tomatoes, pies and lettuce. All they needed was the bacon and I would have had a full breakfast!'[44]

It is notable that Hunt has every clichéd epithet hurled at him along with the groceries, and that the anecdote has apparently been tailored to lead up to its punchline – but this was not the end of the evolution of Frank Hunt's homecoming story, which was to undergo yet another modification in 2015. Steve Strevens' *The Jungle Dark*, which purports to be 'the powerful true story behind the classic Australian song *I Was Only 19*', presented the most comprehensive version of Hunt's life story to date. By now, the tale of the students and the food had shrunk in focus so the only victim was Hunt, the group of students had been formalised as a 'protest', and Hunt's assailant had become a woman. Strevens wrote, 'A couple of passengers helped the nurses lift the chairs into a tram and then out again at their stop, but on the street they found trouble. Here in the middle of Melbourne a small protest happened to be passing as the veterans and nurses made their way along the footpath. One of the protesters stopped and abused the vets, who didn't say much although they wanted to. After a minute or so Frank could not hold back: "Piss off and find out what really fuckin' happened," he yelled. To that a young woman chanting slogans looked at Frank and came closer, rubbing her half-eaten pie in his face and hair. Frank laughed as he cleaned it off: "You forgot the fuckin' sauce."'[45]

What is to be learned from Frank Hunt's startling turnabout? In 1983, the VVAA was a protest movement with some support from former anti-war protesters. Its grievances largely centred around Agent Orange and its effects on the mental and physical health of veterans. This was palatable for left-wing activists, as the message seemed to be that if Agent Orange deformed those who sprayed it, the consequences must have been many times more terrible for those on whom it was sprayed. This was Hunt's story before and immediately after the Evatt Commission and in the year of the Australian Vietnam Forces Welcome Home Parade and National Reunion. After the practical defeat of the case against Agent Orange at the Evatt Royal Commission – but, more particularly, after the 1987 welcome home parade – the story changed so that the actions of protesters gained a prominence which by 2005 had become a pre-eminence. The demonstrators were the story of the homecoming, and veterans were reviled as 'child killers' and 'rapists'. This was the consensus when Paul Ham was researching *Vietnam: The Australian war*, and it was a standpoint reflected in that book. It was the belief when I interviewed the VVMC and it was propagated in my own words. Since then, the popular story has become even more fixed: organised protests were everywhere, unpoliced, uncontrollable and unreported, and young women would humiliate veterans in the most cruel ways imaginable.

In 1983, when memories of the protests were fresh and Hunt was touring Australia with communist musicians, it would not have been possible to tell the stories he was telling in 2005 and 2015, by which time the historical memory of the Vietnam years had become so corrupted by mythology that anyone – even somebody who had been interviewed countless times in the past – could suddenly come up with a new and incredible story about the treatment he had received upon returning home and nobody would ever think to attempt to contradict or corroborate it.

This would all make a nice, neat story if Frank Hunt had spent his later years maligning the militant left, allying himself with conservative causes, and supporting any war that came Australia's way. In fact, Hunt joined the ALP and marched with the anti-nuclear movement. In the face of facts such as this, our strange contemporary picture of the war years seems little more than a mistake of memory and a genuine confusion of real life with the movies – no matter what political usages might have been found for it.

Food is a favourite motif in some veterans' stories. As we have seen, Hiddlestone's Veteran 27 remembers being pelted with lunch at a parade where only confetti was reported thrown. In fact, there are no reported incidents of food being thrown at returned men during the war years, although the men of 3RAR happily admit to hurling fruit – as well as blazing flags – at anti-war marchers in Adelaide in 1970. The act of attacking veterans with food seems clownish, farcical and unlikely – but not impossible. *The Australian* records an incident in October 1966 when

Tom Hughes, a decorated Second World War veteran and the Liberal member for Parkes, New South Wales, was 'showered with fruit and paper darts' at Sydney University when he refused to debate the government's conscription policy with student Richard Walsh.[46] On 1 May 1969, it was widely reported that Governor-General Sir Roden Cutler, who won the Victoria Cross in the Second World War, was pelted with tomatoes at Sydney University.[47] If that happened to politicians and dignitaries who were veterans, it might have happened to veterans who were not politicians or dignitaries. The only point to make is that – like the spitting – it did not happen at the times it has been said to happen. And when it did happen, it did not perform its function in the myth – that is, it was not directed at soldiers returning from Vietnam, in order to shame them for atrocities they were supposed to have committed.

A certain kind of Australian writing about the Vietnam War is rich with anecdotes from men who remember being called 'rapists'. However, as far I could tell from reading of the press – left, right and centre – the idea of military rape had almost no resonance in Australia in the 1960s and early 1970s, and appeared to play little part in Australian anti-war propaganda, even after the reporting of the My Lai massacre.[48] During the research for my doctoral thesis, I repeatedly asked myself, *What are the veterans remembering?* I think the answer lies largely in Ann Curthoys' essay of 1994, in which Curthoys interrogates former RAAF fitter Barry Pedrana's memory (as published in Gary McKay's *Vietnam Fragments* in 1992) that, as members of an armed party at the Shrine of Remembrance, Pedrana and his comrades were 'verbally attacked by a bunch of women calling us murderers and rapists'. Curthoys writes, 'The reference to rape leads me to think this is not a memory concerning protesters in the 1960s at all, but of a much later generation of feminist activists using Anzac Day to highlight the issue of rape in war generally, as they did for several years in the mid-1980s. References to rape in war were minimal in the Vietnam war period itself, being rarely discussed before the advent of Women's Liberation in 1970, and even then not substantially till after 1975, with Susan Brownmiller's *Against Our Will*, published in that year, being an important influence.'[49]

If we look at the history of Australian feminist demonstrations against rape in war, which would seem to begin in the late 1970s and fizzle out towards the late 1980s, we see incident after incident in which Vietnam veterans (among others) met with protesters whose slogans implied that they were all complicit in rape. The protesters were all women, and they confronted the men on Anzac Day. There were clashes between veterans, protesters and spectators, and large numbers of demonstrators were arrested. The media was always present – as the demonstrations were designed to attract national attention – and stories of the protests often appeared on the front pages of metropolitan broadsheet newspapers. Striking photographs exist of even the most unlikely incidents, such as the moment when a man who identified himself as a wounded Vietnam veteran took off his artificial leg and threw it at demonstrators.[50] The demonstrations are remembered by the women who took part in them, as well as the men who faced them. All this would have been true of the mythical airport demonstrations and many of the other folkloric outrages – such as the picketing of veterans' funerals – if those outrages had actually occurred.

The protests are a part of Australian history – but the social history of the 1970s and 1980s, not the history of the Vietnam

War. Clive Hamilton's coffee table book *What Do We Want?: The story of protest in Australia* includes a two-page photograph of a group of demonstrators in Sydney on an occasion identified as Anzac Day 1977. The protesters are all women, their faces are visible, they are clearly identifiable, their hand-painted banners are legible. Their slogans included 'U.S. SOLDIERS ADMIT TO MASS RAPE IN VIETNAM', 'WAR IS THE BIGGEST GANG RAPE OF ALL', 'WAR MEANS RAPE TO WOMEN', 'DISARM ALL RAPISTS', 'WOMEN LOST EVERY WAR' and '300,000 WOMEN RAPED IN BANGLADESHI WAR'.[51] There are no similar pictures from the Vietnam years because such demonstrations did not take place in the Vietnam years and such slogans did not exist in the Vietnam years. In her groundbreaking study *Against Our Will: Men, women and rape*, feminist pioneer Susan Brownmiller wrote, 'In one respect, of course, this war was no different from others – rarely, if ever, was rape considered newsworthy enough to find its way into the dispatches of a foreign correspondent.' In the final years of US involvement in the war, Brownmiller says she received many requests to bring along her 'sisters' to anti-war demonstrations to show their solidarity with the peace movement: 'My response was that if the peace movement cared to raise the issue of rape and prostitution in Vietnam, I would certainly join in. This was met with stony silence on the part of antiwar activists whose catchwords of the day were "anti-imperialism" and "American aggression," and for whom the slogan – it appeared on buttons – "Stop the rape of Vietnam" meant the defoliation of crops, not the abuse of women.'[52]

In Australia, Curthoys wrote, women's groups developed side by side with the Moratorium movement in early 1970. Curthoys quoted the feminist Kate Jennings at a pre-march rally at Sydney University on 8 May, demanding of male students, 'How many of you, who can so clearly see the suffering and misery in Vietnam ... would get off your fat piggy asses and protest against the killing and victimisation of women in your own country?'[53]

The awakening of a feminist consciousness about rape in war was a global phenomenon, but its first public manifestations in Australia seem to have occurred in 1977. If the picture published in Hamilton's book is correctly dated, then there was a small demonstration on Anzac Day in Sydney – and a woman was arrested at the dawn service in Kings Park, Perth, when she tried to lay a wreath 'to commemorate all those women raped by soldiers'. The woman – who said she had changed her name by deed poll and was simply called 'Val' – claimed she and other women had been intimidated by police, who had torn up the wreath. She was arrested for hindering police.[54]

In 1978, women protesters turned out at Anzac Day services in at least four major cities. About 30 women dressed in black were permitted to lay a wreath in Sydney. In Brisbane, women carrying a wreath with the dedication 'In memory of women raped in war' entered the Shrine of Remembrance. In Canberra, where a statue near the Australian War Memorial had been splashed with orange paint the night before (but cleaned up before the dawn service) a group bore a banner reading 'Rape is war against women'. And, according to one report, 'Women, who said they were protesting against the rape and killing of women by soldiers, broke into the ANZAC march in Perth.'[55] The raised awareness of rape in war was part of a broader feminist focus on rape, which had led to the foundation of the first rape crisis centres in the 1970s.

In 1979, nine women from the Melbourne Rape Crisis Centre arrived at the Melbourne Anzac Day service wearing black robes and the slogan 'Remember Women Raped in the War'. They were permitted to lay a wreath. In Sydney, four women aged between 18 and 25 were arrested and charged with malicious damage after they painted the same slogan on RSL clubs in Woollahra–Paddington and the City of Sydney[56] – although this would have no bearing on Vietnam veterans to the historian who accepts the proposition that Vietnam veterans were somehow banned from metropolitan RSLs.

The folk singer Judy Small remembered attending a 1981 protest in Sydney, carrying a banner reading 'In Memory of Women Raped in War'. She said she was approached by an ex-serviceman who 'hissed': 'We should've let the Japs in. Then you'd know what rape is about!' In response, she wrote, recorded and released a song, 'Lest We', with lyrics that made reference to 'the countless children burned alive in napalm's fire' and 'the faces of the women raped and shattered to the core'.[57]

While the 'ex-serviceman' hissed to Small about the Japanese in the Second World War, Small wrote about the Vietnamese in the Vietnam War, referencing napalmed children ('baby killers!') and rape ('rapists!') in the same chorus. According to Adrian Howe, the song was 'usually sung during these marches' thereafter.[58]

Also in 1981, about 250 women joined the tail end of the Canberra parade and were blocked by police and told they could not march. Sixty-four people – 'mostly women' – were arrested for trying to break through police lines. Police acted under Section 23A of the Traffic Ordinance, which had been gazetted the previous Thursday, under which it had become an offence to disturb or disrupt an Anzac Day parade or ceremony. When the ceremony was over, the remaining women, who had gathered a number of supporters, marched to the Stone of Remembrance to lay wreaths 'in honour of all women from all countries raped in all wars'. According to the *Canberra Times*: 'There they were blocked by a small group of men and women who stood in a line silently in front of the Stone. When asked to allow the women to place the wreaths, they did not respond or move. One of the wreath-layers, however, saw a gap in this line and went through it to place the wreath. The other two were not then obstructed. Members of the line which had blocked the wreath-layers did not give their names but said they were not members of any organised group.'[59]

The *Sun-Herald* called it 'the mini-battle of Canberra'.[60] The next year in the ACT, more than 500 women – 'some carrying banners and singing softly' – turned up on Anzac Day and staged their own march against rape in war 90 minutes before the official procession.[61]

In April 1983, the Labor Party's Bob Hawke was prime minister of Australia, and the Labor Party's Neville Wran was premier of New South Wales. The NSW police had been granted an application to the Supreme Court to prevent an Anzac Day march organised by the Sydney Women Against Rape Collective on the grounds that they feared violence if the march were allowed to proceed. When it became apparent the women would march anyway, members of Special Branch and the elite Tactical Response Group were deployed to deal with the threat. The women held their own ceremony then began to march along the official parade route, and 168 of them were arrested. According to the *Sydney Morning Herald*, the women 'put up no resistance and sang as they were driven in police wagons to nearby police stations'.[62]

Anzac Day 1984 had even more of a chaotic feel, as 17 protesters against rape in war were arrested in Melbourne for 'offenses ranging from refusing to leave the Shrine reserve to assault on police, possession of an offensive weapon, resisting arrest, indecent language and offensive behaviour',[63] and three members of the Gay Ex-Services Association were refused entry to the Shrine to lay a wreath. Anti-rape protesters staged protests at the dawn service in Brisbane's Anzac Square and at the official parade in Adelaide. In Sydney, a prison officers' band, which had somehow been given a place in the march, was flour-bombed by a hitherto-unknown group calling itself Prisoners' United Militant Activists. A Sydney march against rape was again banned by the courts, but about 350 women walked towards George Street and 'halted at the barriers erected for the Anzac Day march and very slowly turned their backs on the waiting police. A white floral wreath shaped in the form of linked woman symbols was hastily passed from the back of the march to the front again. The "Unknown Victim of Rape", dressed in black and swathed in white lace, lay perfectly still on her stretcher while she was turned around. The women then marched back up Bridge Street and turned into Macquarie Street, but halfway down Macquarie Street they reversed direction. Once more the wreath was passed over the heads of the marchers to those at the front. At Hyde Park the women held hands and formed a ring around the Pool of Remembrance at the War Memorial before floating their wreath in the pool.'[64]

In Perth, the Tobruk War Memorial was defaced with slogans such as 'Women Against War', and large posters reading 'Remember Women Raped in War' were 'smuggled in' among the wreaths. However, according to a newspaper report, 'A big group of women staged a rival anti-rape sit-in which has split the Perth feminist movement. A spokeswoman from Women Against Rape said she was disgusted at the defacement of the memorial and said the rival group was singling out ex-servicemen and labelling them as rapists.'[65]

In Canberra in 1984, 'about 60 Women Against Rape laid Anzac Day wreaths' before the Stone of Remembrance, and were jeered and told to 'shut up' by others in the crowd when they sang:

> I walk for the women, for their pain
> is my own
> And though I come to lay this wreath
> I spit on your stone.

This is the most unambiguous reported instance of spitting on the service of Vietnam veterans that was recorded during or after the war years. The spitting was figurative, but it was there – and, if there was any doubt who it was meant for, the *Canberra Times* found an 'onlooker' who said he could not take sides since 'his father had fought for Australia but "would no sooner rape a woman than fly to the moon". On the other hand, he knew two soldiers who went to Vietnam and did rape women.'[66]

With all the obvious caveats about the virtually insurmountable difficulties that would have faced Vietnamese women if they had tried to report an assault – and with the exception of the unlikely allegations levelled pseudonymously in Rintoul's book – there have been few suggestions that Australian troops commonly raped women in Vietnam. One account of rape is included in Siobhan McHugh's *Minefields and Miniskirts*, in which entertainer Maureen Elkner reports she was raped at the age of 16 by 'sneaky little Michael', an Australian soldier in Saigon,[67] but the threat of rape is rarely mentioned by the heavily interviewed cohort of Australian women who went to Vietnam.

On Anzac Day in 1985, there were three arrests of Women Against Rape in Sydney, and parades throughout the country were marred by eclectic controversies involving Indigenous veterans; two rival groups of Turkish people; Armenians; and the corrupt Queensland Premier, Joh Bjelke-Petersen. In Melbourne an event occurred that I would surely have considered folkloric if it had not been reported and photographed, and the photograph printed on the front page of *The Age* with a helpful graphic of an arrow to clarify the position of the flying limb as 'a Vietnam veteran threw his artificial leg at a group of 60 women protesters after the Anzac Day march ... he jumped on a truck carrying women from the Anti-Anzac Day Collective outside Young and Jackson's hotel, hurled his leg at them, and was answered by shouts of "You haven't got a leg to stand on."'[68]

On Anzac Day 1986 in Melbourne, two women from the Anti-Anzac Day Collective were arrested by plain-clothes police after a 'scuffle' that broke out near the Shrine of Remembrance. According to *The Age*, 'About 80 women took part in the protest, which began near the Shrine at 11.30 am. It featured speeches and songs on what they see as the inherent sexist, racist, nationalistic and militaristic aspects of war ... the women were hemmed in by police, media crews and spectators, some of whom hurled comments such as "Who'd want to rape you anyway?"'[69]

In Sydney, according to the *Sydney Morning Herald*, a 'bemedalled veteran' wound down the window of his RSL cab, leant out and shouted 'Stuff the lot of you' at the Women Against Rape women, who answered by raising banners such as 'Warrior culture breeds rapists'. The report continued, 'The now-traditional Anzac Day confrontation between the men wearing rosemary and the women wearing armbands was marked this year by a lack of violence, the women preferring to "mourn" silently rather than wail around the Pool of Remembrance ... Instead of the black garb they have worn for the past three years, this year's was red overalls and red jumpers.'[70]

The next year, 1987, was the year of the Australian Vietnam Forces Welcome Home Parade and National Reunion and, as Jeffrey Grey noted, 'The radical contestation seemed to fade as suddenly as it had erupted, and by the end of the 1980s was no more than an occasional bitter recollection.'[71] By 2010, however, when a veteran of 1RAR's first tour told the *Geelong Advertiser* that 'someone from Women Against Rape in War threw red paint all over our commanding officer',[72] the Anzac Day marches of the 1980s had become the welcome home parades of the 1960s, and Nadine Jensen in 1966 had been inducted into an organisation that was not to exist until more than a decade later.

I believe the Women Against Rape demonstrations are, in fact, the airport demonstrations. One of the difficulties faced by veterans in remembering the protests for what they were (that is, post-war anti-rape demonstrations directed at parades of long-returned men) rather than what they were not (that is, wartime anti-war demonstrations directed at recently returned men) is that to stand up as an opponent of anti-rape demonstrations might seem a small step from standing up for rape. Certain cultural battles have been won resoundingly and are unlikely to be rekindled in the near future. One of these is the women's movement's struggle to make an issue of rape. A popular historian would be treading dangerous ground to ridicule the women's movement's emphasis on military rape, whereas the anti-war movement remains fair game.

If I were a more poetic soul given to less prosaic conclusions, I might be drawn to the inference that the unkempt spitting female protester is a proxy for feminism itself. I might feel emboldened to argue that the Vietnam-era national serviceman symbolised a certain kind of tough, disciplined, militarised masculinity that fell out of favour in the 1970s, as boys began to dress like girls and wear hair down to their shoulders, and many veterans felt bewildered and estranged by the new social mores.

I might conclude that an articulation of this alienation is much of the meaning of many of the myths: that the later drafts of soldiers felt that Australia had shifted socially while they were away in Vietnam, and altered even further once the war ended, and one of the hardest transformations to accept – for men who had just lived through the most intense experience of their lives in the virtually all-male environment of the Australian Army – was the changing role and status of women.

8
'You calling me a liar?' Myth vs history – conclusions

One of the best-known myths of the First World War is a myth in the most literal and widely accepted sense, in that it involves the intervention of supernatural beings in the lives of men. When British troops in Belgium retreated with heavy casualties from the Battle of Mons in August 1914, an angel was said to have appeared in the sky to protect them as they withdrew. The idea that this could have happened came from a piece of short fiction, 'The bowmen', published in September by the sometime journalist and gothic-fantasy author Arthur Machen, in which the ghosts of British archers who fell at the Battle of Agincourt in 1415 returned to the earthly plane to unleash magical arrows at German soldiers. The cultural historian Paul Fussell wrote, 'Within a week Machen's fictional bowmen had been transformed into real angels, and what he had written as palpable fiction was soon accepted as fact. He was embarrassed and distressed at the misapprehension, but he was assured, especially by the clergy, that he was wrong: the angels – in some versions, angel bowmen – were real and had appeared in the sky near Mons. It became unpatriotic, almost treasonable, to doubt it.'[1]

Machen himself gave a good account of the evolution of his story, and the process by which his 'light fiction' was taken 'as the solidest of fact': 'If I had failed in the art of letters,' he wrote, 'I had succeeded, unwittingly, in the art of deceit [and] the snowball of rumour that was then set rolling has been rolling ever since, growing bigger and bigger, till it is now swollen to a monstrous size.'[2] The story of the bowmen-cum-angels was accepted and dissected by publications such as *Truth* and *Town Topics*, the *New Church Times* and *John Bull*. In 1915, Machen wrote, 'People send me cuttings from provincial papers containing hot controversy as to the exact nature of the appearances; the "Office Window" of *The Daily Chronicle* suggests scientific explanations of the hallucination; the *Pall Mall* in a note about St. James says he is of the brotherhood of the Bowmen of Mons – this reversion to the bowmen from the angels being possibly due to the strong statements that I have made on the matter.'[3]

The tale of the angels turned up everywhere – but not, once the war was over, as a true story in serious history books.

In some clear ways, the spitting protester and the airport demonstrator are Angels of Mons, fictions consciously popularised by movie-makers and subsequently mistaken for facts. The myth of the airport demonstrations and the spat-upon veteran may have its roots in the movies but its meaning lies in the disenchantment of the veterans. The homecoming stories, while they may be false, are not without value. As the oral historian Alessandro Portelli wrote, 'interrogating the wrong memory, especially when it is so widely shared, is a way of interrogating the meaning of the remembered event. [However] in order to do this interpretive work on false narratives, we must be able to prove that they are indeed false. Thus, the oral historian's work includes a careful check of the facts to the best of our abilities, so that we may distinguish between factually reliable narratives, which are the majority, and the significant cases of creative error and myth. Only after we have done this work, by cross-checking false memories with the reconstruction of the events, we are able to gauge their impact ... At this point, even error, invention, misunderstanding, even lies, especially when they are socially widespread, become precious symptoms of such important historical processes as memory and desire.'[4]

This process of cross-checking and reconstruction has not occurred with the claims of various Vietnam veterans. Gerard Windsor wrote that 'an interviewer is not an interrogator, much less a court of law, and if a man says that this is his memory, then that's the way he gets quoted'.[5] This is a fine sentiment, but it cannot be accepted as the credo of a historian. As Frank Bongiorno wrote, 'From its origins as a recognisable branch of literature in classical Greece, history has defined itself as a form of truth-telling in the face of myths' power over the imagination'.[6] In accepting myth as memory as the raw material of military history, we essentially abandon the writing of history – except as a history of myth.

The pervasiveness of myth in certain narrative recollections makes it tempting to reach damning conclusions about so-called 'oral history'. Perhaps the best counsel is to bear in mind the words of CP Stacey, the official historian of the Canadian Army in the Second World War, who wrote, 'One very seldom encountered a deliberate liar [but] there were considerable numbers who lied to me while honestly believing they were telling the absolute truth.'[7]

It might also be useful to consider the unusual position of Western Australia. Hal Colebatch's memory of blood thrown by clergymen originated in WA, as did the book *Desperate Praise*, with the first published airport demonstration story. The pseud-onymous 'Mike' of the 1970 airport riot came from WA and his story was published in an anthology of the homecoming memo-ries of WA veterans. And it is anyone's guess what SAS veteran Barry Standen meant in a book by Gary McKay, when he accused protesters in Perth of 'throwing horse shit at the SAS marching down St George's Terrace'.[8] Perhaps there is something about the remoteness of the state that is particularly conducive to the devel-opment of a collective memory.

Our overwhelmingly negative picture of the homecoming may have been used for political reasons. In the United States, writes John A Wood, 'The late 1970s also saw the emergence of the belief that GIs in Vietnam were denied victory by the actions of antiwar protesters and then literally spat on when they came home. This narrative gained strength in the 1980s, and propo-nents of America's first war with Iraq used it to silence peace activists in 1991. The populace was warned that if they did not "support the troops" in the Middle East, they would be just as cruel as the radicals who allegedly victimized GIs in the sixties and seventies.'[9]

When John Howard asked critics of the Second Gulf War to 'please vent your anger against me and towards the govern-ment'[10] rather than the troops, he was probably not calling for mass demonstrations against himself. He wanted no demonstra-tions at all.

However, the widespread acceptance of the homecoming myth in Australia emerged through the uncoordinated, uncon-scious efforts of historians, veterans and political activists, both on the left and the right. It was not the result of a conspiracy. Its propagators, for the most part, had no goal but to accurately represent the experiences of both soldiers and civilians, or to give a voice to those who had previously been unheard. It has come about largely because people with an understanding (however facile) of the methods and operation of the military tend to have little understanding of the methods and operation – or even the purposes – of the radical left, and vice versa. As a result, authors have tended to adopt a simplistic or folkloric analysis of either one group or the other.

There is still much interesting and important academic work to be done. No broad history of the often mythology-ridden and mistakenly triumphant anti-war movement has yet been written, for example. Just as crucially, there has been no published study of what might be called the 'pro-war movement' and no explanation offered for its mystifying disappearance from history. It seems inevitable that civilian supporters of the war would have a mythology of their own – if only to explain why they did not volunteer – and it would no doubt be fascinating to read.

Jeffrey Grey once wrote, 'Had Australian military involvement in the Vietnam War consisted of regulars and volunteers, as in Korea and Malaya in the 1950s, there is little reason to believe that anti-war opposition would have been any more widespread than it had been during these campaigns. For many Australians conscription for overseas service was the issue, the nature or conduct of the war being entirely secondary ... as evidenced by the almost complete collapse of the anti-war movement after the withdrawal of Australian forces was announced.'[11]

It would seem that any exploration of this hypothesis would itself be hypothetical, were it not for the existence of New Zealand, whose government chose to fight the war without the use of conscripts. It might be thought that the deployment of regular troops alone might have taken the heat out of opposition to the war, but a comparative examination of the New

Zealand experience reveals some fascinating parallels and contradictions. More people attended Moratorium demonstrations in a Christchurch without conscription (7000–8000 out of a population 260 200) than an Adelaide with conscription (6000 out of a population of 792 000), and more took to the streets in Wellington (5000) than the much larger city of Perth (3000).[12]

A comparison of the Australian anti-war movement with the New Zealand anti-war movement – especially bearing in mind the disrupted Auckland welcome home parade of 1971 – would make for an interesting study.

Whatever work is to follow, it must be guided by sounder principles than have been applied (outside of the Official History) in the past, when uncorroborated oral histories, anonymous and pseudonymous unverifiable testimony, and the lure of accepting a lurid story have contributed more than rigorous analysis or even basic fact-checking. Sources of all kinds must be more thoroughly interrogated; the dates and locations of alleged events must be established; service records must be examined; stories must be confirmed. The standards that would be applied routinely to the military history of more historically distant wars must also be brought to bear on the Vietnam War.

I seem to have spent an enormous amount of time trying to prove that there were no protests at Australian airports against homecoming troops where spitting women called returning men 'rapists'. However, I also do my best to detail the demonstrations at Anzac Day celebrations where women sang about spitting and called returned men rapists. What difference does it make? To veterans, probably none. But it is important to history that things that did not happen are not recorded on the same pages as events that manifestly did occur. Beyond that, it is important because the idea of Australia during the Vietnam War as a society where radical grouplets held such power in the streets that they could murder uniformed men or throw them off trains, picket funerals with impunity and assault disabled veterans, turns history on its head. In this fantasy Australia, the troops are the only dissidents. During the later years of the war, they are told over and again that to fight in Vietnam is to be a rapist and a baby-killer, and yet still they go. Everybody damns them, nobody supports them, they are doused in blood and garbage, even by clergymen, and yet stubbornly, wave after wave of them lines up to rape women and kill their babies. They must be, at best, fanatics, or at, worst psychopaths. It is no wonder that, once they come home, they are a menace to society, prone to extreme violence and waging war on small country towns. And the most fanatical of them all are the national servicemen who, when offered a clear moral choice between draft evasion (which has the support of the community) or serving in uniform (which is spat on, both physically and met-aphorically), not only choose the latter but then volunteer *to a man* to go to Vietnam.

These ideas are pernicious because they obscure the truth that Australia in the Vietnam years was a conformist, conserva-tive society, which repeatedly elected conservative governments, and the young selected for national service were among the fittest and the brightest of their generation. The values held by national servicemen – and regular soldiers – were, broadly speaking, the values of the society that raised them. To argue otherwise is to blame the soldiers for the war.

9
'Interviews with a vampire'
The myth of my dad and other final thoughts

Warning

I suffer from a complete loss of mental stability, and become very violent with the slightest provocation.

The Department of Veterans Affairs has determined that either mental or physical harassment of my body may be extremely hazardous to your physical health and well being.

*SO STAY THE f!*k OUT OF MY FACE!!*

– Calling card given to the author by a Vietnam veteran and former national serviceman

The end of any substantial writing project brings with it a tremendous emptiness: a vacuum because the work is over; and a hollowness because the result seems so small. I studied national service and Australia's Vietnam War for more than six years – first for *The Nashos' War*, then for the doctoral thesis that forms the backbone of this book – and I sometimes wonder whether it was worth the pain. Because it was painful – not in the tramping-through-the jungle sense, of course; not in the stepping-on-a-mine sense; not in the going-home-with-your-arm-blown-off-and-your-best-friend's-body-in-a-coffin sense, but in the mildly troublesome if-that's-all-you've-got-to-complain-about-I'm-going-to-turn-up-the-telly sense. It was painful in the writers' sense. But I'll get back to that.

I interviewed about 160 people, mostly former national servicemen, for *The Nashos' War*. The dialogues became an addiction, and I was reluctant to stop the research after the book was published. When veterans who had read *The Nashos' War* contacted me with additional information, I wanted to interview them, to learn from them, to know them. Once or twice – as with Patrick Davoren, the Ordnance Corps soldier who resisted his posting to Vietnam – I did so, and every man carried within him further answers to questions that had troubled me before I even knew there had once been a national service scheme in Australia.

At the beginning of this book, I sought to explain why I had written about the Vietnam War. In this end piece, I will try to describe why I chose to immerse myself in old men's recollections of national service – and what I came to understand about history, memory and my father.

My dad, Gerry Dapin, was a national serviceman in the British Army between 1949 and 1951. When I was a boy, he would tell me bedtime stories about his days as a cheery, diffident conscript. He died when I was relatively young, and the few memories he had shared with me became unspeakably precious. After his funeral, I visited his second wife, and she gave me his superficial, inscrutable service record and a photograph I had not seen (where had he kept it all these years?) of the grinning young soldier who would grow up to be my father. I asked her why my dad had enjoyed the army; why he liked being told what to do.

'Because your father didn't know what to do,' she said.

My dad was a recently orphaned, illiterate factory worker by the time he was conscripted at 18 years old. He was posted to a logistics unit, where instructors taught him how to drive a truck. During the Korean War, he was stationed in Nottingham and, briefly, Germany – although other wretched British conscripts were sent to fight in Korea. My dad was a garrulous teetotaller, a politically conservative English Jew, and a mystery to me.

It was always national service that interested me as much as Vietnam. When I spoke to the veterans I was in dialogue with my dad. After *The Nashos' War*, I began work on *Jewish Anzacs*, a history of Jews in the Australian military. The book was not my idea – I was approached to write it – but it fed the same personal hunger as *The Nashos' War*. It gave me a delicious excuse to meet even more former national servicemen – and, better still, men whose backgrounds were closest to my dad's.

I had already spoken to a handful of Jewish veterans for *The Nashos' War*. I had found my first Jewish interviewee, David Roubin, by chance, and my next, his younger brother Loris, through David. The elder Roubin reminded me of my dad. He even looked a little like him and had served in the Ordnance Corps. David (unlike my dad) was a national service officer, a Scheyville graduate from the first intake, who had signed up with the Regular Army and made the military his life, eventually retiring as a major in 1989. From the beginning, I was interested in soldiers who did not fight, men who were stationed in Vung Tau and who essentially performed civilian jobs in a garrison town in a war zone. In their lives, I could imagine my dad.

I was also drawn to the dissidents, the disaffected, the subversives, the leftists, because in them I felt that I could see myself. With uncanny symmetry, David's brother Loris turned out to be a former anti-war protester who had entered the Army under extreme sufferance, had an awful time in the Medical Corps in Vietnam and viscerally despised the military.

The secret personal reward in my research was the chance to hear different stories of dissimilar men from diverse Army units and ask myself each time: What would I have done if I were him? And what would my dad have done?

This involved questions of both principle and practice. I remember sitting in a café in Brighton, Victoria, with Michael Frazer, a journalist, Vietnam veteran and author of the 1984 novel *Nasho* (who has previously been incorrectly identified as a conscript 'who did not see service in Vietnam'[1]), who told me he found basic training 'really hard ... because I was a journo and a drinker before I went in. Looking back on it now – if national service ever came back in – you'd get off the drink for months and you'd get yourself enormously, enormously fit and enormously strong, and cut your hair back to absolutely nothing, and then you're basically on the right boat.'

Yes, I thought to myself, *that's exactly my plan for when they bring back national service* – despite the fact I would be over 50 years old, a father of two, deaf in one ear, and probably not a first-team pick for the Australian Army.

However, as an author, I had to empathise with all my characters, not just those who happened to be journalists, drinkers and novelists. If I failed to make any of them real – to the reader or myself – their words and mine would lie lifeless on the page. So I listened closely to bellicose patriots, opportunists and authoritarians, as well as disenchanted pacifists, bewildered victims, poets and cranks, and I tried to understand them. For the first 80 or so interviews, I asked every man the same questions, about where they were born, where their parents worked and where they went to school. As each man described his circumstances and upbringing, I came to realise that, given a similar background, I would probably have done the same thing as they did. This held true for almost everyone except the war heroes and the SAS guys. I knew I could never have become them, no matter how hard the Christian Brothers had belted me, or what my parents had told me about communism.

In the beginning, when I still believed the myth of the ubiquity of the anti-war movement, I found it difficult to comprehend why some of the more reluctant soldiers I interviewed had not simply registered as conscientious objectors, like the student protesters I had heard so much about. It was Gus Howard, who spent his national service operating the movie projector at 3RTB Singleton, who first explained to me that students had 'the same social level as dole bludgers'. It was a typically lucid piece by conservative commentator Gerard Henderson that clarified what should always have been obvious to me: that 'the overwhelming majority of students then (as today) had little interest in politics' and the radicals were 'quite atypical'.[2]

In the early stages of my research for *The Nashos' War*, I interviewed former protesters and anti-war movement leaders, largely to discover where they stood in relation to the conscripts. I abandoned this when it became apparent that – apart from SOS – they did not really stand anywhere. The left had no discernible strategy to deal with national servicemen who obeyed the draft and went to Vietnam, and no burning interest either in confronting them or comforting them. They did not blame them for the war – to an extent, they considered them irrelevant to it.

Much of the muddiest thinking about Australia's Vietnam War seems to be rooted in a mischaracterisation of domestic opposition. The veteran/author Ambrose Crowe wrote, 'The war polarised society into two groups: those in favour of conscription and Australia's involvement in Vietnam and those against it. There was no middle ground.'[3] This is a spectacularly incorrect statement. The agglomeration of the various nuanced debates about national service and the Vietnam War into a single black-and-white question with a yes or no answer has no resonance historically. As I hope I have shown, attitudes to conscription were generally positive across the political spectrum. Even some prominent Sydney Trotskyites were to adopt a position that 'opposed the total abolition of conscription' since 'in a future workers' state, conscription might be necessary and desirable'.[4] But the depth of Crowe's fallacy might best be illustrated by the example of one middle-aged, middle-class woman who advocated 12 months' national service training for all 18-year-olds, 'and girls too'. She suggested female conscripts could do clerical work, driving, nursing and 'code operations' for the Army. She said she had discussed her view with her husband, who agreed with 'most of it'. She was against the Vietnam War but believed that if the government wanted to fight, it should 'call for volunteers'.[5] That woman was Margaret Whitlam, the wife of federal Leader of the Opposition Gough Whitlam, speaking in November 1969, less than two weeks after news had broken of the unspeakable cruelties at My Lai.

In the face of overwhelming societal approval for conscription, the choice to defy the National Service Act – the very idea that non-compliance might be a course a young man would elect to take – simply did not exist for the great majority of youth, particularly in the early years of the scheme. In Australia in the 1960s, people respected authority reflexively. Most young men's fathers – and many of their mothers – had served in the military during the Second World War. Although many of them may not have relished the experience – and 27000 were killed – they had helped save the world from fascism with their machine guns, mortars, discipline and courage. While peacetime soldiers may have been regarded as otherwise unemployable – the typical nashos' response to taunts from Regs was, 'We joined the Army to do a job; you joined the Army to get a job' – the military itself was still the cradle of the Anzacs. Many boys dreamed of marching with the diggers on Anzac Day, with their heads held high and their medals on their chests.

In my preface, I touched on the Hollywood-inspired myth that Vietnam veterans are aggressive, unbalanced, anti-social misfits hell-bent on wreaking revenge on society. To an extent, this stereotype is perpetuated by veterans themselves, even as they drift towards arthritic and whispering old age. The man who gave me the calling card quoted at the head of this chapter was polite, courteous and composed, but he certainly enjoyed the idea of himself as a human time bomb – as I suspect various members of the Vietnam Veterans Motorcycle Club did, too.

Even my doctoral supervisor, the late Professor Jeffrey Grey, was surprised that so many veterans had been willing to talk openly with me for *The Nashos' War*, bearing in mind I was not a national serviceman, I had never been in the Army and I did not fight in Vietnam.

Jeff, whose father, General Ron Grey, was a commanding officer of 7RAR during the Vietnam War, told me a joke:

Q: How many Vietnam veterans does it take to change a lightbulb?
A: You wouldn't know because YOU WEREN'T THERE!

The accepted wisdom has it that Vietnam veterans will not talk about the war, for all kinds of dark and terrible reasons. And there was probably a time when they would not have spoken – just as a silence of returned men follows every war. The troops who came back from the world wars might never have talked about Kokoda, El Alamein or Changi with their children, but they often opened up in retirement, to their grandchildren. But when Vietnam veterans did not immediately tell their stories, it only served to intensify suspicions that they must have something awful to hide.

I began my research for *The Nashos' War* with no clear plan. Since my earliest experience of veterans was with the VVMC, which included men who had served in all three services and throughout the war, I had a vague, misguided idea that most Vietnam veterans somehow knew one another. I assumed I would find one and he would lead me to the rest. As a research technique – if I can dignify it with that title – this is known as 'snowball sampling'. I quickly came to realise that few former fighting men had friends in other units. Among the infantry during the war, men barely even had contact with soldiers in the same company of the same battalion. They lived and died with their platoons.

Many of my friends knew a Vietnam veteran – one of my friends actually turned out to *be* a Vietnam veteran – and I started the project by interviewing them, along with some former soldiers I met at the National Vietnam Veterans Museum on Phillip Island. I eschewed regimental associations and, in the beginning, veterans' organisations, because I (wrongly) assumed they attracted a particular kind of veteran. My snowball sampling was successful to an extent but, once the snowball reached a certain size, it would generally melt away.

So I started to look for men in the phone book. I isolated certain incidents, contacts or units that I hoped to investigate further, found the names of the soldiers involved in news stories or history books or lists on the internet, then searched for them in the White Pages by their home state (with national servicemen, this was distinguishable from the first digit of their service number: the number 1 indicated NSW; 3 was Victoria; 5 was WA and so on). If they had a moderately distinctive name, they were generally easy to track down. If they had a common surname but had returned to the town where they were born (as indicated on the Nominal Roll) it was not hard to find them either.

Then I called them, out of the blue.

A typical conversation would go something like this. First, I would introduce myself, then:

Me: Is that John Alphabet?

John Alphabet (slowly and suspiciously): Ah, yeeeeeah, mate.

Me: The John Alphabet who served in Vietnam?

JA (hesitantly): Ah, yeeeeeah, mate.

Me: I know this is a bit of a strange phone call to receive out of the blue on a Thursday afternoon, but would you be willing to help me with a book I'm writing about national service and the Vietnam War?

JA: Ah, yeeeeeah, mate.

Me: Would I perhaps be able to interview you?

JA: Ah, yeah, mate, but I'm off to the bowlo just now. Call me back in a couple of hours and we can have a yarn. Are you in Mukinbudin yourself? Do you want to come around to our place? We can fix you up with a feed.

Only half a dozen men declined to talk. Most of the others acted as if they received a call from a historian every day of the week and had already put the kettle on.

Some veterans believed unusual things – one man assured me that Vietnam was a Muslim country, for example. Another veteran, sadly, appeared to be actively mentally ill, and the curious statements he made were perhaps distorted by his mania. Two men seemed to have been pretending to have been to Vietnam. Neither of their names were on the DVA's Nominal Roll, and both also pretended to have been attached to the SAS. Their claims were made in preliminary conversations and I chose not to interview them further. I eventually decided not to believe anyone who told me their role in Vietnam was 'still secret', although some veterans may well have believed this to be true. I also declined to speak further to a man who told me on the phone that he had been inside an army base in Australia when he was hit by a bucket of red paint thrown by a protester on the other side of the fence. With those exceptions – and another person who sent me a series of emails I could not fully fathom – I spoke with anyone willing to talk to me, as I found every story equally interesting.

If it were at all possible, I would conduct the interview in person. I would be invited into the veteran's home, which often had some kind of elaborate security system, where I would be introduced to the veteran's wife, who was invariably concerned about whether I had eaten. She would make me a cup of tea and hand me a slice of cake, then generally leave the room, perhaps returning later with a cheese and tomato sandwich. In the absence of a spouse, the veteran might give me a slice of cake. I ate a lot of cake.

In a couple of cases, we met at a pub or a bar, but it was usually too early in the day for most men to have a drink. Many veterans kept a small war room – or war alcove – in their homes, with a regimental crest on the wall and Paul Ham's *Vietnam: The Australian war* on the bookshelf. Most talked easily and fluidly and seemed to enjoy the conversation. At the end of the interview, they would usually put me in touch with a friend who, they thought, would be happy to talk to me – and he nearly always was.

I did not ask my interviewees about their lives after the Army, although many of them told me anyway. I did not ask any how they felt about the Vietnam War in retrospect. I felt there was something voyeuristic about exploring their feelings today, something pornographic and mean. A cowardly journalist saves the toughest question until last: 'So, looking back, knowing what you know now, was a lost war really worth the death of your best friend ...?'

My first Jewish veteran, the late and lovely David Roubin, told me he had agreed with the Vietnam War in the 1960s and he would let me know what he thought of it now when I, inevitably, raised the question. I never did – although he later said he believed it to have been a just war. The first two SAS men I interviewed both said they would have supported Ho Chi Minh had they been Vietnamese. This echoed a conversation I'd once had with a British former-SAS trooper, author 'Gaz Hunter', who had served in Northern Ireland with the Royal Green Jackets and told me he would have joined the IRA if he had been an Irish Catholic. Scheyville graduate and former artillery officer Noel Turnbull, who had been president of the Liberal Club at Melbourne University but had marched in the Moratoriums after he returned from Vietnam, told me, 'Having been there and having been around Bien Hoa and mixed with the Americans and seen what was going on, I thought this was a dreadful, dreadful mistake. It wasn't specific horrific things, it was the sense they had no idea whatever about the country: firepower, bombing, didn't win any hearts and minds. After I'd seen the astonishing inequalities in wealth, the prostitution and all the other things, I thought, "Ho Chi Minh might have some better ideas than these guys have got." It sort of radicalised me, and I got involved in left-wing politics, or what some of my peers in the military would regard as left-wing politics.'

However, of those who expressed an opinion – on or off the record – the majority remained in favour of both national service and the Vietnam War. Some believed the war should have been fought to the last man, and every Australian of military age should have been mobilised and deployed. Most would not go that far but were broadly nostalgic for some kind of conscription scheme to help young men grow up strong, fit and honourable. Another of my favourite veterans, who was twice blown up by mines in Vietnam, assured me that national service had never done him any harm.

When a man made a statement that I thought was factually wrong – either during the interview or afterwards – I occasionally sought to clarify their testimony but rarely attempted to correct it. Once or twice, I thought it might make veterans feel better to be reminded that the majority of people supported them but, in fact, it just seemed to annoy them. It was as if they felt I was missing the point. It was part of their identity that they had been rejected.

Only two men mentioned airport demonstrations. One said he and the rest of his flight from Vietnam were held inside the terminal at Sydney Airport because a large crowd had gathered outside and it was not clear if they were friendly or hostile. He remembered the date because it was Armistice Day in 1969. I looked up the newspapers and there was, of course, no protest recorded on 11 November 1969. The second man told me he had faced a 'huge' protest at the airport. When I repeated 'Huge?', he said there were about three people. When I asked if he was sure it was a protest, he said they might have been waiting for a plane. I was astonished at how quickly he recanted. The former Maoist Michael Hyde told me he would happily have attended a protest at an airport, but the comrades had never suggested it.

Two men said they had been deliberately spat on. The first thought he had been targeted from above while walking beneath a balcony in Kings Cross. The second was a vehemently anti-war veteran who only mentioned spit while he was driving me home after our interview was over. I did not record his statement and I did not press him to elaborate. Another said a man in his unit had been spat on in Sydney, but he could not say when or where or in what circumstances.

I was always absorbed by military sociology and the administrative functioning of a war-fighting organisation, but when my partner read the early draft chapters she focused immediately on the battles. After that, I began to spend more time tracking down fighting men. I moved towards shorter telephone interviews aimed at eliciting specific information to fill the gaps in my research.

It is difficult to conduct a detailed interview on the telephone and some men retreated into a formulaic storyline that ran something like this: everyone supported us at first, then the wharfies blacked our ships and posties refused to deliver our mail, we got no parade when we came home, a woman called me a baby-killer, and we were banned from the local RSL.

Some parts of this narrative are untrue, and some other parts are unlikely, but none says anything much about a man's individual experience of war. The standard account robs veterans of their own stories. The myths gag them, silencing their authentic voices and leaving both us and them bereft of real history.

I used to believe that oral history had a kind of transcendent value, although my preference was always more aesthetic than political. I knew that most people – especially older, less educated people with a practised command of the vernacular – could tell their own story with more colour, precision and flair than any journalist could muster. I now think that, in some cases, this is oral history's only worth. When I wrote earlier that my research had been 'painful', I was referring to the difficulty of reconciling the accounts of men who trusted me with conflicting evidence which I knew to be true. And it was not just the veterans whose accounts could be unreliable: a one-time leader of the anti-war movement told me one of the most ludicrous, improbable stories I have ever heard as a journalist or a historian. That was the point at which I stopped interviewing former protesters.

I find it hard now to credit my own petulant naïveté, but halfway through writing *The Nashos' War*, I gave up. I remember plaintively appealing to Bruce Horsfield, director of the excellent 1994 documentary *Long Tan: The true story*, 'What's the point of asking people questions when they don't tell you the truth?' Wisely, Horsfield replied, 'They do tell you the truth about some things.'

There is more to any book than the words that end up on the printed page. One man told me – when the recorder was turned off – that he had seen an Australian soldier shoot dead a civilian just for the fun of it. One man told me that his own widely read memoir was, in part, an agglomeration of the experiences of other troops. One man, whom I knew quite well, asked me to withdraw part of his story just before the book went to press. He had killed a man, and I did as he asked. As I mentioned in Chapter 5, one man renounced his early testimony that he had not seen women and children killed at Binh Ba, but I had finished recording and was not sure if he was speaking on the record so I chose not to quote him. One man who had refused to go to Vietnam told me he sometimes wondered if he had made the right decision. Again, I was no longer recording, but I think he would have been happy for me to include his doubts. In retrospect, I wish I had. It would have added another layer of nuance, a deeper level of truth.

Some stories I heard were not necessarily true, but they were too good to leave behind. They ended up forming the basis of two novels: *R&R* and the upcoming *The Harold Holt Surf Life Saving Club*. But I wrote fiction about Vietnam primarily because I was interested in exploring the characters of certain types of soldiers, particularly those who had enjoyed the war in a good-natured, laconic, take-whatever-comes-and-make-the-best-of-it style. I was also fascinated by the way some men remembered their younger selves as fathomlessly ingenuous, ignorant of the world and willing to believe whatever they were told.

However, I made the mistake of saying publicly that the novels were inspired by my interviews with national servicemen, which created the mistaken impression that they were supposed to be realistic – or, at least, plausible – dramas about life during wartime, when I meant them as gruesome parabolic comedies. While the period detail is largely accurate, the narratives themselves are as ludicrous as, for example, *First Blood*. Although I was aware how profoundly the truth about Vietnam had been corrupted by post-war fiction, I never anticipated I myself would become part of the process. Yet, after the publication of *R&R*, I received two messages from veterans saying, *Yes, that's exactly how it was in Vung Tau in 1967.*

I was part flattered and part appalled. I feared a wave of veterans' memoirs which, like *R&R*, told stories of disinterred corpses going out drinking in Vung Tau bars. I need not have worried – hardly anyone bought the book.

Another source of (mild, empathetic, writer's) pain was the crying. About 60 veterans wept at some time during our interview. As one eye welled up, they would tip back their face and pretend nothing was happening. The tear would grow and they would lean away still further, in the hope it might stay in place until they had finished speaking. But the weight of sadness would increase until it pulled down their heads and the tear would roll, free and unacknowledged, from cheek to chin. I was moved to see an Afghanistan veteran cry this same way on the ABC documentary *Afghanistan: Inside Australia's war.*

When my interviewees cried, I felt as though I were bringing tears into their lives. It was as if I was a vampire feeding on their grief, sucking out their small stories to polish them and package them and make them into one big story for me. The crying became so commonplace that I began to warn men it might happen. Invariably, they smiled and assured me that it would not. Then, halfway through their story, they would tip back their head ...

Sometimes, they would be talking about the death of a mate or some other terrible trauma, but more often it was the recall of simple facts about ordinary life that seemed to sadden them. At other times, it was other people's hurt.

Probably the most significant effect of my Vietnam War studies on my life is the way they have stolen my trust in my own memory. I was indignant when my aunty, Gloria Yates, published a book about her life and defended it as her own truth. I did not believe there was such a thing as an aunty's truth: reality was immutable; facts were facts; what happened had happened.

I used to imagine I recalled things as they had occurred – beer, whisky and wine permitting. Now I am less certain. I had already had an intimation of my limitations in 2004, when I wrote a memoir, *Sex & Money,* and two friends contacted me to correct passages I had misremembered. To my particular surprise, I had reconstructed the hours around one dramatic sequence – in which I had woken in an alley to find myself beaten up, broke, unshod and in the wrong country – in entirely the wrong order. In another part of the memoir, I had attributed to my mum something that had happened to my aunty. Much later, while writing this book, I realised that something I had always believed had happened to me had in fact happened to a fictional character played by Tim Roth in the 1982 skinhead movie *Made in Britain*: this was a significant consolation to me, as I had often wondered why I had done it.

I came to wonder if it was even necessary to write the truth. I began to think the veterans were entitled to their own idea of history. Why should they be encouraged to believe something that compromises their hard-won sense of self? Does it matter that the airport demonstrations did not happen? The veterans are not libelling anybody: no protester – or even group of protesters – has even been named as having taken part. Why not just let people be?

In 2014, I spoke with Peter Cochrane at the *Griffith Review* about using my early research in an essay about the myth of airport demonstrations. Decades before, Cochrane had published a piece in the anthology *Vietnam Remembered* in which he had written 'at the airport ... soldiers arrived to face demonstrations'. He was surprised to hear I thought the protests had never happened and – understandably, but unbeknownst to me – subsequently put out a call for information from any veterans who had 'experienced anti-war protests at an airport when leaving or returning from Vietnam'. I found out about this when a response to his email was forwarded to me by another of my favourite veterans, Loris Roubin. The reply was from an Ordnance Corps veteran who wrote: 'Yes we arrived back in November 68 to this crap. I have forwarded a couple of poems written about that time from that arsehole Denis Kevans which came from the Green Left Weekly October 15, 2003 "The Slouch of Vietnam" and the reply, "The Slouch Hat of Vietnam" written by Peter Scott in April 2012. Not sure if you have seen this before but it also tells a story as well in poetic form. We have long memories.'[6]

'The Slouch of Vietnam' is a poem written in 1962 by Denis Kevans, from the point of view of an Australian soldier asking why he should go to Vietnam and make a 'suckers' sacrifice' that would have him 'hunt down peasant kids' and 'share the napalm guilt of Uncle Sam', just because a 'brass hat' orders him to fight. Peter Scott's 'The Slouch Hat of Vietnam' calls Kevans a 'mongrel' who pissed on diggers and branded them all as murderers, while the postal workers cut off their mail. In addition, according to the poem, Kevans and his friends had thrown blood over returned servicemen and passed the hat around for Ho Chi Minh, who used their money to make grenades to kill Australians – so they could shove their Moratorium up their arse.

Loris was saddened by one of the poems, and I felt his distress was my fault – I had, inadvertently and indirectly, introduced a new source of angst. I was also concerned that Cochrane had put out a call for testimonies as I had no approval from the UNSW ethics committee to gather information in this way. I had lost battles with the ethics committee to use 'snowball sampling'; to approach veterans for interview personally or individually; to use the names of interviewees; and finally – since we could not agree on ground rules – to interview veterans at all.

As a result of the emails, I felt I had to withdraw my offer of the essay, but I learned something from the fact that the emailer felt it was sufficient to answer the question with a poetic response (and one which made no reference to airport demonstrations), bearing in mind the airport demonstrations themselves apparently are a poetic construction. At the same time, I was disturbed by an acrimonious exchange of emails with another historian – whom I knew slightly – which I have agreed not to publicise without his permission. Obviously, some people had a huge investment in these stories, so – again – why not just let them be?

In 2017, I wrote an essay for *The Honest History Book*, questioning some of the wilder claims made about the early relationship between Vietnam veterans and the RSL. In my chapter, I wrote that history is a dish best served cold, by uninterested wait staff, long after the banquet of lived experience is over. I was criticised for this – and, I think, rightly so. At the time, I had begun to think it would be better to publish my research when the last veteran had passed on. But that was cowardly. Of course, the more embittered men have every right to tell their own stories to explain themselves – after all, everybody else does – but historians have no right to treat their claims as history if there is no evidence to support them. It is the practices of historians that must change, not the memories of soldiers.

When I began this project, I had no sympathy with the idea of national service, but no intention of writing a polemic against it. I felt there was no need. If I simply recorded the facts, they would scream for themselves. Robert Menzies, the prime minister who introduced a selective service scheme that would compel conscripted men to fight overseas, had himself declined to volunteer to fight overseas in the First World War. John Howard, who, at the dawn of national service, was a lawyer aged 26 – comfortably within the age range many lawyers would later have been scheduled to begin their national service – was a passionate defender of conscription who had chosen not to join the Army himself. It seemed clear to me that national service provided a tool for powerful men to compel less powerful men to go to war – and, perhaps, die – while they stayed at home benefitting from peculiar justifications for their own indemnity.

Even now, I return often to the idea of the Menzies 'family conference'. The title sounds imposing and official, but what does it actually mean? How does a 'family conference' differ from a conversation at the dinner table? If the decision of a 'family conference' is sufficient to shelter a man from the obligation to go to war, where would that leave boys like my dad, who had no parents by the time he was 18? In its early years, by its very nature, the national service scheme captured men who had no long-term plans – men, like my dad, who did not know what to do.

I thought there was no need – intellectually, artistically or politically – to propagandise but, some way through the project, I began to wonder if I were simply arguing with my dad and trying to invalidate his experience in some way: another small betrayal of a man I had come to believe I had let down when he was alive.

During my research, I saw many men cry, but I cried only once, in an interview with Jim Booker, who had served with Barry Heard in 7RAR. I did not use that section of Booker's interview in *The Nashos' War* because it related to his life after national service. Booker was a beautiful man, too young and sweet for the army. When he was drafted, he was still playing with Meccano. He was posted to infantry but trained as a hygiene dutyman. In Vietnam, they called him 'Blowfly', because part of his work was to clean the toilets and keep the blowflies away. He was proud of his nickname – it made him feel like he belonged – and disappointed when he learned other men with the same job had traditionally been called 'Blowfly' too. His wife, Carol, was within earshot in another room as he told me, 'We were down in Melbourne for a few days for a battalion reunion, and I caught up with Barry Heard for the first time since Vietnam. I wasn't really pleased with the way I was just whisked home for my discharge. I never had the chance to say, "How can I contact ... " But at the reunion, I met guys I hadn't seen for ages, and ...' As his breathing quickened, Booker's voice began to crack, but he struggled to keep talking. '... Barry did say that he was hoping to catch up with me at the reunion, so that was good. We gave each other a big hug. There were a couple of other guys, and they said to Carol, when she was introduced, "Here's Jim. When we came back to the camp after operations, we'd say, 'Here's Jim. Oh, good.'" I always had a cheery face for them.'

Tears spilled down Booker's cheeks. He asked Carol to join us and explain. 'He was just moved by the fact people recognised him,' she said. 'More than one said, "We looked forward to coming back to see you. You were always so kind." You feel very humble in the ... hygiene area.'

I do not think I had ever met such a modest man. I cried with him because of what he was, I think, as much as what he was telling me. He had been a reluctant, incompetent infantryman who ended up cleaning toilets for better soldiers to sit on, and in the years between he had thought he had not mattered to anyone – but, finally, he knew he had been appreciated.

And maybe I was also crying for my dad, for the awkward, gangly, uniformed youth in the photograph given to me by his second wife. My dad did not drink, and he was proud of the fact. It was one of the things that made him respectable. The only comment on his service record was the quickly scrawled assurance that he was 'of sober and honest habits', which satisfied me that the army had at least noticed something about him.

Later, I learned that was what the officers wrote about everyone.

Notes

1 The myths I helped to make

1. A Portelli, *The Death of Luigi Trastulli, and Other Stories: Form and meaning in oral history*, State University of New York Press, New York, 1991, p. 76.
2. All the above quotes are from M Dapin, 'Uneasy riders', *Good Weekend*, 18 August 2007.
3. KS Inglis, *Sacred Places: War memorials in the Australian landscape*, Melbourne University Press, Carlton, 2008, p. 481.
4. A Portelli, *The Battle of Valle Giulia: Oral history and the art of dialogue*, University of Wisconsin Press, Wisconsin, 1997, p. ix.
5. M Dapin, 'The war within', *Good Weekend*, 24 March 2012.
6. Quoted in B Thomas, 'The agony no family should suffer', *Sun-Herald*, 21 August 1988.
7. M Dapin, 'Straight shooter soldiers on', *Sydney Morning Herald*, 9 February 2013.
8. Quoted in N Giblett (ed.), *Homecomings: Stories from Australian Vietnam veterans and their wives*, 2nd edn, Australian Government Publishing Service, Canberra, 1990, p. 23.
9. Aristotle (translated by Samuel H Butcher), *Poetics*, Dover Publications, New York, 1997, p. 17.
10. Portelli, *The Death of Luigi Trastulli*, p. 50.
11. G Wilson, *Dust, Donkeys and Delusions: The myth of Simpson and his donkey exposed*, Big Sky Publishing, Newport, NSW, 2012, p. ii.
12. D Faulkner, 'Normie Rowe shakin' all over again', *The Saturday Paper*, no. 63, 6–12 June 2015.
13. C Stockings, *Anzac's Dirty Dozen*, NewSouth, Sydney, 2012, p. 2.

2 The myth of the volunteer in Vietnam

1. D Horner and J Bou (eds), *Duty First: The Royal Australian Regiment in war and peace*, Allen & Unwin, Sydney, revised edn, 2008, p. 159.
2. *Sydney Morning Herald*, 31 March 1966.
3. *Sydney Morning Herald*, 21 April 1966.
4. H Armfield, 'National Servicemen and Vietnam: A case by the experts', *The Age*, 26 April 1966.
5. Horner and Bou (eds), *Duty First*, p. 159. In an unpublished paper, Morris states he has an email from Horner accepting his information 'may be incorrect' (EB Morris, 'Volunteers for Vietnam', unpublished).
6. S Langford, 'Appendix: The National Service scheme 1964–72', in P Edwards (ed.), *A Nation at War: Australian politics, society and diplomacy during the Vietnam War 1965–1975*, Allen & Unwin in association with the Australian War Memorial, Sydney, 1997, p. 363.
7. J Grey, *The Australian Army: A history*, Oxford University Press, South Melbourne, 2001, vol. 1 of *The Australian Centenary History of Defence*, p. 208.
8. P Ham, *Vietnam: The Australian war*, HarperCollins, Sydney, 2007, p. 170.
9. AW Martin, *Robert Menzies: A life, Vol. 1, 1894–1943*, Melbourne University Press, Melbourne, 1993, p. 30.
10. J Howard, *The Menzies Era: The years that shaped modern Australia*, HarperCollins, Sydney, 2014, p. 20.

11.   Martin, *Robert Menzies*, p. 29.
12.   Commonwealth of Australia, *Parliamentary Debates: House of Representatives Official Hansard*, no. 46, 15 November 1939, p. 1133.
13.   *Parliamentary Debates: House of Representatives Official Hansard*, no. 46, 16 November 1939, p. 1195.
14.   D Day, *John Curtin: A life*, HarperCollins, Sydney, 2015, p. 543.
15.   KS Inglis, 'A war against the tide of history', *The Australian*, 26 March 1966.
16.   Day, *John Curtin*, pp. 550–51.
17.   NAA P617, 419/1/24, 'National Service – Staffing – Lower Establishments – Lower Establishment Training', HQ T Command, 'Notes for National Service Lecture, Organization of 18 Training Company', p. 2.
18.   NAA A5954, 1884/3, 'National Service File No.1 – Report by the Defence Committee March 1950', p. 17. Although from the start it was secretly acknowledged it was 'not practical for the Army to train personnel who do not live within easy reach of Citizens Military Force training centres'.
19.   'Youths liable to fight abroad', *Argus*, 18 October 1951.
20.   NAA P617, 419/1/24, 'National Service', p. 4: 'The first output of National Service trainees must leave the continuous training period as missionaries for the National Service scheme ... They will be in the CMF for three years after that; make them keen to remain on as volunteers'.
21.   Quoted in D McCarthy, 'The once and future army: An organizational, political and social history of the Citizen Military Forces, 1947–1974', PhD thesis, University of New South Wales (accessed at UNSWorks on 22 May 2016), 1997.
22.   *Sydney Morning Herald*, 10 September 1954.
23.   A Palazzo, *The Australian Army: A history of its organisation 1901–2001*, Oxford University Press, South Melbourne, 2001, p. 237.
24.   *Sydney Morning Herald*, 10 September 1954.
25.   *Daily Telegraph*, 10 September 1955.
26.   NAA M4299, 5, Personal Papers of Prime Minister Harold Holt, 'Press statement by the Rt. Hon. HE Holt, MP, Minister for Labour and National Service', 3 December 1957.
27.   McCarthy, 'Once and future army', p. 103.
28.   T Shields, 'National Service training, 1950–59', in RK Forward and B Reece (eds), *Conscription in Australia*, University of Queensland Press, St Lucia, 1968, p. 77.
29.   NAA A4940, C162, Part 2, 'National Service – Policy, 1964–1967'.
30.   NAA A463, 1964/5143, Part 1, 'National Service Training Scheme – Policy, 1964', speech by R Menzies on Defence Review, 10 November 1964.
31.   Australian Gallup Polls, no. 1789–1803, Oct–Nov 1964.
32.   G Woodard, 'Australia's war in Vietnam: Debate without end', *Australian Journal of International Affairs*, vol. 71, no. 2, 2017, pp. 225–27.
33.   Edwards, *A Nation at War*, p. 27.
34.   P Edwards, *Australia and the Vietnam War: The essential history*, NewSouth, Sydney, 2014 p. 107.
35.   Australian Army, 'Information booklet for National Servicemen', Australian Army, Australia, 1965, p. 13.
36.   *Sydney Morning Herald*, 14 May 1966.
37.   *Courier-Mail* (Brisbane), 29 June 1966.
38.   *The Australian*, 29 September 1966.
39.   M Towers, *A Jungle Circus: Memories of Vietnam*, Allen & Unwin, Sydney, 1999, pp. 38–39.
40.   NAA B2458/3798268, Wittner, David Maurice, letter from Andrew Peacock to Private Wittner, 31 July 1970.

41. 'A person who fails to comply with the requirements of a notice under section twenty-six of this Act and is committed to the custody of a prescribed authority shall, upon being taken into custody by a member of the Permanent Forces under subsection (4.) of this section, be deemed, for the purposes of this Act, to have presented himself for service in accordance with a notice served on him under section twenty-six of this Act': National Service Act 1964 (NO. 126, 1964).
42. The Centennial Supper Club, Centennial Vineyard, 4 February 2016.
43. 'Letters: Australian racism in Vietnam', *Sunday Australian*, 7 November 1971.
44. EB Morris, 'Remembering Vietnam: Official history, soldiers' memories and the participant observer', MA thesis, University of Wollongong (accessed at University of Wollongong Research Online), 2014, p. 42.
45. See M Dapin, 'Myth-making and memory: Australia, the Vietnam War and national service', PhD thesis, University of New South Wales, 2018.
46. Bob Whittaker, email to Anzac Day Commemoration Committee, 28 July 2018, sighted by author.
47. M Dapin, *The Nashos' War: Australia's national servicemen and Vietnam*, Penguin, Melbourne, pp. 384–85.
48. Morris, 'Remembering Vietnam', p. 40.
49. P Rees, *The Boy from Boree Creek: The Tim Fischer story*, Allen & Unwin, Sydney, 2001, p. 46.
50. A Reid, 'Madam, he does not have to go to Vietnam!', *Bulletin*, 15 October 1966.
51. *Parliamentary Debates: Senate Official Hansard*, no. 40, 6 October 1971, p. 1181.
52. Sir Allen Fairhall – interviewed by Ken Taylor, tape 10, side 1 – Parliamentary Library interview with Sir Allen Fairhall, 3 September 1983.
53. *The Australian*, 21 August 2015.
54. NAA J1687, 3005974-6, Katter, Robert Carl [born 1945] – National Service Registrant.
55. *Parliamentary Debates: House of Representatives Official Hansard*, no. 8, 14 June 2011, p. 5912.
56. For example, see NAA B2458, 214669, Army Personnel Files, Braun, John William. Braun joined the Army in 1962.
57. *Parliamentary Debates: House of Representatives Official Hansard*, no. 2, 15 February 2006, p. 105.

3 The myth of the rigged ballot

1. ABC *Media Watch* broadcast the segment 'Normie's dodgy draft mystery solved' on 2 June 2008. See <https://www.abc.net.au/mediawatch/episodes/normies-dodgy-draft-mystery-solved/9975278>.
2. T Fischer, 'Reflections on conscription in Australia: It should never be selective national service ever again: either all in or none in!', speech presented at Military History and Heritage Victoria conference, 30 May 2015. Portions of the proceedings can be accessed at <www.mhhv.org.au/wp-content/uploads/Reflections-on-Conscription-in-Australia-It-should-never-be-selective-National-Service-ever-again-Either-all-in-or-none-in.pdf>.
3. 'Was war service ballot totally fair?', *Canberra Times*, 2 December 2014.
4. 'Mythical marbles', *Canberra Times*, 6 December 2014.
5. 'To the point', *Canberra Times*, 6 December 2014.
6. Langford, 'Appendix: The National Service scheme', in Edwards (ed.), *A Nation at War*, pp. 371–79.
7. Fischer, 'Reflections on conscription'.
8. D Walters and K Laws, *The Doug Walters Story*, Rigby, Adelaide, 1981, p. 34.

9. NAA A463, 1964/5143 Part 1, 'National Service Training Scheme – Policy – 1964', letter from HA Bland to FW Jennings, 22 February 1965.
10. McCarthy, 'Once and future army', p. 51.
11. The ubiquity and dedication of SOS meant that most national servicemen had some exposure to a public demonstration by anti-conscriptionists, and the SOS pickets are probably at the heart of a great number of misremembered anecdotes. National servicemen who recall seeing unreported female protesters when they came home and left the Army almost certainly saw widely reported female protesters when they left home and entered the Army.
12. *The Age*, 9–10 March 1966.
13. *Canberra Times*, 13 July 1966.
14. NAA A5909, 320, Cabinet Minute – Reduction in Period of National Service, 26 July 1971.
15. Australian Gallup Polls, no. 2335–2338, Apr–Jun 1972.
16. Australian Gallup Polls, no. 2362–65, November 1972.
17. Langford, 'Appendix: The National Service scheme', in Edwards, *A Nation at War*, pp. 369–70.
18. Australian Gallup Polls, no. 2388–90–92, March 1973.
19. A Mallett, *One of a Kind: The Doug Walters story*, Allen & Unwin, Sydney, NSW, 2008, pp. 63–64, 73.
20. *Daily Telegraph*, 15 May 2008.
21. *Herald Sun*, 22 May 2008.
22. S Rintoul, *Ashes of Vietnam: Australian voices*, W Heinemann Australia and the ABC, Melbourne, Vic., 1987, p. 5.
23. M Anderson and P Ashton, *Australia in the 20th Century: Working historically*, Macmillan Education Australia, South Yarra, 2008 reprint, pp. 215–16.
24. R Donnelly, *The Scheyville Experience: Officer Training Unit 1965–1973*, University of Queensland Press, St Lucia, 2001, p. 85.
25. Tub Matheson interviewed by Rob Willis, Rob Willis Folklore Collection, National Library of Australia, Caloundra, 14 February 1994.
26. Tim Fischer, interview with the author.
27. Ian Sinclair, email to the author, 16 April 2013.
28. 'Ballot is a mockery he claims', *Australian*, 19 April 1966.

4 The myth of no welcome home parades

1. *Canberra Times*, 7 February 1987.
2. *Sun Herald*, 4 October 1987.
3. *Canberra Times*, 7 October 1987.
4. S Garton, *The Cost of War: Australians return*, Oxford University Press, Melbourne, 1996, pp. 10–15.
5. P Hasluck, *The Government and the People, 1942–1945*, in *Australia in the War of 1939–1945: Second World War Official Histories, Series 4 (Civil)*, Vol. II, 1st edn, 1970.
6. 3RAR Association website history page, <www.3rar.com.au/3rarhistory.html> (accessed 1 February 2015).
7. 'Troops back from Malaya greeted with "ticker-tape"', *Sydney Morning Herald*, 1 November 1957.
8. W Crouch, 'Australian war in Vietnam', *The Australian*, 16 April 1966.
9. *Sydney Morning Herald*, 3 June 1966.
10. *The Australian*, 9 June 1966.
11. 'Lord Mayor gives them the choice', *The Age*, 9 June 1966.
12. *The Australian*, 9 June 1966.

13. *The Australian*, 9 June 1966.
14. 'Protest's over: Woman charged', *Sun*, 9 June 1966.
15. 'March girl fined $6, demonstration aimed at gallant men – SM. "My own idea"', *Sydney Morning Herald*, 9 June 1966.
16. J Cunningham, 'Big crowd cheers the "Tigers"', *Sydney Morning Herald*, 13 May 1967.
17. *Daily Telegraph*, 13 May 1967. There is a curious footnote to 5RAR's welcome home story. Although no newspaper reported any protesters on the scene, the Fairfax Syndication library holds a photograph captioned, 'Vietnam War Protests. Aerial view of crowds a [sic] demonstrators disrupt Australian troops returning from Vietnam marching through Sydney, 13 May 1967.' (Fairfax Syndication Archive, image FXJ173483, <www.fairfaxsyndication.com/archive/Vietnam-War-Protests.-Aerial-view-2F3XC5NER70L.html>) The picture is very difficult to make out: although it might show a single protester, it might equally well show an apprehended well-wisher or, indeed, almost anything else. It looks very like a cropping of the picture used on the front page of the paper under the headline 'Troops come home from the war BIG CROWD CHEERS THE "TIGERS"'. As far as I am aware, no 5RAR veteran has ever recalled the protest, and the filing efficiency of Fairfax Syndication is thrown into doubt by pictures in the collection which purport to show protesters arrested at a welcome home parade in Sydney in September 1970 but are actually photographs of a Moratorium demonstration: see, for example, Fairfax Syndication Archive, image FXJ319649, <www.fairfaxsyndication.com/archive/Protestors-are-arrested-at-the-2F3XC526BONA.html>.
18. C Mollison, *Long Tan and Beyond: Alpha Company 6RAR in Vietnam 1966–67*, Cobb's Crossing Publications, Woombye, Qld, 2005, p. 355.
19. *Canberra Times*, 27 April 1968.
20. *Sydney Morning Herald*, 27 April 1968.
21. M O'Brien, *Conscripts and Regulars with the Seventh Battalion in Vietnam*, Allen & Unwin in association with The Royal Australian Regiment Association Inc., Sydney, NSW, 1995, p. 142.
22. G Windsor, *All Day Long the Noise of Battle: An Australian attack in Vietnam*, Murdoch Books, Sydney, 2011, p. 221.
23. See R Nott and N Payne, *The Vung Tau Ferry: HMAS* Sydney *and escort ships Vietnam 1965–1972*, Rosenberg Publishing, Kenthurst, NSW, 2008, pp. 170–73.
24. 'Vietnam gives new meaning to Anzac', *Sydney Morning Herald*, 26 April 1967.
25. M Dapin, '"We too were Anzacs': Were Vietnam veterans ever truly excluded from the Anzac tradition?", in D Stephens and A Broinowski (eds), *The Honest History Book*, NewSouth, Sydney, 2017, pp. 77–91.
26. *The Australian*, 3 June 1967.
27. 'Sydney march', *Sydney Morning Herald*, 26 April 1968.
28. J Hiddlestone, 'An uneasy legacy: Vietnam veterans and Australian society', PhD thesis, James Cook University (accessed at ResearchOnline@JCU), 2004, p. 75.
29. 'Cheery welcome to Vietnam veterans', *Courier-Mail* (Brisbane), 14 June 1968.
30. Australian Gallup Polls, no. 2087–2104, November 1968 – February 1969.
31. '3rd Bn. cheered in rain', *Advertiser* (Adelaide), 3 December 1968.
32. 'Welcome home to the Fighting First', *Daily Telegraph*, 1 March 1969.
33. 'Restrained welcome for veterans', *Sydney Morning Herald*, 1 March 1969.
34. 'A warm welcome disrupts plans by Viet protesters', *Courier-Mail* (Brisbane), 31 May 1969.
35. See JB Prentice, 'The Brisbane protests 1965–1972', PhD thesis, Griffith University (accessed at Griffith Research Online), 2005.
36. J Doherty, 'Welcome marred: Melee as troops parade', *Advertiser* (Adelaide), 10 December 1969.

37. E Stewart, 'Welcome home: Vietnam vets return from war', *Wartime*, March 2009, pp. 10–13.
38. *Advertiser* (Adelaide), 10 May 1997.
39. *Tribune*, June 1968.
40. WJ Edgar, *Veldt to Vietnam: Haleians at war,* Old Haleians' Association, Wembley Downs, WA, 1994, p. 240.
41. 'Ticker tape welcome', *Sydney Morning Herald*, 11 March 1970.
42. *Sun-Herald*, 10 May 1970.
43. Ham, *Vietnam*, p. 563.
44. 'Tears and cheers for a city's fighting men', *Courier-Mail* (Brisbane), 13 November 1970.
45. *Sydney Morning Herald*, 19 June 2003.
46. 'Tears and cheers for a city's fighting men', *Courier-Mail* (Brisbane), 13 November 1970.
47. O'Brien, *Conscripts and Regulars*, pp. 247–48.
48. 'Big crowd sees city march', *Sydney Morning Herald*, 11 March 1971.
49. L Mann, 'Attitudes toward My Lai and obedience to orders: An Australian Survey', *Australian Journal of Psychology*, vol. 25, no. 1, 1973, pp. 11–21.
50. Ham, *Vietnam*, p. 518.
51. C Hamilton, *What Do We Want!: The story of protest in Australia*, National Library of Australia, Canberra, 2016, p. 22.
52. 'City greets troops after tour in Vietnam', *Townsville Daily Bulletin*, 2 June 1971.
53. DF Ryschka, *Too Young to Vote but Old Enough to Kill*, Xlibris, Gold Coast, Qld, 2012, pp. 541–42.
54. Hiddlestone, 'An uneasy legacy', p. 75.
55. 'The trouble with students: An Australia-wide survey', *Bulletin*, 5 July 1969.
56. *Canberra Times*, 19 August 1971.
57. 'Troops home today', *Advertiser* (Adelaide), 16 October 1971.
58. 'Johnny sails home and there's bedlam at the dockside', *Sunday Mail* (Adelaide), 16 October 1971.
59. *Advertiser* (Adelaide), 17 October 1971.
60. Hiddlestone, 'An uneasy legacy', p. 75.
61. J Cunningham, 'City warms to the men from Vietnam', *Sydney Morning Herald*, 19 November 1971.
62. 'Welcome home from Vietnam', *Townsville Daily Bulletin*, 18 December 1971.
63. G McKay, *Delta Four: Australian riflemen in Vietnam*, Allen & Unwin, Sydney, 1998, p. 192. The idea that postal workers boycotted servicemen's mail or went on strike against the Vietnam War recurs in memory and memoir, perhaps kept alive by recollections of the 'Punch a Postie' stickers produced by John Bullen and Mike Nelson at Vung Tau (A Ekins and I McNeill, *Fighting to the Finish*, Allen & Unwin, Sydney, 2012, pp. 77–81). While the Army may have blamed tardy mail deliveries on the unions, there is no evidence that this was the intention of the Amalgamated Postal Workers' Union (APWU) – and certainly no evidence of any official or unofficial action taken by workers to specifically prevent or delay deliveries to Vietnam. None is mentioned in the official history of the union, *Postal Unions & Politics*, which includes an account of the mail drivers' dispute of 1968 that seems to be at the base of Bullen's antagonism towards postal workers. According to Waters, this was 'the longest stoppage of work ever seen in the Australian Post office. The wheels of the Australian postal machine came to a virtual halt for almost two weeks' (F Waters, with D Murphy (ed.), *Postal Unions & Politics: A history of the Amalgamated Postal Workers' Union of Australia*, University of Queensland Press, St Lucia, Qld, 1978, p. 180). The strike was not about the Vietnam War but about a salary claim for mail drivers. According to the press at

the time, striking postal workers formed a committee to ensure mail was delivered
to groups who might suffer hardship without it, which specifically included 'mail
to Australian Servicemen in Vietnam'. In fact, the union collaborated closely with
the army on this issue: 'An Army spokesman said the PMG Department and the
APWU had arranged for Forces' mail posted at city suburban and country post-
offices to be collected and taken to the Redfern Mail Exchange. A spokesman for
the Post Office told the Army that the daily collection of Service mail from post-
offices probably would continue during the strike. It would be dispatched by the
first available aircraft' ('"Hardship" mail to be delivered', *Sydney Morning Herald*,
17 January 1968, p. 4). When students joined workers on picket lines a few days
later, the press reported 'the Redfern picket line had let through, unmolested, a van
carrying mail for Australian troops in Vietnam. The mail should have left Sydney
by air yesterday' ('Students in mail union picket lines', *Sydney Morning Herald*,
22 January 1968, p. 7). A curiously organised passage in Paul Ham's *Vietnam* seems
to have helped compound the historical confusion about the mail drivers' dispute:
'Union bosses ordered their members to strike in protest at My Lai. In November
1969 the Sydney branch of the Waterside Workers' Federation refused to reload
the *Jeparit*, the military supply ship that shunted between Sydney and Vung Tau ...
Vital supplies were delayed. The postal unions also urged their members to take
industrial action. (The army got its revenge against mail and waterside strikes: in
1968 John Bullen's tireless topographical unit printed the first "Punch a Postie"
leaflets. Thus, "Soldiers of Australia!/Unite Against Postal strikes!/Punch a Postie
on RTA [return to Australia]/Sock it to 'em diggers!" "Wallop a Wharfie" soon
followed. "Contemptible", "despicable", "in the worst possible taste", retorted the
Postal Workers' Union. The press leaped on the story, and the Task Force, from
the commanders down, were elated at "a huge and most successful joke"' (Ham,
Vietnam, p. 520). The passage requires close reading. Although Ham states the
postal unions 'urged their members to take industrial action' in 1969, he doesn't
actually claim they took any action. In his next sentence, he writes, 'The army got
its revenge against mail and waterside strikes ... in 1968'. If he had been talking
about the same strikes as the rest of the paragraph, the revenge would have been
both percipient and pre-emptive, but he isn't. He is talking about the earlier mail
drivers' dispute. But the earlier strike – unlike the later, unanswered call for
industrial action – was unconnected with the Vietnam War.
64. 'First World War homecomings', NZ History, <https://nzhistory.govt.nz/war/first-
world-war-homecomings>.
65. P Diamond, 'New Zealand's Vietnam War Oral History Project', in M Crotty
(ed.), *When the Soldiers Return: November 2007 conference proceedings*, Brisbane,
University of Queensland, School of History, Philosophy, Religion and Classics,
2009, p. 76.
66. *New Zealand Herald*, 13 May 1971.
67. C Hall, *No Front Line: Inside stories of New Zealand's Vietnam War*, Penguin,
Auckland, 2014, pp. 275–76.
68. See footage of the event on YouTube at <www.youtube.com/watch?v=YQOQQZt_
Rjw>.
69. For a full account, see Major JM Masters, MC, RNZA, 'A stunning study in
surrealism – no case to answer', in B Barnz (ed.), *Voices: From Vietnam*, Willson-
Scott Publishing, Christchurch, NZ, 2008.
70. G Windsor, 'Conscripts who served', *Sydney Morning Herald*, 7 February 2015.
71. M O'Brien, *Conscripts and Regulars*, p. 141.
72. G Windsor, 'Conscripts who served', *Sydney Morning Herald*, 7 February 2015.
73. EP Thompson, *The Making of the English Working Class*, Penguin, London, 1968,
p. 13.

5 The myth of Australia's My Lai

1. K Maddock, 'Atrocities and culture: Revisiting the Vietnam War', in A Pawley (ed.), *Man and a Half: Essays in Pacific anthropology and ethnobiology in honour of Ralph Bulmer*, Polynesian Society, Auckland, 1991, p. 296.
2. E Norden, *American Atrocities in Vietnam*, reprinted by Vietnam Action Committee, Sydney, 1966, pp. 2–4.
3. *The Age*, 9 September 1966.
4. *The Age*, 20 September 1966.
5. 'A letter from Vietnam', *Daily Telegraph*, 24 November 1966, p. 7.
6. 'Research', <www.baker.edu.au/Assets/Files/BHRI_Annual_Report_1966.pdf>, Baker Medical Research Institute, Alfred Hospital, 1966, p. 14.
7. *Ormond Chronicle*, Ormond College, University of Melbourne, no. 46, 1966, p. 10.
8. RG Wyllie, *The Truth of Viet Cong Terror*, Ministry of Information and Chieu Hoi of the Republic of Vietnam, Saigon, 1967, p. 15.
9. Wyllie, *The Truth*, p. 14.
10. Wyllie, *The Truth*, p. 7.
11. Ham, *Vietnam*, p. 67.
12. M Russ, *Happy Hunting Ground*, Atheneum, New York, 1968, p. 185.
13. A Ekins, '"Not one scintilla of evidence"?: The media, the military and the government in the Vietnam water torture case', *Australian Journal of Politics and History*, vol. 42, no. 3, August 1996, p. 352.
14. Brian Timberlake, interview with the author.
15. Walter Beattie, interview with the author.
16. A Carey, *Australian Atrocities in Vietnam*, RS Gould, Convenor Vietnam Action Campaign, Sydney, 1968, p. 8.
17. Carey, *Australian Atrocities in Vietnam*, p. 3.
18. Letters to the editor, 'Vietcong atrocities', *Sydney Morning Herald*, 4 December 1969.
19. Column 8, *Sydney Morning Herald*, 8 April 1971.
20. P McCarthy, 'Ambush not like My Lai: Cairns', *The Age*, 4 August 1976.
21. EB Morris, 'Remembering Vietnam: Official history, soldiers' memories and the participant observer', MA thesis, University of Wollongong (accessed at University of Wollongong Research Online), 2014, pp. 65–66.
22. Morris, 'Remembering Vietnam', p. 54. Finally, the Bamboo Pickers ambush returned to the newspapers in 2014 when the Sydney *Daily Telegraph* published a front-page story based on Morris's research, headed 'Bombshell claims army covered up truth about Aussie massacre in Nui Dat in Vietnam in 1967' (M Benns, *Daily Telegraph*, 12 October 2014). This headline has to be parsed carefully, because the truth the Army had supposedly covered up was not that civilians had been killed but that, according to Morris, his company commander had suggested he should have planted enemy weapons on their bodies to make them look like Vietcong. Morris claimed his record of this conversation had been edited out of his after-action report. However, the weapons were never planted, and the 'cover up' in the headline was a cover-up of the assertion that the company commander had suggested a cover-up! The headline notwithstanding, Morris hoped to make the broader point that if he could be advised to drop weapons on civilian corpses to make them look like VC, this might have been standard practice.
23. 'Killen says no Vietnam inquiry', *Canberra Times*, 6 August 1976. EB Morris has stated that he tracked down the co-pilot of the RAAF aircraft through the Nominal Roll of Vietnam Veterans, and he had 'confirmed the gist of the allegations' (Morris, 'Remembering Vietnam', p. 60).
24. R Strathdee, 'Binh Ba – village of the dead', *Sydney Morning Herald*, 9 June 1969.
25. 'Army denies TV charges of Vietnam massacre', *Canberra Times*, 1 July 1980.

26. Quoted in F Cranston, 'Veteran denies Binh Ba massacre', *Canberra Times*, 2 July 1980.
27. Barry Heard, interview with the author.
28. Rintoul, *Ashes of Vietnam*, pp. 5, 34.
29. Archives of the Flight Stewards' Association of Australia, BM Roberts, letter to FSF SAA, 16 March 1970, says flights in the Northern winter left Sydney on Tuesday and would therefore arrive on Wednesday.
30. Rintoul, *Ashes of Vietnam*, p. 170.
31. S Brownmiller, *Against Our Will: Men, women and rape*, Penguin, Hammondsworth, England, 1976, pp. 91–92.
32. I McNeill, *To Long Tan: The Australian Army and the Vietnam War 1950–1966*, Allen & Unwin in association with the Australian War Memorial, Sydney, 1993, p. 252.
33. D Pike, 'The Viet-Cong Strategy of Terror', US Mission, Saigon, 1970, p. 60. The event is also described in 1961 as having happened under slightly different circumstances, in a feature printed in the *Arkansas Catholic* <arc.stparchive.com/ Archive/ARC/ARC07141961p03.php>.
34. Rintoul, *Ashes of Vietnam*, p. 148.
35. B Oswald and J Waddell (eds), *Justice in Arms: Military lawyers in the Australian Army's first hundred years*, Big Sky, Newport, NSW, 2014, p. xcviii.
36. Oswald, *Justice in Arms*, p. xcviii.
37. For example, 'We pulled her pants down and put a gun to her head. Guys are taking turns screwing her. It was like an animal pack ... she was crying. So a guy just put a rifle to her head and pulled the trigger just to put her out of the picture' (M Baker, *Nam*, Berkley Books, New York, reissue, 1986, p. 191); 'Having sex with a woman then killing her made one a double veteran': Baker, *Nam*, p. 298.
38. Rintoul, *Ashes of Vietnam*, p. 166.
39. Tran Quoc Trung, 'A page of history one should not take pride in', in K Maddock and B Wright (eds), *War: Australia and Vietnam*, Harper & Row, Sydney, 1987, p. 90.
40. Maddock, 'Atrocities and culture', in Pawley (ed.), *Man and a Half*, 1991, p. 296.
41. *Sydney Morning Herald*, 27 April 1987.
42. J Rowe, *Vietnam: The Australian experience*, Time-Life Books, Sydney, 1987, pp. 128–29.
43. D Tate, *The War Within*, Murdoch Books, Sydney, 2008, p. 264.
44. Hall, *No Front Line*, pp. 214–16.
45. Hall, *No Front Line*, p. 222.
46. Hall, *No Front Line*, p. 37. This story is possibly adopted or adapted from an anecdote in Mark Baker's *Nam*: 'You sit there at night with the infrared scope from a scout sniper's rifle and watch a Charlie come through four rolls of concertina wire. He started just about ten o'clock and he didn't get through the last strand of concertina wire until almost four o'clock in the morning. It took him six hours and we had every possible kind of trip wire you can think of inside there, along with mines, finger charges and Claymores. He came through and then we shot him. You go out there to take him off the wire the next morning, and it turns out to be the barber who's been shaving you with a straight razor for the last two months': Baker, *Nam*, p. 92.
47. Hall, *No Front Line*, p. 224.
48. T Bower-Miles and M Whittaker, *Bomber: From Vietnam to hell and back*, Pan Macmillan, Sydney, 2009, pp. 104–105.

6 The myth of airport demonstrations

1.   P Cochrane, 'At war at home', in Pemberton (ed.), *Vietnam Remembered*, p. 179.
2.   Wilson, *Dust, Donkeys and Delusions*, pp. 108–28.
3.   Ham, *Vietnam*, p. 560.
4.   A Kitchen, 'Qantas and Vietnam', in Rodney Nott (ed.), *Vietnam Logistics and Support 1962–1975: The long haul*, Vietnam Logistical Support Veterans' Association Qld, Kenmore, Qld, 2004, pp. 11–12.
5.   *Sydney Morning Herald*, 24 April 2003.
6.   Notes of a conference with Sir Henry Bland, Archives of the Flight Stewards' Association of Australia, 1 April 1966.
7.   P Searson, Report of Saigon Flight QF 178183, Archives of the Flight Stewards' Association of Australia, 14 May 1969.
8.   Mollison, *Long Tan and Beyond*, p. 369.
9.   T Spriggs, 'Vietnam – So what?', in John Coe (ed.), *Desperate Praise*, Artlook Books, WA, 1982.
10.   *Sydney Morning Herald*, 18 May 1970.
11.   Coe, *Desperate Praise*, n.p.
12.   H Colebatch, 'Fourteen tell how Vietnam was for them', *Bulletin*, 24 August 1982, p. 70.
13.   Captain P Kelly, 'Book reviews', *Army*, undated.
14.   'Chilling look at Vietnam', *Daily News*, 21 April 1982.
15.   N Jillett, 'Turgid and passionless writing on Vietnam', *The Age*, 29 May 1982.
16.   R Gerster, 'Occidental tourists', in P Pierce, J Doyle and J Grey (eds), *Vietnam Days: Australia and the impact of Vietnam*, Penguin, Maryborough, 1991, p. 233.
17.   Rintoul, *Ashes of Vietnam*, p. 182.
18.   Australian Department of Veterans' Affairs, *Australia and the Vietnam War*, Department of Veterans' Affairs, Woden, ACT, 2007, p. 86.
19.   Giblett, *Homecomings*, p. 23.
20.   PF Perry, *The Rise and Fall of Practically Everybody: An account of student political activity at Monash University, 1965–72*, self-published, Balaclava, Vic, 1973, p. 33a. Perry's arch and interesting memoir of Monash University includes a comprehensive list of Monash University student demonstrations in 1967–72. While Vietnam and conscription-related issues account for about 25 per cent of the protests, there were many others whose targets ranged from 'library inadequacies', 'Easter' and, in 1969, 'car-parking' (Perry writes, 'With the anti-war scene hotting up it is hard to credit what happened next. Car parking became a cause célèbre', p. 33a) to 'liquor regulations', 'Snootiness' and 'Springboks' (p. 102). The existence of Perry's meticulous register should make it difficult to argue demonstrations are ephemeral and forgotten, or to invent new, previously unrecorded events – at least in regard to Monash University.
21.   Ham, *Vietnam*, pp. 560–73.
22.   G Blinco, *Down a Country Lane to War*, Boolarong Press, Morooka, Qld, p. 169.
23.   S Jobson, 'A debate about the Vietnam Moratorium', *Sydney Morning Herald*, 30 April 1970.
24.   Mollison, *Long Tan and Beyond*, p. 369.
25.   'War protesters marched in peace', *Sydney Morning Herald*, 1 July 1971.
26.   Ham, *Vietnam*, p. 562.
27.   *Sydney Morning Herald*, 9 January 1970.
28.   G Smith, *A Pogo's Perspective: A non-combatant soldier's Viet Nam experience; its affects and aftermath*, Sid Harta, Hartwell, Vic., 2007, pp. 132–33.
29.   'At the city "gate"', *Sydney Morning Herald*, 8 April 1971.

30. '5 mothers are jailed', *Sydney Morning Herald*, 9 April, 1971.
31. R Meehan, *Many a Long Road Travelled: The meaning of 'Duty First'*, Zeus Publications, Burleigh MDC, Qld, 2012, p. 243.
32. I Fitchett, 'Govt. will refuse demand for student statement', *Sydney Morning Herald*, 15 May 1969.
33. D Morgan, *My Vietnam War: Scarred forever*, 2014, ch. 13, Kindle.
34. A Thomson, *Anzac Memories: Living with the legend*, Oxford University Press, Melbourne, 1994, p. 313.
35. D Morgan, *My Vietnam War*, 2014, ch. 13, Kindle.
36. H Colebatch, 'A literature of nothingness – Creative literature generated by the Vietnam War', in Maddock and Wright (eds), *War: Australia and Vietnam*, p. 162.
37. 'Blood on the Stock Exchange was to STOP THIS!', in the National Library of Australia's Riley Collection: Vietnam War and anti-Vietnam War movements in Australia – ephemera material, Brisbane, c. 1972.
38. *Courier-Mail* (Brisbane), 8 July 1972.
39. Garton, *The Cost of War*, p. 19. The only Australian women to serve in the military in Vietnam were 43 Army nurses, although there were also civilian nurses and Red Cross women.
40. D Harcourt, *Everybody Wants to be Fuehrer: National Socialism in Australia and New Zealand*, Angus & Robertson, Sydney, 1972, pp. 70–71.
41. Some actual military battles have been given less space in memoir than Freney's account of the punch-up at the airport: 'I heard someone shout and looked back to see five Nazis in full uniform led by The Skull coming up behind us. He punched a Channel Nine cameraman, who promptly hit him back. I turned to warn those in front of me, when the Skull hit me on the back of my head, sending my glasses flying. I set off after him and without thinking rugby tackled him around the legs. He twisted around and gave me a rabbit punch across my shoulder blades. Others helped push him to the ground and hold him there. I grabbed The Skull's thick lensed glasses. If the bastard had broken mine, I was going to do the same to his' etc., etc. The story continues over a further two paragraphs. Even 'Mrs McGregor' returning Freney's undamaged spectacles is recorded: D Freney, *A Map of Days: Life on the left*, Heinemann, Melbourne, 1991, pp. 288–89.
42. Harcourt, *Everybody Wants to be Fuehrer*, p. 57.
43. I McGibbon, *New Zealand's Vietnam War: A history of combat, commitment and controversy*, Exile Publishing, Auckland, New Zealand, 2010, pp. 523–25.
44. D Challinor, *Grey Ghosts*, HarperCollins, New Zealand, 2009, p. 188.
45. AWM 276, R487/1/1, 'Leave – General – Leave on RTA', accessed at <s3-ap-southeast-2.amazonaws.com/awm-media/collection/AWM2016.747.102/document/6253228.PDF>, p. 45.
46. AWM 276, R487/1/1, 'Leave – General – Leave on RTA', pp. 24–27.
47. J Blaxland, *The Protest Years: The official history of ASIO, 1963–1975*, Allen & Unwin, Sydney, 2015.
48. John Blaxland, email to the author, 28 May 2018: 'In my reading of ASIO records I did not come across records of an airport demonstration for returning Vietnam War veterans.'
49. 'Melee as troops parade', *Advertiser* (Adelaide), 10 December 1969.
50. Flyer in the State Library of Victoria's Riley and Ephemera Collection: Political Ephemera relating to the Youth Campaign Against Conscription, YCAC, 1966.
51. *Viet Protest News: Bulletin of the Vietnam Day Committee*, vol. 1, no. 7, 1966.
52. J Grey, 'Protest and dissent: Anti-Vietnam war activism in Australia', in J Doyle, J Grey and P Pierce (eds), *Australia's Vietnam War*, Texas A&M University Press, College Station, Texas, 2002, p. 60.

53. For a brief summary of the balance between different states' revolutionary movements, and debates on revolutionary tactics, see Edwards, *A Nation at War*, pp. 168–69.
54. R Pollard, *The Cream Machine*, Angus & Robertson, Sydney, 1972, p. 95.
55. Spriggs, 'Vietnam – So what?', in Coe, *Desperate Praise*, p. 37.
56. D Savage, *Through the Wire: Action with the SAS in Borneo and the Special Forces in Vietnam*, Allen & Unwin, Sydney, 1999, p. 197.
57. Hiddlestone, 'An uneasy legacy', p. 77.
58. T Bower-Miles and M Whittaker, *Bomber: From Vietnam to hell and back*, Pan Macmillan, Sydney, 2009, p. 50.
59. RJ Barry, *The 10th: Reflections of National Service and life in the Australian Army, 1967–69*, Narrabri, NSW, 2012, p. 399.
60. B Heard, *Well Done, Those Men: Memoirs of a Vietnam veteran*, Scribe, Carlton North, Vic., 2004, p. 213.
61. *Student Guerrilla*, 2 April 1969.
62. 'Melee as troops parade', *Advertiser* (Adelaide), 10 December 1969.
63. R Stolk, quoted in Teun Voeten, 'Dutch Provos', *High Times*, January 1990.
64. L Arnold, quoted in G Langley, *A Decade of Dissent: Vietnam and the conflict on the Australian homefront*, Allen & Unwin, Sydney, 1992, p. 29.
65. 'Protests to Dr Gough', *Sydney Morning Herald*, 9 November 1965.
66. P Barclay, 'Supporting Information' to an interview with Michelle Cavanagh, author of 'Margaret Holmes: The life and times of an Australian peace campaigner', *Perspective*, ABC Radio, 24 May 2006 <www.abc.net.au/radionational/programs/perspective/michelle-cavangh/3325110>.
67. 'A socialist strategy for the anti-war movement', *Direct Action*, September 1970, p. 9.
68. For example, 'Calendar of anti-war activities', in the National Library of Australia's Riley Collection: Vietnam War and anti-Vietnam War movements in Australia – ephemera material, Vietnam Action Campaign, Woollahra, Sydney, undated.
69. C Mannix, 'A "living room war"? Australian television coverage of the Vietnam War', in K Foster (ed.), *The Information Battlefield: Representing Australians at war*, Australian Scholarly Publishing, North Melbourne, 2011, p. 106.
70. J Lembcke, *The Spitting Image: Myth, memory and the legacy of Vietnam*, New York University Press, New York, 1998, pp. 145–46.

7 Myths of blood, spit and jeers

1. 'Faces of our diggers', *Geelong Advertiser*, 24 April 2010.
2. M Burgmann, 'The Women Against Rape in War Collective's protests against ANZAC Day in Sydney, 1983 and 1984', *Cosmopolitan Civil Societies: An Interdisciplinary Journal*, vol. 6, no. 3, 2014, p. 4222.
3. Fairfax Syndication Archive, image FXJ231668, 7 April 1968, <www.fairfaxsyndication.com/archive/Vietnam-War-Protests.-Jean-Curthoys--2F3XC5UPMUED.html>.
4. 'We cannot support a war against children', in the National Library of Australia's Riley Collection: Vietnam War and anti-Vietnam War movements in Australia – ephemera material, Seamen's Union of Australia, Sydney, undated.
5. Edwards, *A Nation at War*, p. 247.
6. MP Holsinger (ed.), *War and American Popular Culture: A historical encyclopedia*, Greenwood Press, Westport, Connecticut, 1999, p. 363.
7. *Sydney Morning Herald*, 23 February 2013.
8. *Sydney Morning Herald*, 16 August 1981.

9. BG Burkett and G Whitley, *Stolen Valor: How the Vietnam generation was robbed of its heroes and its history*, Verity Press, Dallas, Texas, 1998, p. 305.
10. *Advertiser* (Adelaide), 10 May 1997.
11. Sunday *Herald Sun*, 29 March 2004.
12. G Lennox, *Forged by War: Australians in combat and back home*, Melbourne University Press, 2006, pp. 2–4.
13. 'Present arms' is a form of salute for soldiers carrying rifles, the salute usually given to dignitaries attending formal military parades. The order 'Present arms!' would have had the soldiers holding their rifles vertically in front of their bodies.
14. Lennox, *Forged by War*, p. 252.
15. 'Simon Townsend waves to his supporters', *Sydney Morning Herald*, 11 June 1968.
16. Lennox, *Forged by War*, p. 259.
17. G Kulik, *War Stories: False atrocity tales, swift boaters and winter soldiers*, Potomac Books, Washington DC, 2009, p. 82.
18. Kulik, *War Stories*, p. 89.
19. Rintoul, *Ashes of Vietnam*, p. 189.
20. N Biedermann, *Tears on My Pillow: Australian nurses in Vietnam*, Random House, Sydney, 2004, p. 199.
21. Biedermann, *Tears on My Pillow*, p. 150.
22. G McKay, *Vietnam Fragments: An oral history of Australians at war*, Allen & Unwin, St Leonards, NSW, 1992, p. 260.
23. J Grey, *A Soldier's Soldier: A biography of Lieutenant General Sir Thomas Daly*, Cambridge University Press, Port Melbourne, Victoria, 2013, p. 133.
24. J Grey, 'Vietnam, Anzac and the veteran', in Pierce, Doyle and Grey (eds), *Vietnam Days*, p. 78.
25. *Parliamentary Debates: Senate Official Hansard*, no. 123, 28 October 1987, p. 1397.
26. 'Man of protest', *The Age*, 31 March 1966.
27. *Herald* (Melbourne), 24 November 1966.
28. *The Australian*, 24 November 1966.
29. Quoted in Harcourt, *Everybody Wants to be Fuehrer*, p. 50.
30. Quoted in Harcourt, *Everybody Wants to be Fuehrer*, p. 36.
31. *Herald* (Melbourne), 31 October 1966.
32. *Sunday Australian*, 21 March 1971.
33. 'Soldiers attack city marchers', *Advertiser* (Adelaide), 9 May 1970.
34. *Revolution*, vol. 1, no. 2, 1970.
35. R Lewis, T Harvey and S Horan (eds), *Then There was Nine: 9 Platoon, 3RAR, 1969–2001, Woodside to Nui Dat and Beyond*, self-published, Hawthorndene, SA, 2001, p. 21.
36. In Horner and Bou (eds), *Duty First,* pp. 202–203.
37. R Teague, *Born on Anzac Day*, Rosenberg, Kenthurst, NSW, 2015, pp. 223–72.
38. I McNeill and A Ekins, *On the Offensive: The Australian Army in the Vietnam War, January 1967–June 1968*, Allen & Unwin in association with the Australian War Memorial, Sydney, 2003, p. 279.
39. J Schumann, 'I was only 19 – the John Schumann story', 2006, <www.schumann.com.au/john/articles/i_was_only_19.pdf> (accessed 1 January 2017).
40. Schumann, 'I was only 19'.
41. Russell Braddon film interview with Frank Hunt for ABC TV program *Images of Australia: Decline and fall*, AWM F00272, 1986.
42. Rintoul, *Ashes of Vietnam*, p. 216.
43. *Canberra Times*, 3 October 1992.
44. Lennox, *Forged by War*, p. 314.
45. S Strevens, *The Jungle Dark*, Pan Macmillan, Sydney, 2015, p. 223.
46. *Australian*, October 1966.

47. For example, 'Governor pelted with tomatoes by uni. students', *Townsville Daily Bulletin*, 2 May 1969.

48. A rare exception is the pamphlet *For 'Rest and Recuperation' from Vietnam: They're coming here,* issued by the Queensland Peace Committee for International Cooperation and Disarmament in 1967, and including a reprint of a graphic and pornographic story from *Overseas Weekly*, a newspaper aimed primarily at American troops serving abroad, about the gang rape and murder of a young Vietnamese woman. The pamphlet was published in response to the news that GIs would be permitted to take their R&R leave in Australia. It warned the Americans might be a danger to the women of Australia, and suggested, 'If R & R is real rest and recuperation, why can't these boys be flown home to their families? Better still, fly them all home, for good, and let the Vietnamese live their own lives, in peace.' It also noted, apparently accurately, that the 'brutal rape murder' – which was later to become the basis for the 1989 movie *Casualties of War* – was a 'story the papers here had kept from us'. (*For 'Rest and Recuperation' from Vietnam: They're coming here*, issued by the Queensland Peace Committee for International Cooperation and Disarmament, 608 Ann Street, Fortitude Valley, Queensland. Featuring a reprint from the *Overseas Weekly*, vol. 22, no. 13, Pacific Edition, 2 April 1967.)

49. A Curthoys, 'Vietnam: Public memory', in K Darian-Smith and P Hamilton, *Memory and History in Twentieth-Century Australia*, Oxford University Press, Melbourne, 1994, pp. 127–28.

50. K Kizilos, 'Vietnam veteran makes his Anzac protest', *The Age*, 26 April 1985, p. 1.

51. Hamilton, *What Do We Want!*, pp. 54–55.

52. Brownmiller, *Against Our Will*, pp. 86–87, 112–13.

53. A Curthoys, 'Shut up, you bourgeois bitch: Sexual identity and political action in the anti-Vietnam War movement', in J Damousi and M Lake (eds), *Gender and War: Australians at war in the twentieth century*, Cambridge University Press, New York, 1995, p. 335.

54. 'Women charged over rape wreath', *Sydney Morning Herald*, 26 April 1977.

55. 'Women protest in five cities', *Sydney Morning Herald*, 26 April 1978.

56. 'Number of marchers up 2000 on last year', *The Age*, 26 April 1979.

57. As quoted on Reimagining Peace: The Art of Protest, '"Lest we" women, rape and war Judy Small's song from the 1980s', <reimaginingpeace.wordpress.com/2015/04/19/lest-we-women-rape-and-war-judy-smalls-song-from-the-1980s/>.

58. A Howe, 'Anzac mythology and the feminist challenge', in Damousi and Lake (eds), *Gender and War*, p. 305.

59. 'Women put wreaths on memorial stone', *Canberra Times*, 26 April 1981.

60. 'Anzac marches – peace and conflict', *Sun-Herald*, 26 April 1981.

61. 'Rape victims remembered', *Sydney Morning Herald*, 26 April 1982.

62. M Odlum, '168 arrested as women defy "no march" order', *Sydney Morning Herald*, 26 April 1983.

63. R Reines, 'Sydney anti-rape march peaceful', *Sydney Morning Herald*, 26 April 1984.

64. R Reines, 'Sydney anti-rape march peaceful', *Sydney Morning Herald*, 26 April 1984.

65. '60 women lay wreaths before ceremony', *Canberra Times*, 26 April 1984.

66. '60 women lay wreaths before ceremony', *Canberra Times*, 26 April 1984.

67. McHugh, *Minefields and Miniskirts*, p. 51.

68. K Kizilos, 'Vietnam veteran makes his Anzac protest', *The Age*, 26 April 1985, p. 1.

69. C Botten, 'Police arrest two members of anti-war group', *The Age*, 26 April 1986.

70. L Costa, 'Collective women get a mention in dispatches', *Sydney Morning Herald*, 26 April 1986.

71. J Grey, 'The fall and rise of Anzac day? 1956–1990', in Tom Frame (ed.), *Anzac Day Then and Now*, NewSouth, Sydney, 2016, p. 204.
72. 'Faces of our diggers', *Geelong Advertiser*, 24 April 2010.

8 Myth vs history – conclusions

1. P Fussell, *The Great War and Modern Memory*, Oxford University Press, New York, 1975, p. 142.
2. A Machen, 'Introduction', in *The Angels of Mons: The bowmen and other legends of the war*, GP Putnam's Sons, New York, 1915, p. 10.
3. Machen, *The Angels of Mons*, p. 15.
4. A Portelli, 'A dialogical relationship. An approach to oral history', <www.swaraj.org/shikshantar/expressions_portelli.pdf>.
5. G Windsor, *All Day Long the Noise of Battle: An Australian attack in Vietnam*, Murdoch Books, Sydney, 2011, p. 13.
6. F Bongiorno, 'Anti-conscription in Australia: Individuals, organisations and arguments', in R Archer, J Damousi, M Goot and S Scalmer, *The Conscription Conflict and the Great War*, 2016, p. 90.
7. CP Stacey, *A Date with History: Memoirs of a Canadian historian*, Deneau, Ottawa, 1983, p. 230.
8. Quoted in G McKay, *Sleeping with Your Ears Open: On patrol with the Australian SAS*, Allen & Unwin, Sydney, 2001, p. 281.
9. JA Wood, *Veteran Narratives and the Collective Memory of the Vietnam War*, Ohio University Press, Ohio, 2016, pp. 3–4.
10. 'Transcript of the Prime Minister the Hon John Howard MP address to the nation', Media Collection: media/pressrel/RZU86, 20 March 2003, <parlinfo. aph.gov.au/parlInfo/download/media/pressrel/RZU86/upload_binary/rzu865. pdf;fileType=application/pdf>. Ten years later, Howard wrote, 'Thankfully we did not repeat the shame of 40 years ago, when many of our returning men from Vietnam were the target of some who disagreed with that involvement ... on this occasion dissent was solely directed towards those responsible – the political leaders of the time – and not the men and women who had carried out their orders': *Sydney Morning Herald*, 9 April 2013. Previously, Howard had played variations on this theme. He had written, in his memoir *Lazarus Rising*, 'When our troops returned from East Timor, the Australian public did not need its Prime Minister to exhort them to offer a warm welcome home. The huge turnout for the parade through the streets on 19 April 2000 could not have been in starker contrast to the way in which so many Australian diggers returning from Vietnam were, to this country's shame, almost secreted in cover of darkness': John Howard, *Lazarus Rising*, HarperCollins, Sydney, 2010, p. 358.
11. J Grey, *A Military History of Australia*, Cambridge University, Port Melbourne, 2008, p. 237.
12. According to Edwards (*A Nation at War*, pp. 267–70) the Australian Moratorium marches of May 1970 drew crowds of 70 000–100 000 in the streets of Melbourne; 25 000 in Sydney; 8000 in Brisbane; 6000 in Adelaide; 3000 in Perth; and 2000–3000 in Hobart. Figures for the largest Moratorium marches in New Zealand, which occurred on 30 April 1971, in the midst of US, Australian and New Zealand withdrawal from Vietnam, were 10 000–15 000 in Auckland; 7000–8000 in Christchurch; 5000 in Wellington; and 2300 in Dunedin. Christchurch is considerably smaller than Brisbane; Wellington is much smaller than Perth or Hobart; Dunedin is much smaller than Hobart (RG Rabel, *New Zealand and the Vietnam War: Politics and diplomacy*, Auckland University Press, Auckland, 2005,

p. 309). In 1971, the population of all of New Zealand (2 888 500) was slightly larger than the population of Sydney (2 807 828).

9 The myth of my dad and other final thoughts

1.   P Pierce, '"The funny place": Australian literature and the war in Vietnam', in J Doyle and J Grey (eds), *Australia R&R: Representations and reinterpretations of Australia's War in Vietnam*, Vietnam Generation Inc and Burning Cities Press, Maryland, 1991, vol. 3, no. 2, *Australia R&R*, p. 98.
2.   G Henderson, *Gerard Henderson Scribbles On*, Wilkinson Books, Melbourne, 1993, p. 205.
3.   A Crowe, *The Battle After the War: The story of Australia's Vietnam veterans*, Allen & Unwin, Sydney, 1999, p. 2.
4.   J Murphy, *Harvest of Fear: A history of Australia's Vietnam War*, Allen & Unwin, Sydney, 1993, p. 265.
5.   'National Service for girls, says Mrs Whitlam', *Canberra Times*, 25 November 1969.
6.   Email forwarded to the author by Loris Roubin, 31 July 2014.

Appendix I – Correspondence between David Wittner and Minister for the Army Andrew Peacock

```
                                    11 JULY 1970

PAGE THREE

MINISTER FOR THE ARMY,
MR PEACOCK,

DEAR SIR,

I AM A NATIONAL SERVICEMAN HAVING SERVED FIVE MONTHS OF MY TWO
YEAR PERIOD.  I AM ALSO A CIVILIAN QUALIFIED RADIOGRAPHER AND AT
PRESENT WORKING IN THE ABOVE MENTIONED HOSPITAL.

I WAS TOLD ONLY YESTERDAY THAT I WAS TO UNDERTAKE A BATTLE EFFICIENCY
COURSE STARTING ON THE 20TH AUGUST AND THEN AT A UNSPECIFIED DATE
AFTER THIS MY SERVICES WILL BE REQUIRED IN SOUTH VIETNAM.

HOWEVER, I DEFINITELY DO NOT WANT TO SERVE OVERSEAS.  I HAVE WRITTEN
A LETTER GIVING MY REASONS TO THE COMMANDING OFFICER OF MY UNIT AND
SUBSEQUENTLY I HAVE SPOKEN TO HIM ABOUT THIS MATTER.  HE HAS ASSURED
ME THAT MY LETTER WILL BE FORWARDED THROUGH THE CHANNELS AND AN
ANSWER WILL BE GIVEN IN ABOUT THREE WEEKS TIME.

MY REASONS FOR NOT WANTING TO SERVE OVERSEAS ARE AS FOLLOWS.  I HAVE
ALREADY MADE ARRANGEMENT TO BE MARRIED ON THE 21ST AUGUST.  AT THIS
LATE DATE I DO NOT WISH TO CHANGE THE DATE ALREADY SET.  ALSO I DO
NOT WISH TO BE MARRIED AND THEN LEAVE MY WIFE ONLY A FEW DAYS TO
SPEND A TWELVE MONTH PERIOD IN VIETNAM.  I DO NOT FEE THAT THIS
IS VERY GOOD GROUNDING FOR A MARRIAGE.

PAGE FOUR

I AM PREPARED TO SERVE ANYWHERE IN AUSTRALIA AS LONG AS I DO NOT
HAVE TO BE SEPARATED FROM MY WIFE TO BE.  UP TO NOW, I HAVE FULFILLED
ALL OF THE ARMYS DEMANDS UPON MYSELF BUT I AM FORCED TO REFUSE THE
LAST DEMAND OF A TWELVE MONTH DUTY OVERSEAS.  I FEEL VERY STRONGLY
ABOUT THIS AND IF NECESSARY I AM PREPARED TO GO AWL IN ORDER TO
STAY WITHIN AUSTRALIA AND REMAIN WITH MY WIFE TO BE.

ANOTHER REASON WHY I DO NOT WANT TO SERVE OVERSEAS IS THAT I DO
NOT BELIEVE IN AUSTRALIA'S COMMITMENT IN SOUTH VIETNAM.

I WOULD VERY MUCH APPRECIATE A PROMPT REPLY AND A FINAL DECISION
BEFORE THE DATE SET FOR THE START OF THE BATTLE EFFICIENCY COURSE
AND ALSO BEFORE THE DATE OF MY MARRIAGE.

        THANKING YOU IN ANTICIPATION,

                PRIVATE DM. WITTNER

        ..........

                PLOL

ARMY AAAD125
```

MINISTER FOR THE ARMY

Parliament House,
CANBERRA,   A.C.T.   2600

31 JUL 1970

Dear Private Wittner,

I refer to your letter seeking retention in Australia.

While the Army endeavours to employ every soldier in a location of his choice, this is not always possible and when the requirements of the Army and the soldier are at variance, the needs of the Service must take precedence.

When it can be established that a soldier's movement overseas will involve exceptional hardship to either himself or his dependants, every effort is made to retain him in Australia. However such a step is taken only after a thorough examination of every aspect of the case.

Careful consideration has been given to your case but it does not appear that the circumstances are such as to warrant your retention in Australia on compassionate grounds.

I note that the Army has given you every possible assistance with your forthcoming marriage including deferment of your Battle Efficiency Course.

I trust you will appreciate that retention may only be granted for the most pressing reasons. I am, therefore, unable to accede to your request.

Yours sincerely,

(Andrew Peacock)

3798268 Private D.M. Wittner,
X-Ray Department,
1 Military Hospital,
Kadumba Street,
YERONGA,   Q'ld.   4104

Appendix II – Welcome Home Parades of the Vietnam Years

Note: all figures listed are the approximate number of troops as documented in the newspaper of the host city for each parade.					
Date and location of parade	Battalion	Number of marchers	Estimated size of crowd	Protesters reported in press	Dignitary who took the salute
8 June 1966 Sydney	1RAR	Total: 500. All 1RAR troops.	'300,000 Sydney people came to watch' (*Sydney Morning Herald*).	A few	Governor-General Lord Casey
12 May 1967 Sydney	5RAR	Total: 1000. Troops from 5RAR 'just returned' (550) and other 5RAR (130), other ATF units (200), RAAF (100). (Note: included 300 national servicemen.)	'Hundreds of thousands' (*Sydney Morning Herald*); 'More than 250,000' (*Daily Telegraph*).	Possibly one	Administrator of the Commonwealth Sir Edric Bastyan
14 June 1967 Brisbane	6RAR	Total: 700. Troops from 6RAR (500). Also men from 101 Field Battery and Aviation troops of the 161 Reconnaissance Flight.	'100,000' (*Telegraph*), '2000' at wharf (*Courier-Mail*); 600 met 60 of the 6RAR soldiers on landing at Sydney Airport that evening (*Sydney Morning Herald*).	None	Governor of Queensland Sir Alan Mansfield
26 April 1968 Sydney	7RAR	Total: 2000. Troops from 7RAR (700); 5RAR (900); RAN (280 – naval contingent from HMAS *Sydney* and HMAS *Perth*). Members of AATTV, HQ and ATF.	'More than 500,000' (*Canberra Times*); 'Estimated at about 6000 outside Town Hall alone' (*Sydney Morning Herald*).	None	Prime Minister Mr Gorton
13 June 1968 Brisbane	2RAR	Total: 700. 2RAR and 4th Field Regiment (who had returned by air over the past six weeks).	'Thousands of people'. (*Courier-Mail*); 700 at wharf.	None	Chief of the General Staff Lieutenant General Sir Thomas Daly
2 December 1968 Adelaide	3RAR	Total: 360. Troops from 3RAR.	'Thousands of people' (*Advertiser*).	None	Colonel Commandant of the Royal Australian Regiment Lieutenant General Sir Reginald Pollard
1 March 1969 Sydney	1RAR	Total: 1100. Troops from 1RAR (500), the RAAF (200), smaller units and others (400). (Note: 1RAR included 400 national servicemen.)	'Police officers estimated that more than 300,000 people crammed the pavements … another 100,000 crowded the office windows' (*Daily Telegraph*).	None	Governor of New South Wales Sir Roden Cutler

30 May 1969 Brisbane	4RAR	Total: 500. Troops from 4RAR.	'Crowds lined up to six deep' (*The Telegraph*); 700 at wharf.	None	Chairman of the Chiefs of Staff Committee General Sir John Wilton
9 December 1969 Adelaide	9RAR	Total: 450. Troops from 9RAR.		20 demonstrators	Governor of South Australia Major General Sir James Harrison
11 March 1970 Sydney	5RAR	Total: 1100. Troops from 5RAR (520), RAAF (300) and unspecified others.	'Thousands' (*Daily Telegraph*).	None	Minister for the Army Andrew Peacock
12 December 1970 Brisbane	8RAR	Total: 600. Troops from 8RAR.	'Tens of thousands' (*Courier-Mail*); at the wharf 'more than 100 cheering relatives and friends' (*Telegraph*).	None	Governor of Queensland Sir Alan Mansfield
10 March 1971 Sydney	7RAR	Total: 1000. Troops from 7RAR (700) and other recently returned (300).	'Four deep crowd' (*Sydney Morning Herald*).	Small	General Officer Commanding Eastern Command Major General MF Brogan; Lord Mayor Alderman L Emmet McDermott
1 June 1971 Townsville	2RAR	Total: 500. Troops from 2RAR.	'About 3000' (*Courier-Mail*).	None	Minister for the Army Andrew Peacock; Colonel Commandant of the Royal Australian Regiment Lieutenant General Sir Reginald Pollard
16 October 1971 Adelaide	3RAR	Total: 700. Troops from 3RAR (500) and the advance and rear parties of the battalion (200).	Not mentioned.	None	Lieutenant-Governor Sir Thomas John Mellis Napier
18 November 1971 Sydney	4RAR	Total: 1200. Troops from 4RAR, including 500 'just returned'.	'Thousands' (*Sydney Morning Herald*).	None	Minister for the Army Andrew Peacock
17 December 1971 Townsville	4RAR	Total: 360. Troops from 4RAR, 104 Field Battery Artillery, No. 9 Helicopter Squadron RAAF.	'Thousands' (*Townsville Bulletin*).	None	Defence Minister Sir David Fairbairn. Also present were Minister for the Army Andrew Peacock, Federal Opposition leader Gough Whitlam, Qld Premier Joh Bjelke-Petersen and Chief of the General Staff, Lieutenant-General MF Brogan.

Index